Thoreau, The Kid and Mr. Lou

Photo by Patricia Brothers Salome.

Thoreau, The Kid and Mr. Lou
Book Notes of a Foreign Correspondent

By
Louis J. Salome

Great Life Press
Rye, New Hampshire
2020

© 2020 by Louis J. Salome. All Rights Reserved. No part of this book may be reproduced in any form whatsoever without the written permission of the author.

ISBN: 978-1-938394-40-9
Library of Congress Control Number: 2020901230

published by:
Great Life Press
Rye, New Hampshire 03870
www.greatlifepress.com

Please visit the author's website at:
louisjsalome.com

Book design: Grace Peirce

Unless otherwise noted, all photos are by Louis J. Salome

"So Mr. Lou writes this book about how he wrote this other book. Before you head for the exit, hear me out. Mr. Lou is Lou Salome, a veteran newspapermen, a foreign correspondent, no less, that most noble perch in newspaperdom. From bases in London and Jerusalem, he covered war, and occasionally peace, in Afghanistan, Bosnia, Pakistan, Iraq, Northern Ireland and Russia. He slept in more huts than Hyatts, travelled more by goat trail than by dirt road. And after retiring, he decided to write about it all, in *Violence, Veils, and Bloodlines: Reporting from War Zones*. He holed up in a cabin by a pond in New Hampshire, and wrote for nearly a year. In *Thoreau, The Kid and Mr. Lou* we look into the mind of this writer, and how that first book came to be. We follow flashbacks to his harrowing encounters in war zones, but also see the mundane, and often hilarious: preparing the tomato sauce for that night's pasta, walking miles to find a friendly dumpster in which to dispose of his dainty little trash bags, and his vigilant but fruitless quest to spot a deer in the woods. His year coincided with the World Series victory by the Boston Red Sox, ending the 86-year-old *curse of the bambino*. This fan of the game and especially the Red Sox could not ignore it. (Nor could he ignore his own notable performance at a Red Sox fantasy baseball camp a year later.)

"Mr. Lou's neighbors around the pond in New Hampshire seemingly had little in common with the warlords, fixers, fighters, and herders that had crossed his earlier life abroad. But Mr. Lou lets us see the connections."

—*Tom Giuffrida, Florida*

"Lou Salome reported from Europe, Asia and Africa for almost a decade. He'd been asked the traditional 'where are you FROM from?' question by people from Belfast, from Sarajevo, from Djibouti. He realized the ethnic, sectarian and nationalist clashes he reported on could be distilled in a single concept: tribal.

"Wanting to show how that idea worked, he headed to a cabin in the New Hampshire woods to write a book. He got the isolation he sought, but also memories of people he'd met in war zones, and spontaneous visitors from the not entirely deserted woods. And multiple lessons in how to dispose of eggshells and potato peelings. His reminiscences are whimsical with a side order of profound."

—*Betsy Willeford, Florida*

"Louis Salome's account of his time writing his previous book in a cabin on a lake in New Hampshire offers a unique insight into an author's struggle with the completion of a book. He recounts his experience writing intertwined with some of the events that occurred while he was a foreign war correspondent. Having lived in New Hampshire, I can't imagine much worse than being in a cabin on a lake there in January. He relates his 11-month journey with exquisite imagery and humor."

—*Jane Ewell, Virginia*

"A great read in understanding a writer's mind. Since I read his first book, it was so enjoyable to understand how that book was written. The writing in this book is filled with the author's truth, heart, personality, and humanity. A wonderful read!"

—*Mrs. Blue, Texas*

"'Winter in the woods made me feel as if I were alone again in... Uzbekistan, zooming—siren blaring, emergency light flashing and live grenade lolling under the front seat—with a retired but still toting former Soviet army officer from Tashkent to the old imperial city of Samarkand.' Maybe winter in the woods couldn't make you feel that way, but maybe you never were a foreign correspondent. Lou Salome went to the woods to focus 10 years of notebooks into the fault line that leads to our wars, tribalism. His first book, *Violence, Veils and Bloodlines,* was the result. This book is about focusing to write the first one. Like the first, it is really about the people he met and the places he's been. For example, a security officer put something in his food in Pakistan, but, on the other hand, there was a vegan restaurant near his cabin and—what do you know?—he liked the food. Oh, and there is a lot about baseball, which was inevitable because his Red Sox chose his near year in the woods to win their first World Series since Samarkand was in its glory."

—*Thomas E. Blackburn, Florida*

"Author Louis Salome deals with nature, his Lucas Pond neighbors consisting of the two legged, four legged, and winged (including Ted Williams) varieties, as he lives again in self-imposed isolation in the hinterlands of the ornery live free or die state of New Hampshire. He expects the freedom from interruption, uninvited company, and an always tempting dinner in Portsmouth with wife Pat to provide the discipline and needed time to organize the notes and materials from his previous stay in the New Hampshire woods as he authored his first book, *Violence, Veils and Bloodlines: Reporting from War Zones*. What has resulted is *Thoreau, The Kid and Mr. Lou*, an engrossing and entertaining combination of past and present influences and incidents described with Salome's gift to include the reader as he takes us on the journey that leads to this exceptional read."

—*John F. Coey, Pennsylvania*

"In *Thoreau, The Kid and Mr. Lou*, the author details his time in a remote cabin in the New Hampshire woods, the purpose of his self-imposed isolation to confront the internal demons mocking his effort to write a book and, ironically, to let another internal force, his subconscious, help him complete it.

"Mr. Salome did finish the first book, *Violence, Veils and Bloodlines: Reporting from War Zones* (McFarland, 2010). That history, covering his extensive career as a foreign correspondent, had, at its core, observations about tribalism.

"The author's writing time in his wood-side cabin draws an obvious comparison to Thoreau at Walden Pond. But there is a major difference. Thoreau went to '...live deliberately, to front only the essential facts of life, and see if I could not learn what it had to teach...' Mr. Salome took with him into his cabin a lifetime of memories created in war zones. He had seen tribalism at its worst, the hate, the killing, the cruelty of men. He also recognized that culture and beliefs can ennoble us. The woods offered solitude for the organizing of his stories but those stories were earned by searching for truth and reporting it from places as different from a New Hampshire woodland as peaceful serenity is from hell.

"*Thoreau, The Kid and Mr. Lou* interweaves into one tapestry the experiences the author had with strangers in other countries with his encounters in the 'tribal' region of the backwoods of New

Hampshire. Mr. Salome expertly makes the point, whether in New England or Gaza, tribes are the same because people want the same things in life. But he also points out that tribalism is territorial. It can be simply protective. Who is this man writing alone in a cabin in our woods? Or lethal, politicians and religious leaders manipulating our biological dark side fear of 'the other' to create the ethnic-cleansing slaughter in Bosnia.

"Caring for each other, recognizing we all belong to really only one tribe, the human one, is a recurring theme in Mr. Salome's journal generated book. Another is how through struggle and perseverance, the human spirit can triumph. Sometimes that courage means the difference between life and death. Sometimes it allows a writer to finish his book.

"The writing in *Thoreau, The Kid and Mr. Lou* is excellent, insightful, and often poetic as Mr. Salome describes the changing seasons and how in winter the ice on Lucas Pond is an imposing, majestic presence, dominating the landscape. The following passage is an example of his beautiful use of words:

"'As an adult more than fifty years later, I found the woods in winter spectacular in their simplicity. More gray than brown though sprinkled with green holiday conifers, the woods are lifeless-looking and noiseless except when deep silence peaks through harsh winds, frozen branches chatting or the ice spewing echoes as it expands and deepens in the glacial pond. It's true what they say about silence making noises. Sometimes silence shrieks.'

"Mr. Salome's latest book is a five star read."

—*Alan S. Kessler, author of seven novels, including* Gables Court, Clarence Olgibee *and* Shadow Lands; *Vermont*

To my wife Patricia Brothers Salome and our children,
Margaret, Mary and Andrew Salome

He that would thrive, must ask his wife
Olde English Proverb

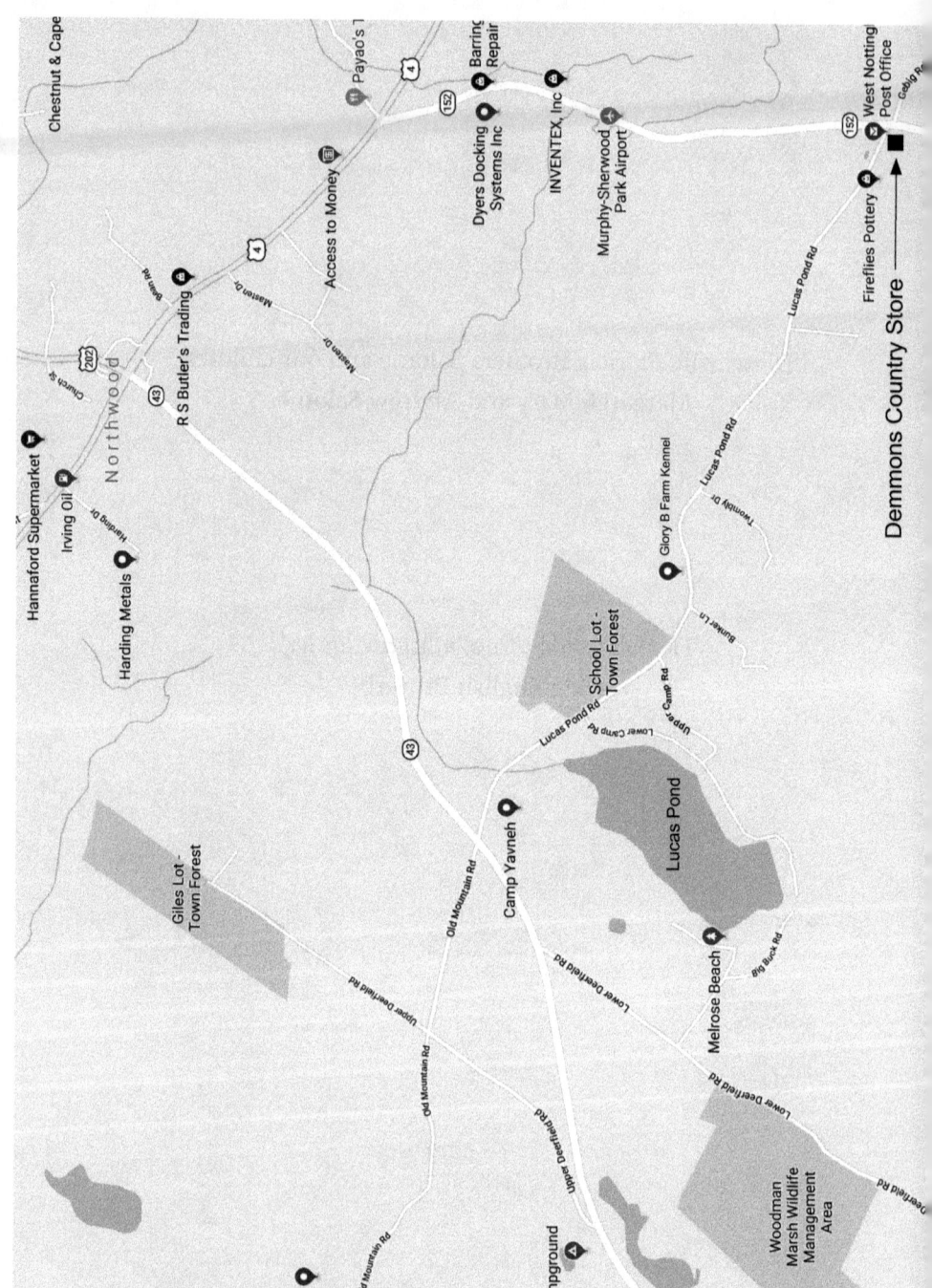

Maps courtesy of Google

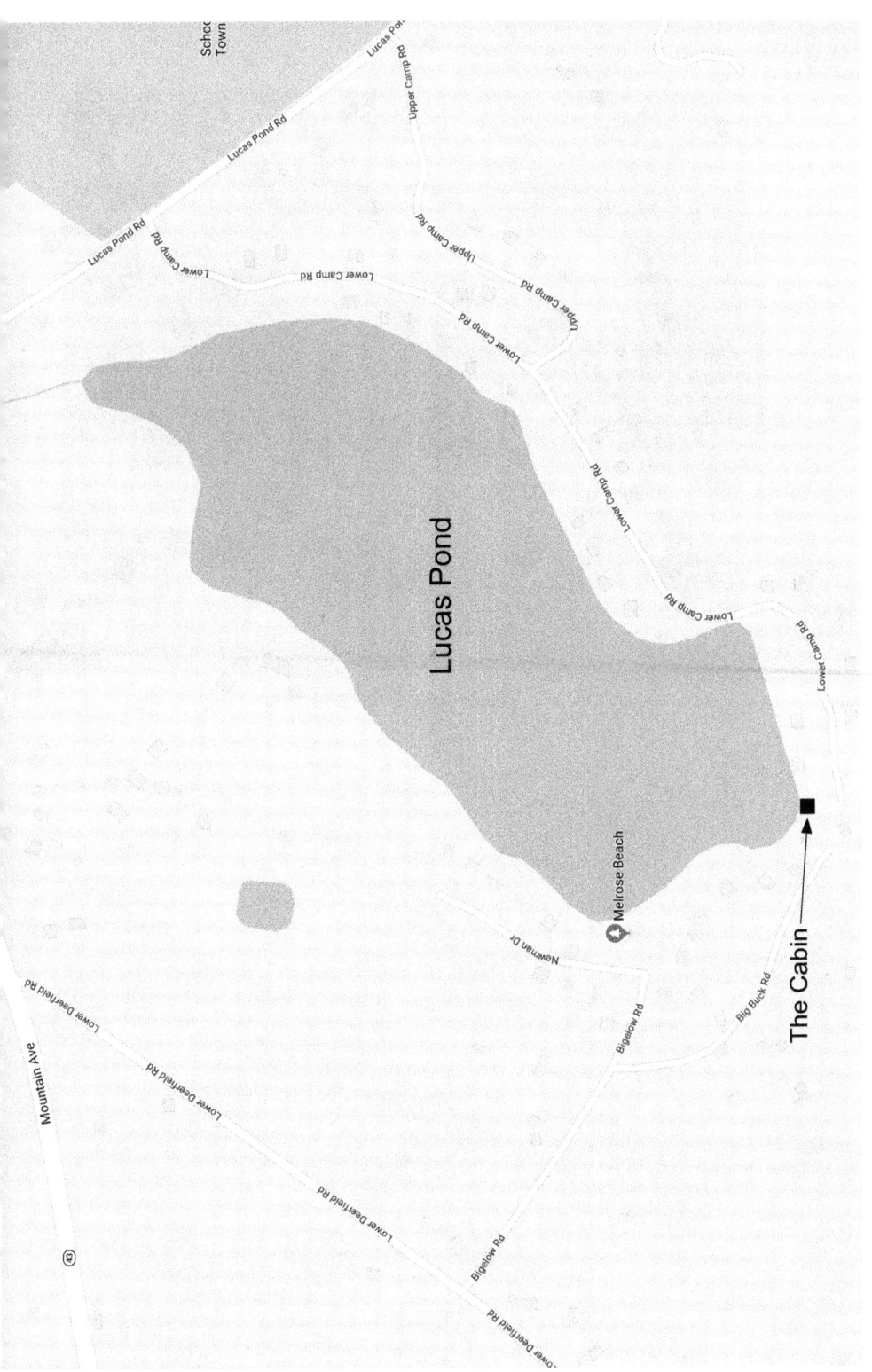

View From The Pond.

Contents

Stop and Go	1
Tick-Tock	7
Writing, On The Rocks	19
Dawn's Early Light	31
Night Life	47
A Superior Being	59
Like Thoreau, Sorta	69
Talking Trash	81
From the Ayatollah to Jesus	105
Seasoned	163
Touch 'Em All	207
Appendix: Cribbage Magic	239
Acknowledgments	242
About the Author	245

Winter's Welcome.

In the beginning, January's snow, ice and whistling wind covered the earth.

Heat was warming up in the bullpen.

In the end, a week before Thanksgiving, my computer crashed but didn't burn.

In between, a captive of seclusion, my writing demons were banished.

Stop and Go

Halfway between ages sixty-two and sixty-three, I kissed daily journalism goodbye after thirty-five years of bickering. A new lover—a book—beckoned. As common as that may sound, for me it was a novel notion. In the woods far behind me, great joys faded—older men on the re-write desk who woke when needed, a veteran World War II writer who skipped from the newsroom nightly for dinner and other services, a cranky cop reporter who climbed on his desk to shout of his refusal to train another city editor, and Don Wright, an utterly superb newspaperman and genius of an editorial cartoonist who each day, five days a week for fifty years, created the most provocative cartoon he had ever drawn. Day in and day out for half a century, Wright's work was so strong that his two Pulitzer prizes and the five times he was named a Pulitzer finalist seem almost incidental.

Special occasions are etched and unforgettable. Slinking low and deep to avoid random bullets, along with Howard Kleinberg, The Editor, and Jesse Jackson, The Reverend, I rode into a blazing riot area to show the wildly disaffected that someone of influence was listening.

Behind me were almost ten years as a foreign correspondent—roaming with strangers to meet killers and kidnappers, and crossing basalt deserts into nothingness. A deep breath before such tempests were a decade haranguing against corruption in lofty moral tones as the editorial page editor at *The Miami* (Florida) *News*, several years covering local, state and national politics, reporting on the dirty tricks of Richard Nixon and cohort during the 1972 presidential campaign, and hunched at a ringside seat in that same year when Florida's contending heavyweight bosses came within an overhand right of duking it out on the floor of the Democratic National Convention in Miami Beach. Such fun. Plus a few more years as an investigative reporter, a label that insiders used to ridicule because they considered it redundant. Question, probe, investigate, after all, is what all reporters are supposed to do. My last five years in the "bidness," as old-timers called it, were as a news editor and dig-deep reporter at *The Palm Beach* (Florida) *Post*.

Tough to leave, newspapers gave me a lifetime of adventures. Where else would I find a woman who offered her body, and a bit of her soul, if I would only bury a story about how she and her husband fleeced a federal social problem? What other job offered an interview with Princess Diana, paid me to stumble into a newsy lunch with a European ambassador in Damascus, swill beer in the parched Sahara with faux teetotalers, sleep with scorpions in Central Afghanistan, and negotiate with kidnappers in Lebanon?

By retiring in September 2003, I left a large amount of money on the table. If I had retired three months later, my bank account would have been several digits thicker. It was the dreams that shoved me out of newspapering and into the forest of uncertainty, haunting recollections of hanging with fascinating strangers in strange lands and finding good luck where bad would have been more probable. Those subconscious realities that nagged when I slept belonged in a book.

After all the paid years of pushing through doors to empower light, I had no complaints. Money and newspapering didn't belong in the same sentence anyway, as one Associated Press reporter used to chirp as often as he cursed, "You can't spell cheap without AP." After my dash from the starting blocks in 1966, I had seen too many desperate newspaper reporters hang on—hostile, worn out and ducking assignments as deftly as they ridiculed new city editors—because they couldn't afford to retire. One reporter of the old school used to mutter, as he belched his breakfast across the bibs of his friends each morning, that he had "f**k you money." That claim was supposed to mean that Mr. Crusty had inherited millions or busted a bank in grade school and could quit any time he wished. No one believed he had cash stashed in a mattress. Hanging on and miserable wouldn't be my fate. Besides, newspapering itself gave me "f**k you money," and I had dreams that barked inside my head day and night and everywhere I roamed.

Distractions—a pool off the patio, banyan trees shading the Intracoastal Waterway a short cast away, and tennis courts a chip shot across a fairway—would have made book-writing impossible in Palm Beach Gardens, Florida. The next move was easy. My wife Pat and I chose Portsmouth, New Hampshire, as our retirement home, a decision that was as easy as visiting Paris in April, on assignment, of course. We both grew up in New England and knew Portsmouth's long history that was rooted in England, where we had lived for five years. A scouting trip clinched the deal after I spied a Persian rug shop in the center of the olde English downtown. Settled around 1623, Portsmouth is a tourist town that locals call home. It retains much of its colonial New England flavor, now spiced with Thai, European and even Nepalese aromas and palate magnets. A small place of about 22,000 people, girdled by borders of smaller New Hampshire towns and by the State of Maine, Portsmouth reminds me of coastal towns in Britain and Ireland—France even—or a neighborhood in any large city. Portsmouth was the draw, but Pat knew I would bolt for seclusion in the woods as soon as a tree house with heat turned up.

During seven days in September of 2003, we sold our condo in Palm Beach Gardens and bought another in Portsmouth. Friends and strangers thought we were loony; we were going in the wrong direction, they said. The day after we bought three beautiful

Persian rugs for our new condo, I began dreaming about a writing cabin in the woods and my search began. For a few moments, I had considered seeking refuge and a new kind of deadline in the North Atlantic, perhaps the far-off Shetland, Orkney or Faroe islands. Really? Yes, really. The idea seemed romantic because I had spent a considerable amount of time reporting in Scotland and its far north. But romantic wasn't good enough. Though patient and forgiving, Pat was slightly cool to the idea, figuring that rowing to help me resupply every month might be more than what she signed up for and well beyond her travel range. Some of Pat's ancestors were fisher folk in Newfoundland and earlier in Ireland, but I was never dumb enough to ask whether she wanted to test her skill in a dory.

Nine small islands off New Hampshire's short coast, squeezed in the mist between Massachusetts and Maine, beckoned but came up barren. A few caretakers filled what little suitable living space there was on those islands in winter. Besides, transportation to and from the islands in January was, to put it coolly, a bit spotty and Pat's car wasn't a duck boat.

Listening with a sympathetic ear, the New Hampshire Parks and Recreation Department was unable to help. Its cabins in winter would kill me with cold before they would keep me warm enough to write. Soon, however, serendipity came to my assistance, the first of many such beneficent strokes to follow. Aid turned up in the form of Mirtha Crisóstomo and Al Dragon, a husband and wife team and longtime friends of my youngest sister Mary Lou Etheredge, and Rob, Mary Lou's husband. Mirtha knew that I was searching for a cabin in the New Hampshire woods; she also knew that Paul and Karen Dale, then her neighbors in Wayland, Massachusetts, owned a cabin about twenty-five miles west of Portsmouth. Kismet, some would say. Sharp scouts, say I. Perhaps both, the elusive New Hampshire deer might answer. The Dales's place in the town of Northwood was perfect for me.

Isolated enough to offer the seclusion I sought, the cabin at Lucas Pond was close enough to Portsmouth to offer the periodic connection I would require. So off I skated in early January 2004 to Big Buck Road at Lucas Pond in the midst of an arctic-like winter that deserved the name like few others in recent history. I would write a book or freeze, just like the ice on the pond. Published in 2010, that book—*Violence, Veils and Bloodlines—Reporting from War Zones*—would give birth to this one, but not without trying years in between.

Like a dream that stretched way into extra innings—first to about six years and then to more than a decade—baseball and the Boston Red Sox became a curious and important extension of my writing time in the woods, and beyond. Book-writing, baseball, getting my book published, stalking the woods, writing daily journals in the cabin, and meeting strangers that tethered Lucas Pond to places like Jerusalem, Ukraine, Belfast, Bosnia, Iran, Afghanistan and Pakistan all simmered in the same pot. This human and geographic blend far surpassed any stew that I could conjure in my little house at Lucas Pond.

Tick-Tock

*T*his book is a twofer. It is the story of how I lived alone in the woods to write one book and, where secluded, gathered material for a second book—this one. Though the raw materials for each book were mined far from each other, many related stories grew together in the same space, a cabin in the New Hampshire woods.

* * *

Slight at first, the aches soon grew more frequent and severe. For six months, I consulted my own doctor—me. Was this chest pain, I asked, mere indigestion or was it rooted in the heart of it all? A week before turning seventy-one, intense pain forced me to dump my own diagnosis. My father died of a heart attack at age fifty-two; his mother, my grandmother, died of a cerebral hemorrhage at fifty-three, and several of my uncles died too young of forms of arteriosclerosis, what was then called, in painfully visual terms, hardening of the arteries. Words such as hereditary, familial and congenital could no longer be avoided. Indigestion belonged on the shelf with self-denial.

Straight ahead, its long, slim hands creeping in a circle yet always moving forward while glaring at me as if shouting a warning, the large clock ticked off its silent alert: time was running out in more ways than one. It was nine-thirty on Tuesday morning, February 28, 2012, and I was talking, live, in the studio of New Hampshire Public Radio in Concord, New Hampshire's capital, when a wave of pain rippled across my chest. Neither fast nor slow, the pain snapped me to attention because it was deeper, heavier and more persistent than usual. We were halfway through the hour-long program, a perfect moment to consider whether the glass was half empty or half full. Glasses-be-damned. Determination to remain upright until the program ended was my only thought. That was and remains a call-in public affairs program, and I didn't want to make news. My in-house treatment called for relaxing, taking deep breaths and refusing to let a silly comment excite me. If my prescription worked, I felt certain the pain would ease before the discussion was scheduled to end at ten o'clock. This was personal, a matter of survival. The war in Syria, the subject of the show, became secondary and more distant than it had been a few minutes earlier. But I said nothing then, later or since to Laura Knoy, the host of *The Exchange*, a five-days-a-week program, or to anyone else, except to my wife Pat. A few minutes before the clock struck ten, the pain had vanished. The next day, my first visit to a doctor in thirty-five years, suddenly couldn't come soon enough.

Unlike mine, the doctor's diagnosis was specific and scientific. She convinced me. Quibbling time had passed. Five days after the doctor uttered hospital, I had open-heart surgery and five arterial bypasses. When the surgeon said my arteries were ninety percent blocked, I calculated the math. That was easy, even for me. Only ten percent of my heart arteries were open sufficiently to allow blood to trickle to my heart and for my heart to pump those drips to the rest of me. One small platelet could have finished me at any moment, a doctor's assistant told my wife. Hardening of the arteries was the antiquated name. Heart attack and death were its names in any age.

Open-heart surgery, and fast, was the solution. Five bypasses would allow blood to flow again as it should, the surgeon said. Only five bypasses, can't we do more? I thought but didn't say. Deflection, stalling, was called for. There would never be a more inappropriate moment to tell my friend Ellis's joke about Italian soldiers being under fire at the front and shouting, "Hurry, bring up the shells! Bring up the shells!" Instead of more ammo, the gnocchi brought the rigatoni. To say the joke was inappropriate does not quite capture the moment. My skilled and gentle surgeon happened to be a true gentleman from Verona. All he did was smile faintly without breaking his scientific stride. My perplexed wife shuddered and her face gave her up, saying, "I don't know this guy. I'm just his driver." On reflection, I figured the surgeon knew that at that moment I preferred diversions to dealing with reality.

There was urgency in all of this, one could say, although I didn't have a heart attack. This time luck, one more time, rode through the thinning passages of my thickening arteries. A floating sliver of plaque would have sent me to another studio where it would have been too late to relax, take deep breaths, tell a joke and let a rigid smile conceal my anxiety.

After ten years of dodging fire from weapons I often couldn't see or identify in places so obscure they defied accurate spelling except in their native alphabets, I had never been nicked. Neither flesh wounds nor broken fingernails marred my battle record. Terrible intestinal distress that I always called dysentery, although I never received a professional diagnosis, was my worst enemy and worst wound. Yet there I was in a calm, sterile place about to have my arteries repaired inside my chest cut wide open because of an inherited wound. It's often said that a person is never more totally alone than at birth and death. Running a close third, I've decided, is waiting to have your chest cut open to save your life.

Open-heart surgery isn't rare now, and the thought of it didn't frighten me before the fact. Too little time passed from the diagnosis to the surgery for anxiety to enter the fray. But after the fact, the thought of lying in surgery with my chest open so my vessels and organs could see outside their comfortable cavity made me just a little nervous, if not dubious, of the process. When it's possible to reflect on how dangerous an event was, that means everything turned out fine. Open-heart surgery seemed a bit like fleeing from helicopter fire in a northern Iraq battle zone and crawling on hands and knees through a minefield in northern Somalia. Things could have gone badly wrong, but they didn't.

Along with an electric razor, toothbrush and toothpaste, I cradled *Voices from The Grave*, a book about the *Troubles* in Northern Ireland, when the hospital's doors opened to me, and my heart. The book's title had nothing to do with me; I only wanted to continue reading the story of mayhem among Northern Ireland's so-called civilized tribes as doctors planned my fate. A book with *Voices* and *Grave* in the title didn't seem peculiar to me as I lay waiting to eye angels in a tunnel. After surgery, while my lungs were flushed of fluid for several days, the book lay on a table at my elbow, although I read nothing more. The title alone must have puzzled the doctors and nurses who checked me for a pulse, leaving them to wonder whose voices I was hearing or where I thought I was headed. No visitor asked about the book, about who spoke from the grave, whether I talked back, or how the mystery turned out. When I was discharged, the book left with me, to the probable relief of doctors and nurses. Still above ground, I was happy to hear my own voice.

Well after my discharge, I wondered what the doctors and nurses thought about the weird patient reading that book. Did they think I strained to hear ghosts while squinting to see lights, angels or the Vestal Virgins in a tunnel during surgery? Weeks after doctors sent this voice home to recover, I finished *Voices from The Grave*, without contributing a personal addendum.

Heart surgery isn't the genesis of this book, but it is worth a few more sentences, even a paragraph or two. At no time during the six hours or so of surgery did an ethereal being woo me into a cavern of sun-drenched light. Not even a bare, cold pathway flashed through the ether and into another world. A few days after surgery, I smiled and said to one of the doctors, "I hope the glue holds." "We don't use glue...." the doctor replied before he stopped, catching the joke.

Eight days after surgery and four days after I reached seven decades plus one year, doctors sprung me. After I saluted and was wheeled from the hospital, my wife, a nurse, drove me home to recover, and to read. Cardiac rehabilitation nurses slipped me a thick packet of information explaining my condition, what happened during surgery and what I should do to live another seventy-one years. "Severe triple vessel coronary artery disease" was the culprit, the prose said, which by this time I had figured out, if only in layman's terms. Inherent in my diseased arteries were plaque and calcification, which together with "disease" formed an enemy tripartite. Pat said the happy hunting ground, with or without a light to guide me through a tunnel, would have been my next stop if luck had not blocked plaque from blocking an artery. A Mulligan, a do-over, was my happy alternative. From that moment on, I convinced myself that heart disease would not kill me. An unforeseen foe would have to intervene.

With the help of a vein taken from the underside of my right knee and lower thigh, five arterial diversions were constructed to circumvent the three clogged arteries; I have the diagram, and the pulse, to prove my case. As if to bolster my morale for the recovery period, the literature left in my lap said that I was young—young at heart being too subjective a phrase—and that my heart "actually behaved quite well." To me, "quite well" meant that my heart could have behaved better, but I didn't seek a more refined medical definition. After reading the medical report, the doctors may have been implying that the rest of my behavior—my kidneys or something—left much to be desired. But then, in what some might describe as a radical misdiagnosis, the doctors wrote that I was "pleasant."

Recovery seemed normal, neither slow nor fast, something like a rookie surfer riding rookie waves; some rides left me exuberant while others left me feeling empty or washed up. Eight years since surgery, the pattern continues, although the ups last longer and are now batting, to use a baseball term, better than five hundred, which is super Hall of Fame stuff. For many months, recovery left room for little else. Instincts became my armor. Without thinking consciously about it, I crossed my protective arms over my wounded chest when rounding a corner, approaching a door that might spring open in my direction or fearing a wayward object would strike me. Not once since surgery have I walked into a wall and not once has the unexpected whacked me in the chest. When I see, in a film or in real life, another person get injured or be in danger of injury, a cold shiver ripples—usually from bottom to top rather than top to bottom—from my toenails to the follicles on my head. My reaction is totally unconscious, automatic, and probably related to trauma and post-traumatic stress. Empathy is absent. My body had been traumatized and it won't let me forget it.

From all of this, I learned that heart surgery and recovery, properly aligned, can stimulate writing. There must be, however, a faster and less painful process to move the mind and pen. Having one's chest cut open for arterial repair has a way of slowing life to its essentials, staying upright and pumping blood. For two years I wrote zero, which is one way of saying that heart surgery paralyzed my pen. But I read, if at the pace of a child in kindergarten, and made notes from flashes of memory and from earlier journals about what I intended to write when I could. Among the books I read, usually four or five pages at a time, was James Joyce's *Ulysses*, all 732 pages of small type in an unabridged edition. *Ulysses* was with me before the sandman came each night and sometimes during the day when chance intervened. *Ulysses* served as my subconscious, just as dreams did years earlier when I lived and wrote in the cabin. The notes I scribbled while reading *Ulysses* concerned not *Ulysses* but ideas for this book, which originated in journal form several years earlier in the New Hampshire woods. From *Ulysses* flowed uncommon encouragement: if Joyce could write his masterpiece, I concluded, I could write my minor piece.

* * *

Back in 2004, I wrote *Violence, Veils and Bloodlines—Reporting from War Zones* while living alone at Lucas Pond. Tribal behavior, which I observed and survived during ten years of reporting across Europe, Asia, North and East Africa, is the body and soul of that book. While writing about tribalism during the four seasons of 2004, making notes in daily journals about my life alone in the woods became a side job, like a teacher playing in a pickup band on weekends. But those journals are the heart of this book, which wouldn't exist had I not been writing another book, a sister book of sorts, more than a decade earlier.

What's it like to live and write in a cabin in the woods, alone? Having done it, I can report that it is not like living in splendid isolation, a term used to describe British social and political privilege before World War I. My isolation was neither splendid nor privileged. Blindness to the needs of others wasn't my affliction. Writing a book was my only goal. After learning the rigors and benefits of living and writing alone, I promised to tell others. My original intent was to compare the tribal behavior of the people of the New Hampshire woods with the behavior of people in far off places on three other continents. In one way or another, people everywhere belong to a tribe of some sort, shaped to varying degrees by family, clan and territory; by language, history, customs and culture, religion, nation/tribe or various combinations of those ties that bind and separate.

As the weeks passed during my writing year in the woods, one diary fattened to three from early January to late November. Observations about tribal behavior in the neighborhood grew to include musings about my own solitary life without a car or a television. Writing, all consuming as the regimen was, soon became a subject unto itself in which other activities were submerged. Separate but just as worthy were observations of the natural world, my attitude toward the pond, the woods, the cabin and the deer I searched for but never spotted. Even baseball along with boxing and fishing legends entered the picture, tied as they became directly to the pond and later indirectly to book publishing and to the Boston Red Sox winning their first World Series Championship in eighty-six years. Living as a voluntary outcast in the woods is a fine and sure way to connect to worlds unknown. Besides the long and unexpected link to baseball, writing alone in a cabin by a pond also drew the inevitable comparison with Henry David Thoreau and his two-year sojourn at Walden Pond in Concord, Massachusetts, long ago but not so far away from my abode.

My life alone also offered evidence that the big world beyond the woods reveals a small world after all. A beautiful ceramic sculpture that was created in Ukraine, transported to Jerusalem, London and West Palm Beach now sits atop a sleek wood plinth in my Dover, New Hampshire dining room. I bought the plinth at an antiques shop in Northwood, New Hampshire, a short walk from my cabin.

More than a decade before Lucas Pond and I became partners, I brought a couple of baseball bats, baseballs and gloves to Jerusalem. This wasn't exactly like Babe Ruth promoting baseball in Japan in the 1930s. My idea was to introduce the Great American Pastime to Palestinians. It would be an understatement to call my effort a flop. But baseball wasn't through with me. The game swept over me at Lucas Pond like Ted Williams whacking homers out of Fenway Park. And baseball kept flying through my writing life for six years after I moved into the woods until, the provider of more great and good luck, it led to a publisher of my first book.

Centering as it does on the seclusion that helped me write my first book, this book raises a similar question: What path did I follow to write this book?

The answer is less mysterious than my choice to spend most of 2004 alone in the woods. But saying this explains nothing. True, the journals on which this book is based were all written in 2004 in my cabin at Lucas Pond. In 2007, five years before heart surgery, I returned to the same cabin on the shores of the same pond to write a chapter of this book. More writing followed in places as varied as a ship and a house at the edge of a desert. I wrote in my son's house in Albuquerque, New Mexico, at the wonderful Athenaeum Historical Research Library in Portsmouth, New Hampshire, on a ship that sailed, without sails, from Fort Lauderdale to Rome, at my homes in Portsmouth and Dover, New Hampshire. No place was safe from my paper and pen, as I all but stapled a Reporter's Notebook to my hip. None of this is as singularly exotic as living and writing alone in the woods. Yet this book wouldn't exist if I hadn't fled into the woods to begin with.

Life in the cabin taught me that seclusion does not hold solitude in its palm. Even when I was secluded, I wasn't alone. My environment became one with me. And my past—where I had been, what I had done, the strangers I met while reporting, roaming and shredding soles—blended into my life in the woods and became more a part of me than it would have been without such extended and deep contemplation. Strangers, their stories and my paths less traveled, when relived, opened my mind, expanded my oneness. In those moments, things past connected to each other in ways that previously had seemed remote and unconnected. In a similar fashion, stories I heard in the woods about fishing and baseball led to playing baseball in a major league ballpark and to the publication of the book I wrote in the cabin. Strangers remained strangers in the woods, but they also connected to circumstances and strangers I encountered continents from my cabin in New Hampshire.

Cabin, pond, woods and strangers formed the center of my physical world for eleven months. Together, they formed a stack of creative kindling that burst into my first book and ignited this one, a work that has two beginnings. As it turned out, I myself became a kind of kindling, in the varied and mysterious ways that environment and experience shape a person.

As a reporter picking my way through Moscow's beautiful subway stations and streets unknown to me, probing the mysterious

Casbah in Algiers, and becoming disoriented by a blinding blizzard in Afghanistan's Hindu Kush Mountains, roads were there to be taken, however alien and dangerous. Some paths were less traveled, some well worn, others to be avoided at almost all costs. But roads exist because strangers left footprints there, and other strangers followed.

Hoary with antiquity yet sprightly as layers of new limestone pile upon the dust of the long dead, Jerusalem throbs with territorial, tribal and religious conflict. A hilly town on the edge of a desert, Yerushalim, as it's known to Jews, or Al Quds—The Holy—as it's known to Arabs, is like a gnarled olive tree that looks ancient, because it is, yet continues to bear fresh and sometimes bitter fruit. A glacial hole filled with fresh water, Lucas Pond is ancient too, no doubt much older than the human settlement of Jerusalem. The link between the two is derived from the winding roads I traveled in diverse lands, and the many strangers I met along the way: a teacher struggling to resume her career in Afghanistan during a lull in the fighting, a Lakota woman at Lucas Pond who had taught the Inuit in Alaska, an old Bosnian writer and a much younger American army veteran who spoke unknowingly to each other about war and its futility.

Spent all night waking with ideas, popping up and writing them down in the cold. A sign of nights to come.—January 8, 2004

Writing, On The Rocks

Shortly after high noon in early January, the ice froze me dead on the doorstep. There was no high sun, as no such animal exists in New Hampshire's winter woods. This is perfect, I thought. All the while I stood speechless as my cheeks stiffened in the throes of what seemed like incipient rigor mortis. Gasping at the Arctic-like absurdity that surrounded us, my wife Pat had a different concept of perfection. She wouldn't hang around for days to watch the ice melt—inside the windows. This was all my idea, in the beginning, stepping solo into a cabin in Janus's month. Four walls inside and the woods and the pond outside were to act as self-imposed deadlines that would compel me to write. To begin in summer would have been too easy, a perfect preface for failure.

In the din behind me, Lucas Pond's solid water expanded and deepened, alternately roaring and tinkling like a symphony of icy chimes, what kids in New England winters way before the turn of the century used to call season's cracks. Pine needles whistled like an ensemble of flutes and tin whistles blown by the razor-like cold and relentless wind, although Tommy Makem and the Clancy Brothers were no longer in the vicinity. Brittle gray maples, oaks and white birches crackled around my new home and the pond that ruled what would become my corner of a frigid domain.

Numbness dulled the nerves too much to incubate tingling. All lay quiet in the cabin's front room. Then I blinked and focused straight on at the shiftless gray and white owl that would forever hover without winking. That stuffed bird would follow me around the cabin from January through November. My eyelid clicked again at the wall map of New Hampshire and Vermont, all the way north to Canada. Northern New England for sure, I thought, even without Maine. In eternal repose near the map behind the day bed, six trout hung on the knotty pine wall—small, colorful rainbows, brownies and maybe brookies caught by children a few summers earlier and cast for all seasons by the skills of taxidermy. Later on, those fish, their eyes frozen in death, watched me sleep, exercise, cook, eat, read and write. It was as if the wall had eyes. In summer, larger living trout staked out territory in the shallows of Lucas Pond next to my cabin, but never once did I try to hook one for the wall.

View From The Fridge.

To my right stood survival. Silent but real, a small propane gas heater spoke its own language: no heat, no write. No heat, no legend or myth of Ted Williams speaking to me at Lucas Pond. No heat, no strangers to meet in the woods; no kismet to carry me through the woods, to a bookstore, to baseball at Fenway Park, and to a book publisher. That mass of cold metal soon would be the heart of my life, my best and not so inanimate friend once flint revived it. Yawning to my left was a white fridge, a cave for my turkey burgers, eggs, veggies, apples, bread, cheese; frozen salmon, swordfish and tuna steaks, and chicken thighs. A kitchen table and four chairs, stout and looking like antiques, filled the small footage in front of a phalanx of cupboards, a sink, a gas cooking stove with four burners, and the cave. Around the corner and a few feet away, the only place they could be, I figured, were the toilet and *hammam*—the shower; if I was going to write about tribalism in tribal worlds I might as well flip the proper mental switch, hammam being the Arabic word for shower.

Swiveling almost full circle to my right and staring, I caught the full freezing effect of an inch of ice inside—yes, inside—the small bay window, what I hoped would one day be my warm porthole to the pond and the world. Ice on the pond thick enough to support cars and a few cabins might be expected. But ice inside my cabin window jarred and made my teeth chatter. In the sill below the ice, several small black flies lay as dormant as Ted Williams's head frozen in the cryonics process. Unlike the Splendid Splinter's remains, the flies of winter would be revived by a little gas heat well before the springtime sun warmed the panes and signaled "play ball," the start of the baseball season. In a few days, artificial warmth would turn those motionless insects into the flies of summer.

Behind my left shoulder, skepticism erupted from beneath a hood and muffler: "You must be crazy. Are you sure you want to do this? This better be a bestseller." That was Pat, my supportive wife, sharing her doubts and speaking her mind. A bestseller, however, was never part of the deal. A book was. Still, I nodded in silence, my don't-worry shout. Absolutely sure I want to do this, I said to no one but myself, thinking about the temperature that was locked in well below zero. Four seasons of seclusion, time to waste, trick and use were my primal needs. A book was my objective. Here in the woods I camped, a townie, a roamer, eager to morph into a recluse, at least for a year. No more excuses, no further delays, the duels with my writing demons were about to begin. The combat would last, as time and writing permitted, until a week before Thanksgiving, the advent of ice renewal, and the return of flies to sleep until another spring.

As daunting as the cold and ice were, they were stimulating. Writing under artillery fire in Beirut or struggling to ward off asphyxiation in an Afghan mountain tunnel were always more energizing than reporting on Belfast street demonstrations or catching Bill Clinton's go-gettem speech to soldiers in Baumholder, Germany, in early December of 1995. A base in Tuzla, Bosnia, would be the soldiers' next home, but I reached that fog-shrouded city before they did.

There I stood in the early afternoon on January 8, 2004, when my dream touched noses with the cold reality that I wanted and embraced. Friends insisted, even boasted on my behalf, that discipline was my alter ego: How else could I live alone, without a car or television, in the woods to write until I won? At that I laughed. Hell, if discipline were my partner, I wouldn't have to bivouac in the woods to begin with. For much of 2004, this cabin on Big Buck Road, a short stony strip on the southern shore of Lucas Pond in Northwood, New Hampshire, would be my home. My library, reading, writing and exercise space, my day bed, kitchen and dining area all thrived in the same fixed circle. Space in the cabin was tight, sure, but the crowds were elsewhere and I was alone. The propane heater was my fireplace. Two small electric heaters, one of which I moved into the bathroom when I showered, once in a while, were a bonus. The twenty-four foot by twelve-foot main room cradled all of my activities outside of the bathroom. A third electric heater proved too much for the cabin's electrical system, killing the power each time I reached for more heat. But that deficiency was easy to bear because I had no choice.

Hearth and Heart.

The icy greeting was a good sign. If I could weather winter's welcome mat, other seasonal tests would seem as easy as roaming the French Riviera searching for a deposed dictator. Eventually, staying warm wouldn't be terribly difficult either. But warmth didn't mean I could exorcise the writing demons, the internal doubts that made me question all aspects of the project most of the time. Those demons had to be beaten back every minute of every day until I finished. Of all the demons, fear hovered over all others. This was not a physical fear of season, place or strangers. It was fear of myself, and doubts about my writing task. Long underwear, sweaters, gloves, hats and heat were necessary, but superficial, aides. After the writing demons were subdued, I still would have to find a publisher, a process that would keep other demons alive long after they should have been buried in permafrost.

Looking back, the first day was relatively easy. A mere six inches of snow crunched under my old boots. That was enough to send me groveling to the cabin's basement in search of a shovel to clear a path from the ice- and snow-covered road to the stairs that led to the pond-facing second-story deck and what was actually the front door. Only then could I free the car of writing tools, heavy clothes and enough food to last a month. This would be my home for the long haul, so I brought those extra electric heaters, a computer and printer, good literature and notebooks, crossword puzzle books of varying degrees of difficulty, a cribbage board and playing cards—all directly or indirectly designed to inveigle my mind to write something, anything, each day. Before I started the heavy lifting from the car into the cabin, my freezing fingers sent the following message: Light the stove! Nothing will go right, I knew, until the heat was on, which it already was, although that was pressure—heat of a different definition.

This was the first of many moments in the cabin when I would consult someone else's notes. Those sorcerer's instructions belonged to Paul Dale, the cabin's owner. In great detail, Paul told me how to empower the stove and then lure water into the cabin pipes without using a divining rod. I didn't tell Paul, but humanity would have been dining on sushi and steak tartare for eons longer had I been the person needed to master the flint/fire trick.

Expecting an explosion, maybe even hoping for a small one that would sidetrack me, Paul's instructions became my science, and art, too. Turn the knobs on the propane heater, Paul wrote. So I did. Step by step. That meant aligning the large blue button behind the stove with the copper gas line, turning the dial on top of the heater to the left until it clicked, then holding down the dial for at least thirty seconds to light the pilot, a signal achievement. No pilot, no fire. (To be sure the pilot would light, I held the dial down for sixty seconds.) After that, following Paul's instructions, I raised the dial slightly and turned it to the left to light the first row of flames. Paul said nothing about praying or facing east, so I simply crossed two fingers on my left hand. Let there be fire, I murmured, and there was. To light the second row of flames, Paul suggested that I turn the dial atop the heater to the left again and release it. Fingers crossed worked again. My (note the possessive) stove was firing on all cylinders or something like that. At that moment, I felt more like an engineer than someone reading notes dictated by another person who was well-practiced in what I, in an honest moment, would call the arcane art of propane stove abracadabra.

Swollen with success, but humble still, I took a breather from the boiler works. Deciding to give heat a chance, I shifted gears to slide my lifeline supply of food, clothing and accessories from the car to the cabin. After that lengthy chore was completed, the basement—boats, shovels, tools and all—would come into view. There I would wrestle with the more complex but less explosive task of turning on the water and lighting the hot water heater, one truly freezing floor below the main refrigerator I now called home.

Geezers playing movers in winter and sneaking into the woods without snowshoes must have puzzled the few humans peeking from behind curtains in more toasty quarters. And that says nothing of the deer that, I figured, were watching, smiling and motionless from behind stately bright green pines and dull gray oaks. Pat's help eased the burden, which was never easy or rapid due to the ice, the stairs and the weight of books and canned goods that had been stuffed into Pat's small hatchback.

Up and down Pat and I slogged from the car, along the narrow path that I had shoveled through the snow, up and down the down and up staircase, along the cleared pond-facing deck and into the cabin that at first seemed colder than the air whistling across the pond. A few hours after we lugged in my supplies and exercised our lungs, the cabin appeared to be warming. That was a false sensation, of course, our feeling of warmth being due to our rising blood pressure.

We've moved eighteen times during our marriage, several times in Massachusetts, Connecticut and Florida, twice each in Jerusalem and London and twice, so far, in New Hampshire, but this moment was as different as Algiers is from Dublin. After all my baggage was piled into the cabin, the homemaking task was all mine. The fridge and cupboards beckoned, as did three small back bedrooms where my extra clothes and dirty laundry would sleep in cold storage. To keep the heat in my living space and the freezing air out, I piled pillows and blankets in front of the bedroom doors.

Plumbing was more puzzling to me than lighting a gas stove, although a mite less dangerous. A gas stove could explode in my face, but drowning might be my fate if the plumbing adjustments went badly awry because I can't swim or even float except in salty confines such as the Dead Sea. But I can wade, which in a basement made me feel safe enough. Exaggerations, perhaps, but the mind plays strange tricks on strange occasions.

Before heading down to the pipes and water works, I returned to Paul Dales's engineering directives. First, turn on the black switch near the floor behind the toilet upstairs. Here was that old upstairs downstairs trick, which is anything but intuitive. This clever twist triggered the water pipe heaters in the basement. Without this tactic, water would have frozen in the pipes in an instant. The key to powering this engine, however, was to first turn on the electricity, the box for which was in the basement. There, at the same time, I pulled down on two copper-wire switches to awaken the hot water heater. Two small amber lights flickered on outside the water heater, a sure-fire sign that I was on to something big. To make the water flow, I flipped switches to the right of the water heater and turned on the large spigot hidden behind a slab of plywood next to the heater. Converting my fresh notes—the same cabin bible according to Paul Dale as translated by me—into action was easier for me then than it would be now.

January in the New Hampshire woods was the month of the Big Cold in 2004. Outside my cabin door, the temperature didn't rise above zero for two consecutive weeks. A small thermometer that dangled from my belt told me so. Temperature differences, while sometimes small, came to represent large seasonal gaps. Elsewhere, in town for example, zero would have seemed an Arctic figure. But in the woods, zero seemed warm compared to minus-ten degrees. And minus-fifteen felt cozy compared with minus-twenty-five degrees. Wind roaring across the pond made a temperature of zero seem like it would have been more at home in the Himalayas. A windless temperature of plus-ten degrees felt South Florida balmy. There were many small storms but no big blizzards during my year in the woods. The deep cold often sucked up the snow between storms preventing it from accumulating to knee-high levels. The snow god, at least, was my friend. Shoveling was easy, too, because the blizzards drifted elsewhere. I never let the snow accumulate on the stairs or deck that faced the pond and led to my front door, which from Big Buck Road looks more like the back door.

My year in the woods reminded me of the winter of 1958, forty-six years earlier, my first year in college. Back then my home wasn't a Lincolnesque log cabin, but I studied with my feet inside our oil-burning stove that was supposed to heat our family house in Millville, Massachusetts. When the blizzards blew, the heat went straight up the chimney instead of into the kitchen and the rest of the house. The stove itself was cold enough to allow me to stick my shoeless feet inside without burning my flesh or my wool socks.

As cold as it was outside my cabin, it was never as cold inside, after I stoked the propane and radiators, as it was in a small Gaza Strip hotel room fourteen years earlier. Fully dressed for winter on that occasion, covered by all the blankets I could find and almost kissing a small space heater aimed at my face from atop a bedside table, my teeth still chattered throughout that night. No shower then either.

Nor was my Lucas Pond igloo ever as uncomfortable or remote as the tiny, cinder block room where I camped for a night in the mountains of southeastern Afghanistan in the late winter of 2002. The mysterious owner of that room promised to leave the flickering electric power on until midnight so I and another American reporter could finish writing our stories. The dim bulb in our room died at 11:30 on that frigid night and we were left with only flashlights to guide us. And that was before I trudged outside in a heavy snow to fish for the Indian Ocean satellite. Without that satellite connection, my story would never have reached Washington and the Cox Newspapers Bureau there.

Days passed before all the machines in my cabin woke from hibernation. Despite my successful tinkering with power, water, wires and switches in the basement, water didn't flow to the kitchen sink or the toilet until eleven o'clock on that first night in boot camp. Almost twenty-four hours later, a few cups of warm water reached the kitchen sink, days before the mice. But the water was more tepid than hot, and soon it turned colder than the water from the cold-water tap. Paul Dale, as genial and cooperative a cabin owner as I could hope to find, set about arranging for a new hot water heater. Installing a water heater wouldn't be easy in mid-winter's freeze. For almost a month, my showers were few and eye-drop quick until a new water heater was installed on February 4. The showers I took after that were more comfortable, but I'm not sure they were more numerous.

How do I remember all the details? They aren't all in my memory. But they are etched in the black-on-white pages of diaries that I kept throughout 2004. Nothing new about that exercise: I filled notebooks for almost ten years while reporting across Central Asia and the Middle East, East and North Africa and Europe. Recording impressions, events and interviews were the raw materials of my life's work. Several boxes of those old notebooks and expense receipts were my sidekicks in the cabin; I couldn't have written *Violence, Veils and Bloodlines—Reporting from War Zones* without them. Daily observations about my life at Lucas Pond would later serve as the raw material for this book.

Pat refused to hang around the freezer after we hauled all of my supplies into the cabin. She was too smart for that. It was too cold, too grim. In the gathering early darkness, I skippered Pat and her silver Honda Civic hatchback up narrow, snow-slick and rocky Big Buck Road to Bigelow Road's asphalt. We embraced, kissed and promised to call every day, before Pat slipped behind the wheel and fled for the heat and other comforts of home. Slipping and sliding back to the cabin, and howling for fun and to frighten the wildlife, I was where I wanted to be. Inside, I stayed bundled while storing food in the refrigerator and cupboards, and tossing clean clothes into one small bedroom before sealing off that and the two other small bedrooms behind my day bed and kitchen.

Day One in the woods was a success. My pulse was proof of that. So was a dinner of sautéed chicken thighs, mashed potatoes, peas, bread stuffing, multigrain bread, and tea. Contentment and comfort spoke from my diary for that day. "Wind howling. Very cold. I have no watch, no TV or calendar. No car. Must lock myself away to write. Water in sink wheezed through pipes; water in toilet did, too. Gas heater still working. No hot water yet. Read Iraqi Kurd notes before I went to sleep. To bed about eleven. That's a guess."

Before diving into the day bed, I realized that my best ammunition against the night freeze remained in Portsmouth. Two sleeping bags lined up at home to accompany me were still lined up at home and wouldn't join me for another month, when Pat picked me up so I could replenish my food supply. Resources surrounded me, however. To replace the sleeping bags, I created my own igloo made of three blankets rescued from one of the nearby bedrooms. Inside the igloo I wore long johns, two tee shirts, a heavy wool shirt, a wool hat and thick wool socks.

My last conscious acts on that first night were to close the blinds at the bay window and slide the curtains across the small window above the kitchen sink. Then I stuffed the pillows and blankets more tightly at the entrances to the freezer-like bedrooms behind me. Let the record reflect that the next morning I wrote, "Room is actually warming." I wasn't hallucinating, but I might have been fibbing a little.

Can't hear the propane heater unless I get close to it. Otherwise, I hear only the refrigerator when it turns on or the hot water heater or water pump when I use the water. Otherwise, silence.—March 7, 2004

Dawn's Early Light

My first morning huddled near the propane heater sketched the outline for most of the one-hundred-and-ninety-two mornings that followed. Day after day, my routine remained loosely predictable, but never rigid. Life in winter beyond my artificial sleeping bag wasn't toasty. The daybed slumped five feet from the propane heater and a mere arm's length from the short stool where my laptop lay napping. To face the frigid air I bolted straight from the blanketed igloo into exercise mode. This was the quickest way to stay warm and hype the mental juices.

Wool socks, which during many months I changed now and then but never removed until summer, warmed my toes. A thick braided rug covered much of the main room. In short order, the rug became my exercise mat. It also shielded me from the frigid air that blew up from the basement and flew between the spaces in the wide, wood planks. Before long I stuffed rolled up newspaper pages into the spaces between the floorboards not covered by the rug. As clever as the squirrels that vanished into dead tree trunks in winter, I realized that air-conditioning was no asset when the temperature outside my self-made sleeping bag seemed colder than ice. The newsprint proved as useful as the wood from which it came. Lying on the rug and atop an exercise mat that I brought from home, my body took charge: a series of stretches, sit-ups and push-ups. They took forty-five minutes. Two twenty-pound dumbbells, found me later, at no set time, but before I fell back into the igloo, which was often close to midnight. My dumbbells and I proved a perfect match.

Sometime each day, or every other day, another series of strength exercises added vigor to my routine. By repeatedly stretching five tightly wound metal springs with plastic handles on each end that I had bought in Islamabad, Pakistan, in the spring of 2002, I maintained strength and flexibility. Those exercises also reminded my subconscious and conscious selves about the book I was writing. Odd as this might seem, it was a Pakistani employee at an American-owned hotel in Islamabad who helped me stay strong at Lucas Pond. Through the years, I had snapped several sets of these springs that had, by 2002, become antiques. I could no longer find any like them in the United States, England or mainland Europe. With this new set of springs, Pakistan's capital stretched all the way to the New Hampshire woods, another example of how the past informed my writing present, and how travel introduced me to strangers who remained forever familiar.

As I walked by the hotel gym in Islamabad, I spied a set of these springs and became more excited than if I had seen a Saudi woman without a veil. Well, almost as excited. Despite my pleas, a man who worked in the gym said he couldn't sell the hotel's springs but could acquire another set just like them—five shiny silver springs, more tightly wound than any I had ever owned. Each thirteen inches long, the springs were attached with metal clips to two blue four-inch-long plastic handles. Each spring could be attached separately to each handle, which meant that I could stretch between one and five springs at once. Although I'm no muscle man, I had trained myself to stretch all five springs at the same time. I thought of this accomplishment as one great feat for one man, if not for mankind.

My Pakistani ally and I arranged a secret meeting outside the hotel for the following Friday night, when the man promised to bring a fresh set of springs. A furtive rendezvous was necessary because Pakistanis aren't allowed to be in Western-owned hotels unless they are working. Nor are they allowed to do personal business on company time. Because of those restrictions, we met in the shadows at nine o'clock outside the hotel grounds on the man's day off. Any observer who watched this transaction might have wondered where the bodies were, or the hashish, but all we were doing was trading in a set of rare exercise springs that cost ten dollars. I gave the man twenty dollars because that was the smallest bill I had. Besides, a ten-dollar tip for the man's troubles and risks, and for such a rare find, seemed fair enough. The simple but mysterious-looking deal took mere seconds in the gloaming of shadowy Islamabad. True to the form of such arrangements, I never saw the stranger again.

Those springs remain memorable beyond measure, like the piece of a chalked cement baseline that I lifted from the abandoned officers' club tennis court at the old military base at Wuensdorf in the former East Germany just after the end of communism when Soviet troops had pulled out. That was long after the base was controlled by Frederick Barbarossa and later by a singular tyrannical killer named Hitler. Those memorabilia rest in my office with a cluster of raw cotton that I had plucked from a field in Uzbekistan in 1992, on the road from Tashkent to Samarkand. The cement baseline and the cotton balls pose next to the small reddish-colored rock that I rescued in 2002 from the rubble of the gigantic 1,400-year-old Buddha statues which the Taliban destroyed during a venomous rage of religious and tribal hatred in Bamiyan, Afghanistan. The past was indeed past, yet its memories enlivened my presence in the woods, and my writing there.

Memories from the New Hampshire woods also live on, tangible as they are and impossible to forget. A walking stick, for example, handed to me by a stranger in his yard near Woodman Marsh, stands angled with a spray of umbrellas inside the front entrance to our house. An antiques store in Northwood, New Hampshire, yielded a sleek wooden plinth, atop which sits a sculpture crafted by a master from Ukraine who moved to Jerusalem. The sculpture and plinth now adorn a corner of our dining room. Seclusion and the opportunity to think and write a book—probably the best of all roaming rewards—are rooted in the woods themselves. Those gifts can be the most difficult to measure, but in the end are the easiest to identify.

Rusting and quietly suffering from metal fatigue even in storage, my Pakistani springs are static and no longer appeal. The springs have been replaced in my exercise kit by wide rubber bands that won't overstretch, snap and plunge into my jugular vein. Open-heart surgery played more than a tiny part in my decision to retire the springs permanently.

A careful reader should by now have questioned how I knew dates and days of the week when I had no television and no newspaper delivery at Lucas Pond. When nature and solitude were my bunkmates, I kept a diary, three magical tomes in all, full of observations, ruminations and notes about battling demons plotting to thwart my writing. All I needed to know was one date, which I could get from a newspaper at Irving's convenience store, and I could track the following days in my journal. My unerring calendar was, however, a wireless. The little cabin on Big Buck Road—where

I dreamed what to write and how, kept muscles in tone, cooked and ate my personal cuisine, occasionally showered, and generally huddled in a circle that hugged a propane gas heater and two small electric radiators—came with a secret radio.

Nests of surprises, small and large, greeted me in the cabin's main room on that first morning. Near the ice-covered bay window squatted a square cluster of black plastic. A close look revealed a radio that appeared more sophisticated than it was. After spying that technological marvel, I decided, following much internal debate, to let the radio erode my rules of isolation. There were limits, however. The radio was allowed only as I exercised, prepared and ate my haute cuisine, played cribbage or did crosswords, each of which was designed to give my subconscious time to think and talk to me and, if another secret must be told, to allow my conscious self to dodge the hard job of sitting down to write.

At first I resented the radio as meddlesome, an intruder. The wireless almost convicted me of cheating based on self-incriminating charges that I wasn't as isolated as I should have been or thought I was. Before long, however, I realized that Garrison Keillor would be my friend. A wizard of sorts, he smartly filled in the long periods of dead time; he was my electronic equivalent of reading for pleasure, inspiration and confirmation. One April morning, on his brief but brilliant Writer's Almanac, Keillor quoted the American playwright August Wilson: "Your willingness to wrestle with your demons will cause your angels to sing." Keillor and Wilson remained on my mind and in my pocket as I battled the demons of doubt and stroked the angels, temporal though mine were. After waking each day, I turned on National Public Radio for Maine or New Hampshire, searching for angels. Most often a droning voice eventually told me the hour that I didn't want to know.

News—mostly the police blotter—on the radio never interested me. Decades earlier I had blotted bank robberies, headlines preceded by police sirens, and convenience store holdups from my sight and mind. If I wasn't listening to Garrison Keillor for five minutes on a weekday morning or an hour or so on a weekend, I turned the dial to classical music from Maine Public Radio in the morning. Internet use I limited to basic fact-checking, my standard being to check three sites before I felt certain of small facts.

Even those feints and dodges weren't wasted. They were thinking and writing tools of an unusual order, regular aides for my subconscious writing mind when my conscious mind was wondering how thick the ice was or how the trout managed to leap in winter. From deep in the woods I was able to raise very few stations on the black plastic box with its twin speakers. Fortunately, the regulars were public radio stations in New Hampshire and Maine and, rarely, one in Boston. Come the autumn of 2004, my radio taboo was lifted further so I could hear, barely, whispers of the Boston Red Sox winning their first World Series Championship in a mere eighty-six years. For another moment, my mind wandered wildly: too bad Ted Williams, baseball's grand vizier, and Jack Sharkey, the former heavyweight boxing champ, weren't still in the neighborhood, where they exist together in Lucas Pond fishing lore, closer to myth than to legend.

Early on January 9, the radio genies were having a great day: as I was exercising, Alex Brodie greeted me from a scratchy public radio station in far off Boston, a lobster pot on this side of the great pond. With his authoritative voice striking perfect pitch and power, Alex was moderating a British Broadcasting Corporation program about domestic, as in British, politics. Alex was good, all-around good, at the news game, although his tennis, as I recall from personal experience, was a bit spotty. I knew Alex during my days reporting from Jerusalem in the early 1990s, when I was the Middle East correspondent for *The Atlanta Journal and Constitution* and the then seventeen other daily journals in the Cox Newspapers group. Alex was assigned to the BBC's Jerusalem Bureau, whose every dispatch spelled gravitas.

Alone in the New Hampshire woods—reading, thinking, writing—Sarajevo, Damascus, Moscow, Jerusalem, Karachi and dozens more cities in other climate zones joined me, however idiosyncratically. At the same time, the Caspian Sea, the Mediterranean, the Black Sea and the Baltic flowed through my mind like the gurgling brook that tumbled from Woodman Marsh into Lucas Pond. That's what seclusion, writing, and thinking, did for me; they insinuated the past into the present and the present into the past so people and places merged in the form of words and ideas. This happened to me over and over when I lived at Lucas Pond, writing stories about tribes and voices, peaks and valleys, far away but never really too far away. Via England and Boston, Alex Brodie's public radio voice caught up to me in the woods, but it was the Alex Brodie I knew in Jerusalem whom I heard.

A few days before Alex assumed his post in Jerusalem, his predecessor had tossed a great artifact onto the street outside the Beit Agron press building in that contested city. The BBC teletype machine, printer and instruction booklet—long dormant and no longer needed but of no slight historical value in my mind—were being dumped into history's trash bin before my incredulous eyes. After determining that the machine and its trappings were indeed intended to join the weighty shards of pottery, biblical testimonials, mosaics and other remnants of the ancestral dead and their times, I hauled those pieces of journalistic history to my house in the Ramat Eshkol neighborhood of West Jerusalem. Two years later, I ferried those artifacts to another rented house in the Emek Refaim (German Colony) area of the city. To London, England, Juno Beach and Palm Beach Gardens in Florida, and to Portsmouth, New Hampshire, those tools of journalism past journeyed with me during the next decade. More than twenty years after their rescue, those artifacts reside now, still wrapped and ready to be moved again, at my home in Dover, near New Hampshire's coast. With proper attention, I'm convinced the BBC teletype machine could be brought back to life.

My only concern, however, would be that copy sent via a BBC teletype would end up exclusively in British colonies and protectorates that no longer exist.

Last I read, Alex Brodie had left the BBC several years ago to open a brewery in England's lake district. If he tired of being an instrument that public figures could use to tell varnished truths and unvarnished lies, I understood.

Next to the writing dodge in all its forms, preparing food was my most time-consuming and ceaseless chore in the cabin. A chronic condition called hypoglycemia, or low blood sugar, a flaw familiar to anyone who knows me well, keeps me constantly thinking about my next bowl of pasta or porridge, or an aromatic meatball sandwich loaded with onions and peppers. During one office move at the *Miami* (Florida) *News*, I found four sandwiches—black, moldy and looking like dead rats—in the bottom right-hand drawer of my desk. Remnants of a long ago, all-night work session, I had stashed the emergency rations to ward off a hunger attack at five in the morning, just before deadline. Stuffed under letters to the editor, those sandwiches quickly lost all meaning.

No matter how much food I lugged into the cabin, it never seemed enough. Like a bad tune by a starving country-western singer, food was always on my mind. Always, whether preparing or eating it, walking seven miles to buy salad supplies, hauling a carload of survival protein back from Portsmouth, or writing about it. Compared with endlessly satisfying my food fetish, staying warm became as simple as making a salad—after the cabin's interior thawed and snapped to life from a little heat, a reverse version of the pond's cracking and roaring as the ice deepened and expanded.

My storehouse of basic foods was more than enough to last a month, as it did. Boxes of linguine, penne, shells, ziti and rigatoni, along with shredded wheat were piled high atop the refrigerator. Cans of tuna, baked beans and tomatoes in various sizes and forms—sliced, diced and plum—filled the lower cupboards.

A gallon of olive oil reigned as king of the cupboards. Boxes of instant mashed potatoes, instant powdered milk and instant oatmeal, plus an herbal-garden variety of spices for my special red sauce weighed down the kitchen table. A tiny space—nearest the gas heater—on the table was reserved for my cribbage games. A clearing close to the sink was my dining spot. Mr. Lou's was the name of my red sauce, which, by the way, hasn't been patented.

Here, the truth must be told: I leaned on cribbage for inspiration as others leaned on John Barleycorn. Played solo in the woods, cribbage was a sorcerer's card game worthy of its own appendage, actually an appendix, for its value as a writing tool that defies logical explanation.

If you haven't guessed it by now, if forced to live alone on an island with only one kind of food, I would choose pasta, any version. I could live on pasta and tomato sauce and never miss a meal, although I prefer to enliven the Italian grains with chicken and turkey, along with the tuna, salmon and swordfish steaks that rocked the freezer. It's remarkable what a person can call haute cuisine when that person is his own chef.

Into the gaping fridge I stuffed more vittles—eggs, fake butter, loaves of multi-grain bread, cheese slices and a variety of condiments. Oranges, apples and frozen orange juice added a bit of spice to my diet, if fruits can be spicy. On a small desk, hidden in plain sight outside one of the freezer-like bedrooms, rested a large container of salted peanuts and a sizable bag of popcorn. Those were my snacks. I didn't go hungry, but eating every meal alone has a weird way of making a pantry seem paltry regardless of its size. No matter how hard I tried to make a meal more tasty and exotic, mere repetition dulled them and bored me. But even that couldn't dampen my interest in dining alone, eating being a rather critical component of survival.

Mine was not a sparsely equipped cabin, especially in the kitchen. So many pots, pans, dishes, cups, glasses and utensils hid in cupboards and drawers that I could have lived for a month without washing one kitchen tool. Still, I cleaned up after each meal to avoid being swamped by dishes and pots caked with yesterday's grub. Without taxing my cabin's supplies, I could have had a banquet for everyone living on the shores of Lucas Pond in winter, maybe even in summer with its more numerous visitors. Only a chef would have been required. All of this was in rather luxurious contrast to the small, rectangular blue and brown bag I shouldered over mountains and across deserts in Asia, Europe, and North and East Africa. That overnight bag contained work papers and books, one change of clothes and personal health items designed to last a month. My erstwhile travel companion that I still possess measures nineteen inches long by fifteen inches wide by eight inches deep. Please note that those measurements are in inches. No food was stuffed into that puny bag, not even a snort of whisky. Bottled water, oranges, pistachios and walnuts I carried by hand until they flew from the truck that carried me along the rutted dirt road to the Tigris River on the way from Syria into Iraq in the late winter of 1991. My dining pleasures on the road varied, however, ranging from five-star hotels in large cities to a watery gruel that, despite being famished, I rejected as a matter of survival while reporting on a world-class famine in Somalia's bush country.

But where, writers and newspaper hacks might ask, were the whisky, beer and wine? The hops, where did I stash the keg, the bottles and cans? Surprising and maybe disappointing to some, those oily writing tools never came close to the cabin door, which makes me, in the eyes of many, a lousy loner.

Although never a teetotaler, neither did I ever chug-a-lug a jug of home brew to win a bet. Once or twice I became ill from swilling too much vodka, although drinking foul water in Tashkent was a greater danger than drinking too much vodka and vino at a banquet there. Enjoying a little wine socially was and remains my specialty, although not when I was camping too long in a hangout for journalists in Jerusalem, Beirut or Moscow, or drinking half-pints of Guinness to every two pints poured down by friendly locals in East London's Ferry House pub. Drinking, as some would say, wasn't in me. Living alone also raised fears that alcohol in any measure would become a crutch that I could never toss into the pond. If doing crosswords and playing cribbage stimulated my subconscious, I might have leaned too hard on alcohol to do the same. Abstinence was my solution.

Another question: where was my lumberjack beard? Easy answer. Gray beards look great on other graybeards, but gray reminds me too much of aging. A two-day beard was the most for me. After that, the battery-operated razor that I bought years earlier in Dubai's mammoth duty-free zone buzzed into service to wipe out the whiskers. Tucked between the instant mashed potato and powdered milk cartons on the kitchen table, the razor that fit neatly into the palm of my hand greeted me daily so I wouldn't forget.

After exercises on my first shivering morning, I poured fifty-six ounces of whole plum tomatoes with basil leaves into a King Henry VIII-size pot. Into that I splashed twelve ounces of tomato paste, large doses of garlic pepper, oregano, olive oil from my bottomless jug and enough raw garlic to drive off the shadowy deer or bring them closer. Measuring cups and dainty spoons were foreigners in my kitchen where volume ruled.

Playing grandmother without the tools, I told my diary, "Let sauce simmer to taste." Dump out and start over, others might have said. But I liked my sauce. Why wouldn't I? It was mine, and one pot lasted a week.

Often I lingered over preparations of a mound of grub while I was reading, writing in longhand or otherwise waiting for my subconscious to shout. That was a time-saver, most of the time. Thinking creatively, I brought in a New Hampshire specialty, a three-pound, three-ounce can of New England clam chowder. What a treat, I thought. After I dumped the glob of cement-like chowder into a pan fit for contestants in a twenty-four hour glutton contest, I gagged and couldn't even look at the mess. Down the toilet and into the pond it went. Do trout like clams? I wondered. Maybe turtles do. It was well past my post-cabin life before New England clam chowder crossed my palate again.

Rather than stare at my simmering red sauce on Day One in the cabin, I ate two slices of multigrain toast, a large glass of orange juice, removed from its frozen state, and a cup of tea. Then the phone rang. Paul Dale's local landline, I learned later after running up a huge long-distance phone bill, had a range of something like two towns in the winter, when he and his family camped elsewhere. Beyond that range, all calls were long distance. "May I speak to the homeowner, please?" a male voice said. "Who are you?" I asked, while struggling to grasp the plastic receiver. "New Hampshire Exteriors," the man said. I laughed, thinking of the cold inside and out; to me, New Hampshire exteriors meant sub-zero. "I'm not interested in anything you're selling," I said, before pulling off my gloves, sticking one hand over the gas heater and using the other to grip the phone at the end of an extension line that was long enough to circle the house. I laughed to myself again. Here I stood alone in a rented cabin on the shores of an ice-filled pond in the woods in winter and someone selling shingles and siding for houses rends my isolation.

After I hung up, muttering, I wrote in my journal, "Those assholes catch up to you everywhere." Nothing personal, of course, but one unerring and annoying constant of my time in the cabin was the unsolicited calls from people or machines offering free cruises, selling direct satellite television service or credit cards with low interest rates, tempting me with six days and five nights on the French Riviera, mysteriously looking for someone named Rita, and several callers selling newspapers, one with a wonderful New Hampshire line, "Are you seeing the paper there?"

At 7 p.m. on that same day, another caller sliced through my insular life with one of many familiar and dull interruptions. The caller was selling *Foster's Daily Democrat*, a Dover, New Hampshire, newspaper. Not today, I answered, astounded that someone trying to sell a newspaper in mid-winter was calling a cabin in the woods where humans usually hang out only in summer. No wonder newspapers are taking a dive, I thought, as I grappled with my book about reporting for newspapers from overseas for ten years.

The landline was an ally, most of the time, especially when I wanted to connect my computer to the Internet. Before I realized that my calls were long, long distance and later changed my Internet link to a telephone number closer to the cabin, I ran up a bill worthy of calls from the banks of the Khabur River on the Turkish-Iraqi border. I wasn't just imagining that possibility because, believe it or not, twelve years earlier I had filed stories to my Washington bureau from a pay phone in that remote area using my old handy Tandy 200 computer. After my plea of ignorance about the long, long distance calls, the local telephone company in New Hampshire cut my bill by several hundred dollars, which was almost in half, more testimony to how nice people in small-town New Hampshire can be.

More New Hampshire courtesies fell into my lap on March 4, 2004, five days before my sixty-third birthday. In the mood for pizza and a newspaper, and to run from a blank page, I jogged to the convenience store at Irving's gas station on Route 4, the original New Hampshire Turnpike that links Portsmouth and the coast to Concord, the state capital, about fifty miles to the west. A veggie pizza was on my mind as usual, but the veggie bin was empty. "Oh, no problem," the young woman behind the counter said, "we'll make you a veggie and you'll have it in four minutes." I paid for the pizza and a copy of *The New York Times*. Then I read and read, waited and waited, for my pizza. After I finished reading the paper, I asked the clerk if she had called my number and I missed it, although I didn't have a number because the place was so small that no number was necessary. A delay of any sort was no great inconvenience because I had been reading the paper and was in no rush to face a blank page back at the cabin. "I'm so sorry, I'm so sorry," the clerk said, embarrassed, effusive in her apology and begging for forgiveness. "Please excuse us. We'll have the pizza right away." When she brought my pizza, pronto this time, the clerk returned the money that I paid for the pizza and the newspaper and gave me a coupon for a free sub sandwich. Please come back, she said, as if I might not. With deals like this, I couldn't afford not to return. Besides, my legs and I had few other choices.

On another visit to Irving's, as I waited for two slices of pizza, I was startled to hear a young man lament to a young woman he was wooing, "Yesterday, I was hit and run."

Small courtesies such as those at Irving's, examples of the pleasant behavior and simplicity of life in rural places, buoyed me. They were almost as alluring as the cocoon created by the cabin, woods and pond.

Exercise was another daily companion. Stretches, sit-ups and pushups started my day, not at dawn but whenever nature woke me. After exercising I piled on more heavy shirts and sweaters to replace my igloo made of blankets. What served as pajamas stayed on until I could no longer survive the odor and switched to another set from the pile of very cold clothing waiting in one of the rear bedrooms. A tight-fitting wool hat I bought a decade earlier in Heidelberg, Germany, in preparation for a trip to Bosnia, never left my head in winter, if you don't count time out to shower. I was then, and remain, a religious believer in the scientific dictum that most body heat escapes from the head. Breakfast, there's that ever-present food again, was often quick and easy: oatmeal and multigrain toast but sometimes scrambled eggs and toast along with orange juice usually filled the cavity by ten in the morning. Shredded wheat was a substitute on occasion, but usually I left that for an evening snack. Sometimes breakfast was lunch, or lunch was breakfast.

This book-writing stuff is hard work, I learned, nothing like writing most newspaper stories, opinion columns or editorials. It's difficult because it's always on your mind. It can't be any other way. If it is any other way, I suspect, you'll have no book. It nags. It gnaws. It wakes you at night, even wakes you when you're awake. Couldn't play one-man cribbage or do crosswords, whip through sit-ups and curl twenty pound weights, make a meal, shower, stroll on or around the pond or through the woods, walk seven miles for groceries, talk to a reverend who lived in the woods, visit a vegan restaurant or a country store that dates to 1824, just to hear human voices; search for invisible deer, watch territorial trout harass smaller fish, gaze at pond water reflecting the trees and sky, look in awe at Canada geese cruising over trees and skimming to a silent stop on the inky water, sneak a gaze at the tenderness of a mother duck shielding her babies—without thinking about my book. That meant thinking about war zones, killers and the killed in Asia, Africa and Europe, or about the order and titles of chapters, even the book title itself before the book was even finished and the search for an agent and a publisher began.

Long dream last night. I was reading my notes from Macedonia, exactly as I wrote them, but which I don't have with me. I was driving through Macedonia, meeting people, talking with U.N. and American soldiers, peering across the mountains toward Serbia. It seemed real, which it wasn't because I was dreaming. But it had happened.—February 27, 2004

Night Life

It was the dreams wot did it, a headline writer at a London tabloid might scribble. Every night the dreams that slung tribal arrows at me from Northern Ireland to Bosnia, south to Algeria and Somalia, across the Middle East and Central Asia to Afghanistan and Pakistan revived the stories that belonged in a book. The dreams became regular excursions into my recent past. They stimulated ideas about how to write the stories in a book, zeroing in as they did on religion, tribe, culture, land, history, language and revenge as the deep wells of conflict. Those dreams drove me into the woods in winter to write the book that was ripe to be harvested from my notes, my expense receipts and my memory. With those dreams gnawing at me nightly, the stories swelled and brightened like springtime in Paris. The more I dreamed, the more I wrote; the more I wrote, the more I dreamed. Prodding me with ideas, reflections and recollections of people and scenes, my dreams opened paths to finish stories and chapters, even to solve the puzzle of how to arrange the chapters.

My subconscious clarified my conscious recollections, sharpened and solidified what I was trying to write when I stared at the computer. Clarity of events past came on the wings of my dreams. Not a pure writer, although not impure either, I am foremost a reporter and persistent pain-in-the-arse digger. Within eight hours of landing in a German city, for example, I had located a woman, hitherto unidentified and unknown, who had been raped by several

American soldiers on a U.S. army base. The following morning, I took photos of the room on the army base where the violent attack occurred. Shortly after the formal end of the first Persian Gulf War, I boarded a rowboat that leaked like a spaghetti strainer and crossed the Tigris River from Syria into bleeding Iraq; too many long days after that, I fled with fifteen other journalists from Iraq to Turkey on a less-than-crafty raft that floated too far downstream before making it across the Habur River. On other occasions, if a question hung in the air, unasked, I asked it.

When it comes to writing and other art forms, dreams occupy a warm and well-worn niche. That corner is firmly established in art and history. By his actions and his words, Sam Clemens, better known for commercial purposes as Mark Twain, praised the role of his subconscious, which he also called the unconscious, in his long, brilliant and provocative writing life. When Clemens was stymied for ideas about how to make a story work, his writing tank empty, he went on walkabouts, sometimes putting aside a manuscript for several years. What refilled his tank, Clemens wrote, was "unconscious and profitable cerebration." I can imagine Clemens working on his books when he didn't even know he was doing so until his conscious mind bellowed that the time was right to write again.

Louis Armstrong talked about how one night while touring in North Dakota he couldn't get a song out of his head. The lyrics, he said, "just kept hittin'." His answer was to "put it right," to "do it now while it's on my mind," by getting out of bed at four o'clock in the morning and scribbling the words on paper. *Someday (You'll Be Sorry)*, is the name of that tune. If Satchmo could wake in the middle of a night to write a dream song that just kept on hittin', the least I could do was to wake in the darkness to give life on paper to the women in Somalia who ate strips of rawhide in desperate bids to survive drought, famine and tribal war. In Somalia, I wished that death itself had died, so often were bodies heaped upon one another in shallow graves along a street outside a food pantry. But death doesn't die; it marches on and on, although individual lives do not. Starving Somali women were not alone in my conscious mind or my notes. They lived in my dreams with scores of others like them, including the old man who huddled alone in a hut in a Lebanese mountain village, tending a few vegetables and small fruit trees at his door while rubble from constant bombardment piled high outside his cave.

Dreams are linked to creativity in ways well reported but little understood. Scientists are targeting the brain, a universe of mystery unto itself, for clues about how dreams and creativity cohabitate. Machines may detect dreamlike activity during deep sleep, but no machine I know of can translate the content of dreams as they occur, or even later. Neither can a machine measure precisely why or how particular dreams occur, how exactly the conscious self seeks help from the subconscious, and why the subconscious dreams about certain subjects but not others. Psychologists are also doing their part to probe the relationship among dreams, creativity and individuals. Good luck to them, I say.

Most people don't write entire books, songs or poems in their dreams, but some do. Many more people do solve everyday problems by "sleeping" on them. We've all heard it; when a decision is too difficult to make on the spot, a person says, "Let me sleep on it." That's just another way of saying let me think about it, let my subconscious work on it, give me time, if I'm lucky, to dream about it.

Insomnia was never my problem. A notebook, pen and a small flashlight that lay on the wide, wood planks beside my igloo saved an idea conceived in dreamy darkness from being lost after dawn's early light. Rising quickly to write kept my dreams alive. When a dream woke me, I rose and scribbled the revelations immediately so they would be book notes later, after I broke the fast. Some dreams—vivid, detailed, broad and singly pertinent to important sections of my book—forced me to jump from bed, turn on the lamp over my left shoulder where I sat to write, crank up the computer and begin banging the keyboard for two or three hours. There I wrote until the thread had been exhausted and I could return to sleep, hoping to continue the dream at the point where it had forced me into consciousness. Often that worked.

Winter's Darkness, Framed.

On many, maybe most, occasions, what I thought were diamonds at three in the morning looked like soft coal at noon. What the hell was I thinking? I asked the dormant flies and the spiders hanging out in the frigid corners near the bay window, and the field mice that visited the sink occasionally. Whether the spiders in winter were really alive or simply not quite dead I hadn't yet figured out. What I thought was all that mattered to me anyway because the insects weren't talking or even moving. This much I did know: when I wrote my dreams, I had black on white, which Flaubert told de Maupassant was essential to converting ideas into actual writing, to give life to the blank page. After jotting down my dreams I always had something new to work with, to massage, polish or erase, that I lacked before the night's reveries.

As I came to understand it, dreaming was a way of thinking about what I wanted to think about without consciously thinking about it. Dreams provided the loose, less literal free association of ideas that often escaped my conscious mind. My subconscious carried the nighttime load. While I thought about my book every waking moment, my subconscious did the thinking when I slept, and sometimes even when I was conscious, like dreaming while awake although those weren't the same as nighttime dreams. I became like an urban convenience store, open 24/7 for consciously and subconsciously thinking and dreaming about my book. It's not surprising that nearly all of the dreams I could recall during this time related directly to my all-consuming book. Those dreams happened all the time; I couldn't have turned them off if I wanted to.

One dream I had often in the cabin concerned a respected friend who was reporting from the Middle East. This was pure fiction, even in dreaming terms. The friend in my dream wasn't in the Middle East at all, and never had been. But I lived and worked there. My interpretation of this dream was that I was trying to absorb my friend's writing skills and somehow insert them into my own work. Hell, my subconscious may have thought, my other side needed help and tapping into another person was worth a try. The subconscious, after all, can be devious and serpentine, and deviations gave my conscious mind assistance in its book-writing chores. Nightmarish dreams, which occasionally assaulted me in the cabin, concerned losing my notes a few days before taking final exams in college or forgetting the classrooms where the finals were being held. Those kinds of dreams, I convinced myself, were my subconscious mind's way of giving its book-writing side a rest. Or perhaps my own cooking—a bad batch of homemade spaghetti sauce—had upset my stomach enough to muddle the rhythm of my bookish dreams. Now and then, I branched out into the world of weird dreams. One night I learned that my wife was a bigamist who was also married to an itinerant California vegetable salesman, which Pat vehemently denied. Steinbeck's novels must have been locked deep in my subconscious, or in Pat's, which she transferred to mine.

To help my conscious self, I taped notes of my writing wisdom, or lack of same, on large sheets of paper all around my cabin's main room. This may not seem innovative to others, but to me it was magical. Detail, detail, detail, I wrote. Use humor. Face the blank page. Face the fear of failure. Write something, anything, every day. Read good writing. Tell the truths, the real truths not just the facts. Use understatement. Capture color. Beat the demons of doubt. You can do it. Write anytime, anywhere. Walk in the woods, and think. Walk for groceries, and think. Play cribbage. Do crosswords. Free my subconscious. Don't write myself dry each day. Let today point the way to tomorrow.

The demons, the doubts, were daunting and persistent. But Voltaire traveled with me, too. Thinking of him, I became an optimist who took the long view. It was, after all, Voltaire who wrote, "Doubt is not a pleasant condition, but certitude is absurd."

Though totally psychological, the demons of doubt were as real as the deer I knew were watching me but that I never spotted. Throughout that writing year in the woods, the range of doubts was wide and didn't vanish because the questions of finding a publisher and wondering how the book would be received remained long after I typed the last period. Was the subject worthy? Could I pull the chapters together? Could I write it well enough? Would anyone like my book? Doubts like that, in various forms, haunted me as much as the dreams helped me. Every doubt I had about the value of the stories I was writing was followed by certainty because deep inside I knew that I had compelling and revealing tales to tell. Still, every certainty was trailed by nagging doubts and doubts were followed by certainty. When I wrote senseless sentences, common sense followed—the knowledge that rewriting is essential all the time. One moment I would think that if a sentence were not perfect at first draft, it was worthless. The next moment I buried that thought with another, more accurate, reality: rewrite, rewrite, rewrite, that's the way to go. Before long, I came to embrace rewriting. Still, that circle of doubt followed by certainty dogged me whether I was doing push-ups, cooking penne, playing cribbage, puzzling over crosswords, reading Joseph Conrad while exploring the woods, dreaming of Ted Williams fishing on Lucas Pond or walking my trash without a leash.

From that first night in the cabin the book took over my life, became my life, which was the point. Wherever I went and whatever I did the essential pen and paper walked with me, just like my fingers and toes, so I could record the assistance of my subconscious. Whether I was awake or sleeping, my subconscious worked all the time. Ideas, broad concepts about how to tell the stories and connect them, flowed from my inner mind. Words and sentences usually came later, after I wrote the ideas on paper and began composing on the computer. To remember the ideas that my subconscious poured out I carried a notebook as I wore a hat, always, except during my infrequent showers. Even then I tossed those blank sheets of notebook paper and accompanying ink on the floor outside the small shower stall so I would be ready when my subconscious spoke. Whether in the cabin or outdoors acting like a tinhorn woodsman, a Reporter's Notebook and a pen were extensions of my body. Vigilance was required because my subconscious was always grinding, usually when I didn't know it, until an idea went from mind to pen to paper. My assistants were many, literally everything I saw or did. Motorists who would or wouldn't stop for a hitchhiker, me, proved as useful as great blue heron nesting or Canada geese gliding to the pond, or the invisible deer that left their trails of scat that led me nowhere near the animals themselves.

People and places, those precious veins that I would mine for the book I was writing, were locked in my memory and in the dozens of notebooks I kept during my nearly ten years as a correspondent. Those details of my reporting and traveling life were much more ingrained in me than living alone in the woods during all four seasons of one year. Organizing my thoughts and writing about tribal conflicts in Europe, Africa and Asia were only a few of the mountains I had to surmount. To climb those ridges and cliffs, to cross those rivers and deserts, I knew that I would have to conquer myself, my own varied fears about being able to write a book well enough to entice others to read.

My new neighborhood proved much easier to navigate than I expected. Most people who live far from cities and towns do so because they yearn for separation. Many aren't readily communal or even social, so they don't talk much to each other. They are even more wary of strangers. In Northern New England, a cultural and learned reticence adds to the distance. I walked the narrow line between bothering people and telling them who I was, where I was living and what I was doing. Information, I found, eased fears, led to a few, but not many, questions about my work, and generally convinced people that I was just like them and the rest of their neighbors. I simply wanted to be left alone.

"Hey, mister, we hear you're writing a book. Are you writing a horror story? Are you writing a mystery? Is it a murder story?" The shouts came from several teenage boys, who had interrupted my walk along the top of Bigelow Road, as spring was beginning to silence winter. Rumors had reached their ears, I thought, or maybe their imaginations ran away from reality when they wondered about the stranger writing alone in a cabin in *their* woods. They were thinking gore—a dead body unearthed in the woods or a murder under a full moon in an ancient cemetery. After telling those kids that I was writing about the tribal roots of conflicts around the world, I never heard from the inquisitors again. Young though they were, those kids might have been as open and inquisitive as they would ever be, although the error, I hoped, would be mine.

From living alone in the woods to constantly jotting notes, following my advice taped to the cabin walls, writing my conscious and subconscious thoughts, my schemes were meant for me alone. That is surely a relief to others. My writing eccentricities weren't designed to be a text for how to write a book. If they were, fewer books would be written. There is, for sure, no formula for writing that works for everyone. If a formula were possible, I wouldn't be the person to devise it. As Somerset Maugham said, "There are three rules for writing a novel. Unfortunately, no one knows what they are." Fortunately, I wasn't writing a novel, but I was writing a book and I followed my own rules, a few of which no doubt were novel. I needed all of my tricks to transfer the stories from brain to paper to computer. Even my approach to writing each chapter differed, not because I planned it that way but because that's how it turned out.

Seclusion—fleeing into a forest or cave to write—has proven a necessary starting point for many. But exactly what is seclusion? Is it only physical? Montaigne wrote his famous essays in the library of his own house. He wasn't physically secluded, but he was mentally isolated. Exile offers an extreme and unwelcome form of *isolation*, and it worked brilliantly for Dante. Banished from his beloved Florence for nearly twenty years, Dante managed to cobble together a little tome, *The Divine Comedy*, during his time as an outcast. Volumes have been written in customs houses, fire-watch towers on mountaintops, in prisons, bars and power plants, on rolls of toilet paper, in cars parked in the woods at midnight, in cemeteries, and in small rooms in small houses. Books have been written just about everywhere people breathe, even entirely in the writer's head before a word was put down on paper or anywhere else. Does the latter writer, I wonder, rewrite in his head? If so, how does that work? Does black ink work better than blue ink? My method may add to the list of the idiosyncratic, but I make no apologies for that.

A strict writing schedule eluded me. Look elsewhere for information about the best time to write—such as write from seven in the morning to noon daily, read for two hours each afternoon and take every fourth Saturday off to shower and trim the beard. I had my own personal version of flextime: write something, anything, every day, no matter how jumbled and no matter what time. Whatever I wrote could always be rewritten many times over. My only other writing trick, an old one widely used, was never to write the well dry on any day. The point was to leave something ripe and dangling, ready for harvest, so I would have a good place to begin on the following day. My work habits, such as they were and are, often found me writing late at night so I could keep the promise to myself, to write something every day. I kept that pledge each day I lived in the cabin at Lucas Pond.

Before and after I became secluded in the woods, it was indeed the dreams wot did it. But the dreams did not function in isolation. Without pen, notebook and computer keyboard as accomplices, my dreams would have had no soil in which to flower. If forced to nail my writing commandments to a cabin door, the rules would read like this: hole up alone somewhere, focus all waking hours on your book, on thinking, reading and writing; let your subconscious do its job, and lash paper and pen to your body so you can record the creativity that the deeper self pours into your conscious mind all the time.

Back on January 9, 2004, my first morning in the cabin, I shivered for a time and raised the blinds at the bay window in the main room. A few moments later, I opened the curtain inside the small window over the kitchen sink. The entry of morning light, always dramatic when propelled by the sun, reminded me of a relief pitcher striding in from the bullpen to save the game.

Slivers of light and hope greeted me across the ice-covered bay window. The light reflected blue and white as it angled in weird and conflicting patterns through the ice crystals stuck to the glass. The ice still blocked my view, but my imagination was enhanced. Crosswords to dust off the cobwebs of my mind and one-man cribbage awaited me after I ate a light breakfast and played beginner chef conjuring up my red spaghetti sauce. Word games and card games, walks in the woods and other diversions deflected me from the hard task of writing, which was the real point of fleeing to the woods. But even the diversions prodded my subconscious. As many have noted, the hardest part about writing is, surprise, sitting down to write. The second hardest thing is actually writing, the problem with writing being that there are too many ways to get it wrong, too many combinations of letters and words to create confusion. And that says nothing about plumbing the aquifer for ideas, some worthy, others not.

January 11 was a night of fitful sleep. The hours were filled as much with waking to jot my dreams into a notebook as they were for sleeping. Each time I woke to write notes about my dreams, I was able to return to sleep and continue with the same dreams. This pattern became habit-forming. It continued throughout my writing days in the woods.

Pat called early. The vet said Delilah should be put to sleep. Pat came to get me at mid-day so we could take our Jerusalem cat on her last ride. Very sad. I sobbed until Pat came.—February 7, 2004

A Superior Being

Jerusalem was calling when my phone rang at midday on February 7. I sensed the source because our wild, wise and beautiful cat had been painfully ill. Dreading the inevitable, I felt instinctively that, in some form, our Jerusalem-born cat Delilah was at the other end of the line. Fluffy with big fur but weighing only six pounds, Delilah offered a simple example of how the past is always present, never past, in our conscious and subconscious minds. It is impossible to forget the vengeful critter that urinated on me as I slept in Jerusalem, played feline pitch-and-catch baseball with the best of them in London, and in many a vet's office roared like a lion defending the pride, frightening nearby animals, two-legged and four-legged alike. In her own way, Delilah offered evidence that all living things are connected.

Speaking for Delilah, Pat was on the line, and she didn't speak in tongues. A survivalist born to harass and to last beyond others of her kind, our wise old cat was at the end of her long road on her third and last continent. Kidney failure. Seemingly ageless, Delilah had more frequent flier miles than most humans, but that didn't give her another free ride. For two years we had used a form of feline dialysis to keep Delilah alive and growling. Now, the vet said, Delilah's most humane friend should be euthanasia.

This was Day 26 in the cabin, and only then was I flipping the switch all the way from living in the woods to writing in the woods. Delilah's impending end caused a stutter in my work as it provoked memories of her life and mine. As it turned out, for domesticated cats the dark and thorny woods were out of bounds. Cats, even the wild variety, were like the elusive deer; I never saw one of either species during my year in the woods. Not a puma, cougar, panther, catamount, mountain lion, snow leopard or kin by any other name caught my eye. Not even a smaller fisher cat or a bobcat.

Memories of Delilah's Jerusalem origins and her travels with us fit snugly into my writing life. Her death, however, would be a sad way to remember her exciting years. Delilah was another thread that stretched from Jerusalem to Lucas Pond. She adopted us in Jerusalem, traveled with us halfway around the world and would die with us a world away from her birthplace somewhere along the fractious border between Israelis and Palestinians.

After Pat told me that Delilah was doomed, I sat atop my igloo and mourned alone until Pat arrived from Portsmouth to mourn with me. Alone, I was left to think about Delilah's quirks and to dwell on a universal question that reaches beyond the death of a pet: Is it easier to cry alone or to share grief? The answer, I have concluded, varies with the individuals and the circumstances. Or maybe grieving alone differs so much from grieving with others that a comparison is futile. Pat arrived within two hours. We left the cabin immediately. Back in Portsmouth, Pat and I spent two days reminiscing about Delilah with little relief. This was humbling; a cat dies and humans, supposedly the superior beings, weep for days. Where lies the superiority? Delilah was part of our family, a large slice of the animal part of the human race perhaps. We attached human qualities to her that were better than human. Delilah was, for sure, several pegs up the ladder of life.

Before we drove to the vet's office on Delilah's last day, the afternoon of February 7, Pat and I lay on the floor next to the small, warmed bed where Delilah lay dying. No one had to tell Delilah that her traveling days were over. Weeping like children, we petted and talked to her, and alternated taking photos of her with each of us.

Because she had stopped eating, wise old Delilah knew what we knew. Pat carried Delilah in a blanket as I drove to the vet. No cat carrier on this trip. Delilah turned and snarled one final time when the vet anesthetized her. Then she breathed no more. Still weeping, Pat and I hugged Delilah as her body cooled, and we stayed with her for several minutes after she breathed her last. A vet's office is no place to hang out under any circumstances, so we took our sadness on the road. We pointed Pat's car to the town of New Castle adjacent to Portsmouth, and later swung along the ocean at Rye Beach. Grieving, I believe, it's called.

At home in Portsmouth, we moved Delilah's bed, carrier and the scratch pad she never used to a storage room. Delilah preferred to torment the hands and ankles of humans rather than scratch a pad, an inanimate object that didn't shout or chase her off. Her remains still rest in a small jar on a shelf in our library. For a decade, until we cancelled our landline, the message on our telephone answering machine named Delilah as a family member. After our tax accountant first heard the message, he asked whether we wanted Delilah listed as a dependent for tax purposes. Too late, we told our diligent tax man. We didn't tell him that Delilah was a cat.

* * *

No ordinary feral cat that became domesticated, but never fully so, Delilah's life for us was like a scrapbook bulging with a world of memories. She remained a roamer, which fit our family profile. Strangers were her pals, especially in Jerusalem, which was more good luck for us. Searching for food and friends led Delilah to us. Seldom did she report back with information about her travels, unless she hauled in a battered mouse or a warm chicken breast purloined from a neighbor's grille. She was, after all, only teaching her five beautiful kittens that hunting was essential to their survival. When she moaned loudly like a sick child, an ancestral call of the wild, we knew she was beckoning the kittens to her table and in a small way teaching them to forage and thus invigorate their species. Delilah gave birth in the dark secrecy of a closet my shoes called home, a privilege I accepted with pride.

Queen of the German Colony neighborhood in West Jerusalem, Delilah adopted us in 1992. With beauty enhanced by long, thick fur, Delilah was special and she knew it, so special that our name for her was a natural. She came without identification, and her ancestry remained a mystery. We lived in an apartment near railroad tracks at the time, so we decided to let the Israelis and Palestinians quarrel without resolution over her roots. All eyes and big color—brown, black and white—fierce, gorgeous without primping, intelligent, wily and Miss Personality, Delilah no doubt fingered us at first sight as the best of many worlds, a sure ticket to security and traveling the globe.

Jerusalem is renowned for its hordes of feral cats; Delilah was the queen of the leading pride on her block. Launched from the pit of her abdomen, Delilah's roar seemed to erupt from the depths of a jungle. Her exhale could be heard throughout a vet's office, scaring the hell out of everyone there. Feared and respected, Delilah forced veterinarians and technicians to wear long, thick rubber gloves when she visited.

Shortly after Delilah sniffed us out as easy marks in *her* Jerusalem neighborhood, she learned our routines. Survival was so much easier that way. She was at the door daily to greet Pat in the late afternoon. Her timing was clockwork perfect, much better than mine in the cabin at Lucas Pond. Before long Delilah entered our apartment without us. We left a grated window open so she could come and go as she pleased, which is how she did everything—naturally, and on her own terms.

Delilah traveled by car to the vet's office in Jerusalem when necessary, howling and snarling her way on those foreign jaunts. One of the great moments in her life, but not in mine, struck with malice aforethought while she and I were engaged in a weeks-long and deeply personal medical dispute. Devious and employing a secret weapon, Delilah won that battle. An infected eye compelled me to sneak up on Delilah one day as she slept, shove her into a cat carrier before she realized an enemy got the drop on her, and speed to a vet's office. After removing a blade of grass that had sliced into Delilah's right eye, the vet squirted medicine into the wound and gave me fighting instructions. For Delilah to heal, the vet advised, the same medicine had to be squirted into Delilah's wound every day. Let me repeat that: every day. Fine so far. But I was supposed to act as the vet. Not so fine.

The only way I could do the job was to catch her napping and squirt fast before she woke; Delilah's job was to stop me. I had only one shot to hit Delilah's slowly opening eye before she woke and turned rogue. I missed the target more than I hit it, which shifted the battle once a week to the vet's office to ensure that some medicine entered Delilah's eye. This was combat duty, I was losing and the war went on for three weeks before Delilah threw everything she had at me, or almost everything. To get revenge for my intrusions and to show that she was the boss, one night as I lay sleeping, lots of warm fluid seeped through a blanket and sheet onto my legs. This wasn't a dream. Puzzled about what was happening, I looked up. That's when I spotted beautiful Delilah squatting and strafing my legs with urine. Her message was not difficult to divine. As long as I tried to squirt medicine in her eye, she would bombard, not squirt, my legs with her urine. In cat language that any human could understand, Delilah's message was, "OK, pal, let's see how long you want to continue this battle!" The war ended that night, after I took the sheets and blanket to the washing machine and my body to the shower. Unforgettable is a word that describes Delilah. Who could forget being peed on in the middle of the night, and the cat that did the dirty deed? Vengeance is mine, Delilah chortled, with biblical swagger.

Delilah wore many faces. Her narrowed blank eyes expressed

anger, impatience, irritation and disdain. Her wide eyes and loud chortle meant happiness and expressed a "let's play" attitude. Delilah talked a lot. She was lovable, but she never stopped swiping and nipping, especially after we wouldn't let her escape from our London or Florida apartments. She never learned that we weren't scratch pads.

When we moved from Jerusalem to London in mid-1993, Delilah went along for the ride, to learn a little Cockney. Always different, she crossed the Mediterranean the day before we did. She required different travel plans because British law at the time required visiting pets to enter quarantine for six months. The owner of a cattery in the Cotswolds met Delilah at Heathrow Airport in London. We caught up to Delilah a day later and ensured that she was safely in her temporary home, a three-hour train ride west of London. Always happy to entertain herself by chasing and batting small rubber balls, Delilah soon captivated the cattery owner. Within a few weeks, Delilah was living with the boss in the Big House, away from other cats in stricter quarantine and more restricted quarters. Each time we visited the cattery, Delilah ignored us.

Delilah's privileged London adventure lasted five years. Life was good for two years in North London, but for three years it was even better across the cobblestone street from the historic Ferry House Pub in East London, where real Londoners live. A minor legend in East London, Delilah was bosom pals with young Emma, her cat-sitter, and Emma's parents, Reg and Liza, who operated the pub. From our second-story grated balcony overlooking the narrow street and straight into the pub, Delilah, her head between the bars and her eyes thin, looked like an angry prisoner gazing from the asylum. Inside our flat, Delilah acted like a puppy or a child, playing pitch and catch with small rubber balls. Throw a ball to Delilah sitting on a stairway landing and she would snag it with a paw and quickly shake it back at you. Not just once or twice, but for fifteen minutes at a time. Often she would sit on the stairs and look down, her wide eyes saying, like Mr. Cub Ernie Banks, come on, let's play two. That was the fun part, but Delilah wasn't always pure fun.

One cold night in London, when friends stood too long in an open doorway, Delilah seized the moment and bolted into the darkness for a night on the town. After the night traffic ebbed, I expected Delilah to return, hungry and cold. Knowing her, I also figured that Delilah would leave again to hunt for food if our door were closed when she came knocking. So, with the door half-open, I waited throughout the cold night in the kitchen of our flat on the Isle of Dogs/Docklands, East London, for Delilah's return. Hungry for sure and tired, she walked through the open door at four-thirty in the morning, chortling like a cat turned magpie and went straight for her food. Slam went the door. Pat rushed from our bedroom two floors up to witness Delilah rescuing herself.

After a flight from London to Florida, Delilah found herself in West Palm Beach, South Palm Beach, Juno Beach and Palm Beach Gardens. Delilah's third plane trip brought her to Boston, from where she motored to New Hampshire, in 2003. Life was too good to bail out along the way, although she tried a few times, but never seriously or for too long.

After we flew back to the United States from London in 1998, we searched the grounds of a hotel in West Palm Beach until two in the morning because we thought Delilah had escaped while we were out enjoying dinner with friends. When things quieted down, Delilah emerged meowing from the box spring where she had hidden when hotel employees, strangers, delivered a welcome home gift sent by my Washington office.

With all those memories of Delilah churning, Pat drove me back to Lucas Pond to think, write, play cribbage and dream about my book. With a new twist, my dreams kicked in on schedule. On my first night back in the woods, I dreamt that a kitten was meowing in the cold outside the cabin door. Really. For one night only, Delilah's dream replacement took the place of dreams about my book. Naturally, I rescued the kitten, which looked as much like Delilah as did Delilah.

A few days later, we signed up, in Delilah Salome's name, as contributing members of Maine Public Radio. I told the humorless collector of contributions that Delilah was half Palestinian and half Israeli, but my joke floated unrecognized off the rockbound coast of Maine and up to Greenland. That donation was our tribute to Delilah, a cat we always felt had a lot of Maine Coon in her, even if she hailed from Jerusalem.

Thoreau says all good things happen in the morning. I take them whenever I can get them, any time, day or night, awake or asleep.—February 17, 2004

Like Thoreau, Sorta

Thoreau had three chairs in his self-made one-room cabin in the woods at Walden Pond. He said so, in his own hand. One chair was for solitude, another for friendship and a third was for society. He wrote that, too. Imaginative. Literary. But mainly symbolic. Those labels were Thoreau's attempts to be slightly inclusive in what was supposed to be his solitary world. The solitude, his chair, I can accept at face value for when he was really alone, thinking and writing. But one chair for friendship, for all of his friends, and another chair for Concord's literary lions, his society, appear more figurative than real, and more powerful in the fashion he described.

Thoreau had many friends who knew where he was hanging out in prissy Concord, Massachusetts. The thinker, writer, lover of all things natural, anti-war activist and abolitionist, land surveyor and expert pencil-maker was a Concord recluse mainly in myth. Thoreau's friendship and society chairs, if they had any practical value at all, were no doubt worn smooth by his own and Ralph Waldo Emerson's many pals who were numerous enough to compel them to drag in their own chairs rather than sit on the stoop, if there was one, at Chez Thoreau. Or maybe Thoreau met all of his friends in downtown Concord.

At Big Buck Road, the seating arrangement was more for individual, me, rather than group therapy. Six chairs and a daybed, far superior to Henry David Thoreau's bed of nails, adorned the inner sanctum of my much larger cabin at Lucas Pond in Northwood,

New Hampshire, a few miles from ordinary Concord, capital of the Live Free or Die state. My chairs served a practical purpose. They were all equal, too, although some—such as my dining, reading and writing chairs—were more equal than others. One of my other chairs cradled a printer that was wired to a computer, another served as a hanger for my tan Woolrich winter coat. Its seat tucked beneath the top of my kitchen table, another chair served without complaint as a storage bin for notebooks, a dictionary, thesaurus, gloves and, occasionally, for my ever-present gray wool cap.

Pat, The Enabler, And The Enabled. Photo by J.B. Dobeck.

As Thoreau tells his story, if he had more than two visitors, someone stood. In all my time at Lucas Pond, and this I can say with absolute certainty, I had a total of four visitors, and only one stood. One wintry night, a neighbor whose help I had sought earlier to discuss one of my balky electric heaters stopped by to offer advice: the heater couldn't be saved, he said, while standing. My only other visitors were Pat every four weeks or so, and the Dobecks—Pat's sister, Joanne Dobeck, and Joanne's husband, Bill—who visited just once. After I cleared the chairs of books and boxed food on that occasion, we all sat. Pat and the Dobecks surprised me on

March 9, 2004, my 63rd birthday, which turned into a champagne celebration surrounded by now-warmish knotty pine walls.

Each month when Pat reached Big Buck Road to whisk me home to Portsmouth or to abandon me in the woods she was never tempted to dally. When she picked me up at the cabin, we loaded her car with my dirty laundry, computer and printer plus a few supplies before we fled in a whisker. Upon our return to the cabin, after we unloaded food, my working tools and fresh supplies, Pat's routine was to pat me on the noggin before fleeing again. Her trips were essential, however, because in Portsmouth I bought food to last a month. Those purchases of pasta, salmon, haddock, swordfish, turkey and chicken kept my hefty spending advantage over Thoreau, which would have been as easy as buying a quart of milk, a loaf of bread and a dozen eggs, once every few months.

During his first eight months at Walden, Thoreau spent twenty-seven cents a week on food. He wrote that, so quibbling now is out of the question. Those expenses totaled about $8.64 during that long span, a hot dog, maybe two, and a small soda in the woods today. But it's no secret, wasn't then and isn't now, that he often skipped the short distance into Concord's center to scrounge meals with family and friends. In other words, others would have paid for those meals. That's one way to trim expenses. But I won't hold that against Thoreau for any reason. For nearly two years after those first eight months, Thoreau wrote, he ate rye and Indian meal without yeast; potatoes, rice, and very little salt pork, molasses and salt. Thoreau said nothing about whisky or apple cider. He drank only water. He loved Indian (as in India) philosophy and thus, perhaps, ate rice and Indian (Native American) meal with good cheer. He made bread from rye, salt and pure Indian meal, made genuine hoecakes and baked them in his outdoor oven. When he exhausted his yeast, the naturalist-chef wrote, he stopped leavening his bread.

Thoreau, one might say, also dwelled on his stomach as I did. His diet, however, might partially explain his lean and hungry look. Did he, I wonder, also have low blood sugar? Plagued by tuberculosis all of his adult life, Thoreau wasn't a well man when he lived at Walden. He was, in fact, frail and gaunt. Thoreau died at age forty-four. Camping at Lucas Pond, I was well, or thought I was. My clogging arteries were eight years from being almost fully clogged. What I didn't know in 2004 didn't kill me, although my ignorance eventually brought me too close to joining Thoreau much too soon.

On one of his many scampers into Concord, Thoreau ran into the local tax collector. A bad day was in the stars. You owe six years of back taxes, the revenooer said; fork it over. You'll not get the money from me, answered the anti-war philosopher, who had withheld his taxes as a protest against slavery and war. Off to the gaol Thoreau went, but for only one night. An unidentified sympathizer soon paid the delinquent taxes and Thoreau, no longer a scofflaw but forever a principled protester, was once more free to roam Concord and to live at Walden. Objecting to the war against Mexico, Thoreau refused to pay taxes. I objected to the invasion of Iraq, but I still paid taxes, further evidence that Darwin was wrong.

No back taxes stalked me, not in Northwood, Nottingham, Portsmouth, Jerusalem, London, Florida or anywhere else. Maybe they should have, given the state of war and peace in my time. But I am no Thoreau. In Nottingham, New Hampshire, however, I did converse with a local taxman of sorts. Our talks were all friendly, merely local gossip. I was renting a cabin in neighboring Northwood, so I was out of his jurisdiction and had nothing to fear anyway.

No matter how often he ate in town, and accounting for more than one-hundred-and-sixty years of inflation, Thoreau was his own cheap date. But I wouldn't trade menus, not even to save hundreds of dollars. Food and various other supplies, such as flashlight batteries, cost $1,513 during my mere one-hundred-and-ninety-three days in the cabin, a period that stretched over eleven months and all four seasons. That's a huge cost differential for powdered milk, frozen orange juice, fresh fruit, salted peanuts and popcorn, as well as for frozen fish and poultry, vegetables of assorted kinds, olive oil and Boston baked beans. As long as I had protein and carbohydrates to spare, I was never alone in the woods.

Why, it's fair to wonder, does the renowned Henry David Thoreau appear here and now in my story—he the philosopher, writer and prime mover of the modern environmental movement? Real similarities exist to be sure, although they may appear generic and superficial. He lived in his own cabin engulfed by woods near a pond, Walden, in his own New England town. An outsider, I rented a cabin in alien woods on the shore of Lucas Pond in Northwood, New Hampshire. Thoreau finished one book in his cabin—*A Week on the Concord and Merrimack River*—and started another, his majestic *Walden*. He sought seclusion in the woods for many reasons, but thinking and writing were his prime movers. I wrote one book at Lucas Pond and gathered material for a second book, this one.

But I resurrect Thoreau not because of those similarities. Thoreau is here because so many of my friends and many strangers made the comparison, not because I wish to invite comparisons, small, weighty or otherwise.

You know, friends and strangers told me with history and knowledge on their lips, this cabin-in-the-woods escape has been done before. Ha! Ha! But not by me, I answered, so the rest doesn't matter. Unless I lived alone in a cabin in the woods, I wouldn't get the stories, the book, out of my head. That was my answer to all who wondered and asked. I knew that reality better than anyone.

When strangers learned of my plans to use a cabin in the woods as a writing tool they didn't say I was loony. If they thought so, they were kind enough to remain silent. They professed, instead, to acknowledge my self-discipline. No, I corrected them, if discipline ruled me, I would have been able to write at predictable times in the comfort of home or office. What I needed was pressure to trick me into thinking and writing each day. Living alone in the woods, without a television or a car handy, allowed me endless hours to manipulate my surroundings and myself.

"Oh, just like Thoreau at Walden Pond," friends and strangers said with mock seriousness when they heard of my plans. That was always the exclamation, "Oh, just like Thoreau at Walden Pond!" No other references reached my ears; no one stumbled on Kerouac in a fire tower or Hawthorne in a customs house far from any woods. Any serious comparison with Thoreau, of course, is as wide of the mark as 1845 is from 2004, which is the most obvious difference. Forget about talent, friendly surroundings, experience and results, which is easy for me to do. Comparisons between Walden and Lucas ponds, between Northwood, New Hampshire, and Concord, Massachusetts, are worth a think.

Northwood, New Hampshire, is small, typical in size of many New Hampshire towns. The town's roughly 4,300 people live on a little more than twenty-eight square miles of land and occasionally on slightly more than two square miles of ponds and lakes. My slice of Northwood was just that, a small slice of a small pie. A few square miles were all I could claim, and those only when I walked in the woods, around the pond and along country roads to count birds and snowflakes, to fetch tomatoes, lettuce, cucumbers and garbanzo (not Boston baked) beans, and to search for deer I never spotted. Northwood has nine lakes and ponds, and I was lucky enough to live on one that glistened like a precious gem in the woods and on the land. Northwood was settled in 1763 and incorporated in 1773 when it split from neighboring Nottingham. The area was called, seriously, the Great North Woods when it was part of Nottingham; hence, the town's birth name of Northwood. A linear town, Northwood's main street—aka Route 4 and the old New Hampshire turnpike—is eight miles long.

Besides Lucas Pond, my cabin and the surrounding woods, the distinguishing features of my Northwood were Saddleback Mountain, the town's highest point at 1,150 feet; sparkling Woodman

Marsh, Susty's Vegan Restaurant and three other restaurants, the town's small but elegant stone public library, a supermarket, two gasoline stops and a convenience store, along with a section of Route 4 called Antique Alley.

Without anticipating the slightest blowback, I can say that Northwood measures up to Concord, Massachusetts, only in narrow geographic terms. Northwood's more than twenty-eight square miles exceed Concord's, which fall just short of twenty-six square miles. Concord's contemporary population, however, is almost 18,000, more than four times that of Northwood's. They might be considered similar in another small way: they both have ponds. One is famous in American history and literature; Lucas Pond much less so. Concord, Massachusetts, founded in 1635 and well before Northwood became Northwood, was America's Athens during Thoreau's life.

Curiously enough, Thoreau built his shelter on Emerson's land. I ponder, from this distance, the name of the Indian from whom Emerson bought the land. The meaning being, did Emerson or his forebears buy the land at all? Seventy years before Thoreau built his shelter on someone else's land, Concord gave the American Revolution a rousing start when a small group of ill-garbed farmers with long guns sent the well-dressed Red Coats retreating to Boston twenty miles to the east. The Great War for Independence was on. If you missed that, Thoreau's pal, Ralph Waldo Emerson, put it to verse in the opening stanza of his *Concord Hymn*:

> *By the rude bridge that arched the flood,*
> *Their flag to April's breeze unfurled,*
> *Here once the embattled farmers stood,*
> *And fired the shot heard round the world.*

The Northwood hymn is yet to be written, as far as I know.

As for the liquid and geological similarities, Lucas Pond and Walden Pond were both created by ice. Glaciers cut deep into the earth and then retreated, leaving holes filled with water in their wakes. Walden is called a kettle pond because it's fed entirely by underground water and has no visible outward flow. One main stream feeds Lucas Pond and high water flows out through a small dam opposite the stream.

Walden Pond covers sixty-one acres and its shoreline measures 1.68 miles. Lucas Pond today covers forty acres, although a 1936 survey reported its size as fifty-one acres. Its shoreline is 1.12 miles. A number of cabins and houses lie along or near the shore of Lucas Pond. Construction is banned on Walden's shores. Lucas Pond and Walden Pond are called ponds because they're not large enough to be called lakes, although the dividing line appears more subjective than objective. The same is true of other ponds throughout New England.

Walden Pond is like secular divinity to those who prize nature, pacifism, philosophy and literature. Because of Thoreau's renown as a thinker and writer and his large footprint on the conservation movement in the United States, Walden is a National Historic Landmark and a reservation that is part of the Massachusetts forests and parks system. Walden attracts almost 700,000 visitors annually. While the woods around Walden are protected from development, hiking, boating, fishing and other activities are permitted on a daily basis. The sole building in the state reservation used to be a replica of Thoreau's one-room cabin, which was at the edge of a parking lot and isn't near the site of the original cabin that is marked by chains linked to granite posts.

Powerboats are banned on Lucas Pond, whose forty acres (but no mules) make it seem more like a small lake than a pond. The ponds of my youth were much smaller than this watery expanse of my sixties and seventies. But woodland measurements are alien to me. In such an atmosphere, the noise of silence usually ruled at Lucas Pond, especially in winter, although sometimes cars, engines roaring and echoing through the naked woods, raced across ice that seemed bottomless.

Lucas Pond is considered one of the best fishing holes in southeastern New Hampshire. Unless one considers the possibility that Ted Williams, the ballplayer, and Jack Sharkey, the boxer, performed a mini-historic act by casting lines in search of record trout, Lucas Pond remains just a very nice place to row and toss a line when fishing season opens each April. But no one tallies the number of fisher folk or vacationers who show up there each year.

Thoreau lived in the woods at Walden from July 1845 to September 1847. Frequent visits into town provided the à la mode for Thoreau's garden-variety diet. My life on the shore of Lucas Pond stretched to eleven months. Compressed, that period totaled a few days short of seven months because I left the cabin every four weeks to resupply, and I took July off. A vacation, it's called, was my à la mode. But the distance between Thoreau at Walden and me at Lucas Pond was far greater than the miles or the years. Though loose, the similarities exceed place and purpose.

I wasn't in the cabin to philosophize, create a movement of any kind, or separate myself for the sake of separation. Like a person obsessed with discovering mineral wealth, I was there to find the atmosphere and the tools necessary to force myself to write the book that I wanted to write. Ways to observe and analyze nature and the world spread before me while I lived in the woods. They all helped me and even became part of my working life. I couldn't have escaped the physical confinements and the visible and mental vistas of the cabin, the pond, the woods and the people unless I had shredded my notebooks, blasted my computer and fled for the safety of convention.

Walden was among the books I read while releasing my subconscious to think for me in the woods. My objective was to find and harness the mood. Although I had read it years earlier, I didn't finish the book this time around because my own time and purpose kept intruding.

Maybe it was the pond, the cabin, the woods and the solitude, but I experienced at Lucas Pond many of the kinds of observations and events that Thoreau chronicled in *Walden*. From that perspective, Thoreau's experiences were valuable as a way to illuminate what I saw and otherwise sensed. At the same time, Thoreau waded into activities that I avoided.

During his summers, Thoreau probably bathed, maybe even swam, at Walden. On warm summer days, I would guess, Thoreau also picnicked outside his cabin, perhaps with some of his pals from the city. Bathing in Lucas Pond was as far from my mind as escaping from Iraq by swimming across the Khabur River to Turkey, a swim that I refused to try after the end of the first Persian Gulf War in 1991. I could have plunged into Lucas Pond, but was never even tempted to take a dip because, while I can wade, I can't swim. The water was so cold to my finger that my toe wouldn't touch it. Not once did I enjoy a picnic on the deck off my cabin's front door facing the territorial trout, larger fish that always chased off smaller ones.

Like many philosophers, artists and monks before him and since, Thoreau said he moved into the woods to live deliberately, to reduce life to its essentials and see what life in the raw was like. It's too late to dispute Thoreau's essentials. But here I can quibble. Based on my experience, I suspect that he wasn't telling the whole truth, his cabin also being his writing cocoon. It's no secret: I went to the woods for seclusion, isolation, to provide pressure and artificial deadlines that forced me to think, read and write. Thoreau completed his mission; I completed mine.

Thoreau wrote of a French-Canadian woodchopper he knew: "but the intellectual and what is called spiritual man in him were slumbering as in an infant. He had been instructed in that innocent and ineffectual way in which the Catholic priests teach the aborigines, by which the pupil is never educated to the degree of consciousness, but only to the degree of trust and reverence, and a child is not made a man, but kept a child." I met a man of the cloth at Lucas Pond. He didn't convert me to any faith, nor did he even try.

Writing in *Walden*, Thoreau downplayed the hardships of his spare life alone. After talking to a man who worked hard to keep his family alive, Thoreau wrote, "As I did not work hard, I did not eat hard." In my case, however, I wasn't working hard physically, but I was often hungry and I ate hard because thinking and writing are for me hard work. Besides, there's that low blood sugar again, which often keeps me thinking hard about my next meal.

In his rejection of material goods and desire for simplicity, Thoreau was thoroughly un-American. I went to the woods not for simplicity, although in many ways I found it, along with an active subconscious, a secret weapon that is anything but simple. Life in the woods for me was a diversion from modernity and its pressures. Freedom is what I found, and time, enough free time to waste and still find my small version of a writing life, or at least a writing year.

His seven miles of beans were Thoreau's tribute to himself. I loved the icepack on Lucas Pond, long treks in the surrounding woods, hitch-hiking now and then, meeting strangers in strange places and lugging a few groceries back to the cabin after long walks. I did not plant vegetables of any color, although I was always trying to plant seeds of other kinds. Walking through miles of woods and keeping my eyes peeled for wayward deer, I became a surveyor of sorts. Unlike Thoreau, however, I used only my eyes as instruments for recording unscientific measurements. Far from being a pencil-maker, I used pens, never a pencil, to write in my Reporter's Notebook.

Thinking like a Greek in ancient Athens, Thoreau wrote in Walden, "Not till we are lost, in other words not till we have lost the world, do we begin to find ourselves, and realize where we are and the infinite extent of our relations.... In the long run, men hit only what they aim at. Therefore, though they should fail immediately, they had better aim at something high." Alone at Lucas Pond, I agreed.

Cleaned the toilet for the hell of it. Must continue to confront the demons. The demons that make you want to run away from the writing, the demons that want to make you shave the truth. The demons that want to take you on long walks, or walk to lunch or listen to the radio, anything to avoid spending the time putting black on white.
—April 27, 2004

Talking Trash

A glance at the clock above the sink exposed my memory lapse—time had stopped.

On that day in May, the fire-red metal and plastic timepiece betrayed its purpose. Four months earlier, in the beginning, I had shrouded my mechanical link to minutes and hours under a checkered red, white and two-tone blue dishcloth, with five white stars in the upper left-hand corner. The covered clock became my rebel flag, a sign of control not of surrender. Living alone in the woods made it easy to pretend I was a Micmac Indian, far northeasterners who had no word for time. I am not a Micmac, but I would mark time in my own way, create my own time-culture. A clock I couldn't see helped me erase the tyranny of time and eliminate the need for a schedule. My days would be divided into light and dark, a scheme that encouraged me to write at any time. A clock that I could see would have dictated my reading and writing life.

With hours excised from my life, I would live more like a farmer, hoeing with pen, paper and computer and hewing to the broadest rhythms of nature. Or more, perhaps, like a Bedouin guided by the sun and stars but with no animals but myself to herd in the deserts and oases of words and ideas. After thirty-five years of submitting to newspaper deadlines ordered by editors and production managers, timelessness and solitude were to be my new masters.

Peculiar as my forced self-discipline was, it worked. Honoring my creative goal, I wrote the first draft of a book about global tribalism—not a contradiction in terms, I might point out—while alone in a cabin. With only my goal as a guide, I was naked in the woods, without a car, a television or a clock.

On May 4, 2004, after a daily routine of exercises and breaking the fast, I set about planning my main non-writing activity of the day—dumping the trash.

Winter's arctic ice was behind me. Spring was in the sprouting woods. Writing, it seemed, would never end. Baseball's magic would creep up on me. Ridding myself of a week's trash, I thought, would be a moment of mundane ambition. Ahead lay a calming stroll on a dirt road, maybe a tip of the hat and a crease of the lips to a friendly neighbor or two before a squat neighborly dumpster would welcome my trash. Soon after that, the woods would welcome this stranger to think, stimulate my subconscious, jot book notes and continue my futile search for unsuspecting deer. Reality had a different plan. My day turned into a seminar on woodland etiquette. Until this trash-dumping excursion, I knew little of proper rural behavior. Only the natives knew that dumpsters aren't dumpsters unless they are linked to the possessive, as in his or hers, mine or theirs, and that in the woods possession is ten-tenths of the law.

Wrapped loosely in a life of traveling and reporting hid the essential ingredient of luck, and chance meetings with peculiar strangers who were no more peculiar than I. Allowing for different accents, landscapes and cultural bents, strangers in the New Hampshire woods acted much like strangers I met in Iran, Bosnia and Pakistan.

Circled by twittering birds, scampering squirrels, the buzz of insects, and the hum of warm, still air over flat, dark blue water, I walked with my trash bags across the deck and down the stairs into one surprise after another.

Bright and greening, nature was an imperfect hourglass. The

high sun lit the landscape as six honking Canada geese glided like a fleet of remote-controlled drones to the pond's glassy southwestern corner. This was the season of the hawk and the heron, too, of trees singing in the rain, of menacing Rottweilers and even dingoes, and hammers whacking fresh nails on rising porches.

Dangling two small plastic bags filled with the detritus of a sole and sparse life in the woods, trash that wouldn't survive long enough to interest the laziest archaeologist on the longest leash, I skipped over the rocks and gravel of Big Buck Road, my road. Happy ferns, in no danger, surrounded an archer's target well to the left of the trail. Mosquitoes and black flies were not yet a menace, so it was natural to grovel for flat, smooth, granite-like stones slightly larger than a silver dollar that would fit between my thumb and curved right forefinger. The purpose was to scale those stones sidearm under branches and watch them whiz a few hops and skips across the water before they sank, finally whipped by gravity. Other stones, unsuitable for fine scaling and skimming, I kicked with my worn tennis shoes into the omnipresent dirt as I would have done more than a half century earlier just about anywhere.

In my sights was a trash dumpster at the corner of Bigelow and Lower Deerfield roads on the rim of the Lucas Pond basin. Dumpsters standing within smelling distance of Lucas Pond were small potatoes compared with the large open garbage dump that greeted guests going and coming from a four-star hotel in Karachi, Pakistan. Still, each time I tossed my trash into a dumpster along Big Buck Road, I thought of the garbage festering in Karachi.

Lightweight stuff, my donations to an eventual landfill were egg shells, empty blue boxes of linguine and penne, a couple of smeared, greased copies of *The Boston Globe* and sections of *The Sunday New York Times*, wasted cans of tuna and baked beans, and cans that once housed tasty plum tomatoes and tomato sauce. Age sixty-three at the time, my strange behavior might have added to local suspicions about the *stranger in the cabin*. My canter couldn't have been odd to the natural denizens of the woods, the numerous deer that I felt sure watched my every move although my sight of them was limited to their trails and scat. Canny creatures, deer are much smarter than hunters, otherwise why are they still out there? If deer had guns, it seemed to me, human hunters would be forced to survive on fish and berries.

During all four seasons of 2004, I spent hours, days, trying to spot an antler or a white tail, with no luck and sleuthing skill diminished by growing diffidence. In winter I could understand the difficulty, as a local wit explained that when the snow falls and the ice deepens, deer leave the woods to spend the season socializing behind the local Elks Club. But that doesn't explain my failure during the other seasons. As still as a graying and stunted petrified oak I stood trying to outwit and out-wait a curious buck or doe, but I may as well have worn blinders.

A shortcut through thin brush and small trees beckoned across a ninety-degree bend in Big Buck Road. I took it. A walking stick poking from my right hand and two tan plastic bags twirling from my left, I skipped over a narrow wood bridge that spanned a stream near its entrance to the pond. Back then the bridge was a decaying wonder, a wonder that it held the weight of a car or small truck. Safe passage, however, was guaranteed for one human with two trash bags and a walking stick.

After crossing the bridge, I met a friendly neighbor. Soon after, I received an extended lesson in the proper way to dispose of trash in the woods, what might be called trash protocol or proper etiquette for rural living. In the cabin, I was struggling to write a book about tribal behavior in Africa, Asia and Europe. Trash in hand, I tasted tribalism, New Hampshire style.

Where are you going? my friendly neighbor asked. Just to the top of Bigelow Road, I answered with a compliant smile, waving my trash, where I will put these little bags in the large dumpster by the road. Several times before, I had waved a hearty hello to this woman and other members of her family as I walked alone and they were entertaining themselves with play and yard work. On those occasions, I was off to walk and think in the woods or hike to the supermarket on Route 4, a little more than three miles away. Our chatter was always pleasant, but usually never much beyond hello and how are ya, until this day when I flashed my trash bags and triggered Lesson 101 about the rules of the woods.

Sensing, falsely, no concern about my purpose, I was pleased to reveal my resourcefulness. Do you remember the trash dumpster that used to be in front of the long brown house just up the road? I asked the woman. Well, I used to dump my trash into that cavernous bin, which seemed large enough to hold a year's supply of my small bags. But, I explained, that black dumpster disappeared after the brown house was sold. This should have been my first clue: house sold, house empty; dumpster gone, dumpster somehow tied to house. But the clue eluded me. Instead, proud of my ability to adapt and my desire to avoid littering, I explained that now I simply walked another half mile or so to my new trash-dumping destination at the top of Bigelow Road. My friendly neighbor might have missed my earlier violations, but she wasn't going to miss this one.

Veiling her horror at such a breach of protocol, my neighbor explained that homeowners paid monthly fees to trash collection companies. As part of the deal, my neighbor said, homeowners received the dumpsters for *their own* use, the emphasis being mine. Got that stranger, my neighbor said without accusation. Trash bins, in other words, are for each homeowner's own use, not mine or anyone else's. Dumpsters along Big Buck Road and other roads in the Lucas Pond watershed were always empty. To a townie like me, that meant the dumpsters were part of a town or county trash collection service. Besides, what harm could a couple of small trash bags do anyway, when I gently placed them in a dumpster every two weeks or so? But harm there was, if only to the rules of the woods and the psyche of residents there.

With a goodbye wave, off I strolled, better informed about woodland etiquette but without feeling thwarted. As happy as a deer that had survived the hunting season, I remained secure in the belief that I could dispose of my trash in another's dumpster one more time. After that I would mend my ways, never again to commit such a despicable act. Up to the corner of Bigelow and Lower Deerfield roads I strolled, whistling, whacking my walking stick on the ground beyond where Big Buck's dirt turns to Bigelow's asphalt. All the while I kept an untrained eye out for deer that I knew were snickering, waiting for parts two, three and four of my education in rural living.

As I began to raise the unlocked lid on what had become my favorite dumpster—just an average five-feet-long, three or four feet deep and three feet wide black bin with two green covers—shouts rose from the suddenly opened door of a house about thirty yards from me and *their* dumpster. If this were a chance encounter, the renters of the dumpster must have been taking shifts at the window awaiting a strange and unexpected scoundrel aiming to target their trash bin. What could have been more tedious? A few minutes earlier, I had been warned that my trash-dumping behavior was foul, but I had missed the red flag. Now I was being ambushed, bushwhacked, waylaid, cut off at the pass. Or, I asked myself, what are neighbors for? The early warning system aimed at controlling maverick dumpers seemed wired and working. Thinking back, I shouldn't have been surprised if neighbors warned neighbors about strangers violating the law of the land. Life in the woods is more solitary than communal, yet it is also protective. Along dirt roads and wooded lakeshores, a stranger is often more suspect than welcomed, until the newcomer proves himself worthy with consistent, predictable and proper behavior. In the woods, time is a stranger's best and usually only ally.

The woman of the house emerged first, no gun drawn, no frothing hounds unleashed, but her voice in high decibel. Her anguished warning went something like this. You can't throw your trash in there. It's our trash bin. We pay for it. With a dash of humor that missed its mark, I shouted that my trash bags were too small to harm hers. Then reinforcements arrived in the form of the man of the house. We pay for that bin, he shouted; we pay twenty-five dollars a month for it. His right arm pointing to the left toward adjacent Lower Deerfield Road, the man said that the people in that nearby house also pay twenty-five dollars a month. It's our dumpster and it's for our trash only, he shouted. Across Bigelow Road and behind me, a hound barked and a roaring lawnmower competed for airtime. But I had no difficulty hearing the objections being hurled my way. The barking hound, I chose to believe, was an ally because it was howling on my side of the battle zone. But I couldn't be certain from the inflections of its barks exactly whose side it was on. The lawnmower, I knew, was neutral.

From where I stood, puny trash bags still in hand and looking dumber than the trash bin straight ahead, I shouted back, trying to make light of what seemed a silly situation. "But my bags don't take up much room," I shouted. "My trash is no worse than any other. I'll pay you five dollars, twenty-five dollars, if you let me dump my trash in your dumpster." Here, I thought, was the rural equivalent of what once was the *casus bellum* between an urban apartment dweller hanging intrusive wash on another's clothes line. I tried to understand the rural point of view which, as I saw it, is American to the core, centering as it does on money and the sanctity of private property: the dumpster's mine. I paid for it. Get your own dumpster. And then there's the, "It all adds up" argument: two bags of trash from one townie, two from a vagrant and pretty soon you'd be into real trash with no room for the owner's.

When I offered to pay twenty-five dollars for dumping privileges, the guardians of their very own dumpster, disgusted with me, slammed their door and turned their backs on the stranger on the verge of their property violating local rules. There it was,

American hospitality at its regional finest, inked in laws that sanctify private property, even if it's leased. Nothing like the hospitality shown me in 1992 by a dozen big eating and hard drinking Jews in Tashkent, Uzbekistan, just after the new Russia and many new countries emerged from the vanished Soviet Union. Certainly there was no similarity with the man who, in 1990, bought me an egg sandwich and a bottle of water in Dera'a, the Syrian town near the border with Jordan. A foot of mud after a big rain forced me to stop searching for food when the man in Dera'a, seeing my plight, came to my rescue. Dera'a, by the way, is where the Great Syrian War began in 2011.

When the dumpster guardians turned away, they probably figured that I would dump my trash in their bin and flee. Indeed, I had them cornered, but I acted with the honor of a stranger in the land of others. Instead of dumping my trash in a stranger's dumpster, I walked off, trash bags still dangling from my left hand. My reputation wasn't going to become that of an irresponsible dumper. Content to fume like the angry English king who had great difficulty dealing with the meddlesome archbishop, I walked off. Then, I groused about whether there was a dumpster anywhere that would rid me of this troublesome trash.

Now what? I thought. It would be stupid to return to the cabin, trash still in hand, as if I took the trash for a stroll as others walk their poodles. The invisible, snickering deer would notice and stand in silent ridicule. No, I stammered, I'll spy another dumpster, trash the trash, and swear with my hand on the tribal by-laws of the woods never again to toss my eggshells into someone else's dumpster.

With the fresh taste of rejection lingering, and still mumbling to myself, I trekked down Lower Deerfield Road toward Route 43, where more obstacles awaited.

Since the 1950s, hitchhiking had been a reliable ally. My right thumb took me to and from college, from a hail of missiles in Iraq and into trouble in Kosovo. Lately, I hitched just for fun and games, as a way to measure moral and religious values along New Hampshire's country roads. At this moment, however, sticking my thumb out and begging for a ride wasn't an option. Even I knew that no one, no matter how charitable, would pick up an old guy bearing two very visible trash bags.

After a few cars whizzed by, my hitchhiking idea vanished with them. My ride turned out to be my walk, a shuffle, really, along Route 43 until I reached Lucas Pond Road, which skirts the dam end of Lucas Pond itself. What at that point seemed like a mission to nowhere I decided to anoint with a higher purpose. If I followed Lucas Pond Road I would reach the adjacent town of Nottingham; West Nottingham, to be precise. To be more precise, I would walk right into Demmons Country Store, a landmark in that part of the country. Long before this moment, I had intended to see Demmons for myself. I had heard much about the old-time haven for meetings and gathering gossip, but had never visited. So here was an opportunity for luck to pay a visit. Along the road, I pretended to be marching to Pretoria, crossing from Macedonia to Kosovo under cover of ignorance, sloshing through airless tunnels high in Afghanistan's Hindu Kush Mountains or looking for the remains of the Donner Party; anything for a diversion. A significant bonus along the way would be to spot a fresh dumpster with a dozing watchdog nearby. I would hurl my trash into the bin and vanish.

Up and down hilly Lucas Pond Road I sauntered, light trash still fingered lightly in my left hand. Right away, I saw slices of other worlds: Scottish Highland cattle followed by llamas, or maybe they were alpacas, gazing at me in subtle amusement. A hound howling weakly in the arthritic throes of old age behind an electronic fence was more harmless than the protectors of the trash bin who had thwarted me earlier. Younger, angrier dogs rushed to greet me, and I waved them off with brisk whisks of my trash bags and walking stick. But I never spotted a trash bin.

I passed the entrance to a summer camp, strolled under high-tension transmission wires and past signs that marked out-of-season snowmobile trails. I saw no other walkers, with or without trash. A few motorists passed by, but none laughed, which I interpreted as a good sign, although the reason escaped me. No one got close enough to smell my trash. Past houses and a couple of small businesses I trod on, but not one dumpster did my squinting eyes discern. This was a sure sign of a conspiracy. Nah, there can't be a conspiracy; I've been living alone too long, I thought. My friendly neighbor couldn't possibly have warned the owner of every dumpster in the Lucas Pond bowl.

Oppressive humidity followed by rain-forest rain turned a leisurely walk into a slog for a mile down Lucas Pond Road before I reached Demmons. Tied tightly, my trash bags were unmarred by the deluge. If I had thought that the invisible deer were eyeing me from behind stone walls, I would have been as demented as they. On this and later visits to Demmons, I learned that hunters hauled their deer kills to the rear of the store to be weighed and tallied. From mid-September into December, archery season, hunters paid two dollars to enter a raffle. The pot was usually about a hundred dollars. The prize was split, half went to the hunter who killed the largest doe, half went to the nimrod who felled the biggest buck. Only a deer seriously short of survival instincts would tempt fate by foraging anywhere near Demmons at any time of year. The only deer I ever spotted during my time at Lucas Pond was, however, at Demmons; its dead tongue lolling from its mouth, the animal was hanging on the scale next to the store.

With the innocence of a fawn, I approached Demmons from the rear. Poised as if I were planning to ambush a trash bin, I scanned the area behind the store. Nothing. A very old country store must have at least one very old dumpster. Scarred by failures to that point, I conjured excuses for Demmons: maybe its dumpster was hidden underground to thwart strangers stalking trash bins.

Wood steps leading, I learned later, to a second-floor apartment; a concrete well cover, an official station for weighing dead deer, bits of unrelated rubble, and window frames of faded green highlighted the view from the rear. One sign noted that Demmons was a wild turkey registration station. Out front, appearances improved. On the porch was an ice machine, poised for action on days when the temperature soared to seventy-two. Near the porch was a sign to delight anglers: "Live Bait, Canadian Crawlers And Worms." The hitching posts vanished long ago, but friends and neighbors could fill their gasoline tanks in front of the store. The West Nottingham Post Office, 03291, served customers from the far end of the building. A large container, something like a specialized dumpster, in a parking area beside the post office invited used shoes and clothes. The post office has hung on through the ages. Not so the gasoline. New federal regulations governing gas pumps and lines closed the tap in December 2015. Tens of thousands of dollars would have to be spent to bring the system up to code.

There I was, gazing around, trash bags in hand and right thumb in mouth. Fast thinking was called for because I didn't want to investigate further, create a stir and appear to be some kind of weird small-time thief trading in trash. What a terrible first impression that would have made, I thought. Seeming like a sneaky trash-dumper was burden enough. Without thinking about whether I would be forced to carry my treasure back to the cabin after all, I placed the trash bags to the right of the steps at the store's entrance and leaned my walking stick against the building. Then I strolled inside, smiling like an innocent stranger stopping by for a cold drink. Only I knew the embarrassing truth, that my visit was another reconnaissance mission. This time, however, my hopes of finding a place to dump the trash seemed to be fading faster than the day's light.

Demmons has been a country store on that very same spot since 1824. That's what Jody, the owner who is no Demmons, told me. Demmons has been called Demmons since the 1940s. Jody had been there awhile, so he knows a mite about local history. Age always impresses me, especially as I age. In this case, it meant that I was standing where a country store has stood since James Monroe was president, four years after Maine became a state and only about twenty years after New Hampshire's first turnpike opened to traffic. In the beginning, Demmons was a stop on the original stagecoach road between Portsmouth, on the coast and once the state's capital, and Concord, the capital since 1808.

Artifacts—decades, even generations, old—hang on Demmons's walls and ceiling. The store holds an enviable collection of regional antiques belonging to old-time rural life that is known to few now. A weathered hammer hung on a wall next to a sign that says, "This hammer was built and patented by Lee Wilson, a well-known resident of Nottingham. Ask management for details." A 1991 World Almanac sat on a shelf, fairly current, I thought, considering that the premises had been seeing customers for almost 200 years. Posted on a crossbeam, a vintage paper sign warned, "Do not spit on the floor. To do so may spread disease." No health officer or doctor takes credit for the sign.

My favorite Demmons antique is a fading poster from the Star Theater in Newmarket, New Hampshire, a few towns away. If you liked James Cagney, Katharine Hepburn, Barbara Stanwyck and Jean Harlow, the Star Theater was the place for you, a few decades earlier.

As I gawked and Jody talked, an older woman under a helmet roared up on a motorcycle. Bravo for her, I thought. The customers at Demmons know the clerks and vice versa. Demmons is such a good-old-boy-girl kind of store that it allowed some customers to keep a running tab, as in buy now and pay later; we trust you.

It was at Demmons where I learned that people in New Hampshire sometimes converse without talking. A conversation, a verbal exchange, might be between two people standing opposite each other, but neither talks, except occasionally. Another person walks in, a stranger like me, perhaps, and since no one is talking the stranger thinks that nothing is going on. But the stranger is actually breaking up an intermittent conversation. The stranger realizes this when one of the two other people ups and walks out, saying nothing at all. See you tomorrow, is the unspoken message.

Later sojourns to Demmons also taught me that New Hampshire has 234 cities and towns, each of which thinks it's a state, while the state acts like a small town. Think about that as you vow to remember that in New Hampshire, New Hampshire is pronounced New Hampshah.

To prolong my stay at Demmons on that trash-dumping day, meet a few people and try to fathom a solution to my trash travails that by now had become a problem in West Nottingham as well as Northwood, I ate a hot dog, sat on a small wood stool—the best and only seat in the house—near the newspapers, and chatted with Jody and two of his helpers. Customers come in waves, Jody explained, during the summer when it's hot—which, I later learned, means seventy-two degrees in that neighborhood. That's when people come for ice and cold drinks. In the winter when a big snow falls, people stock up on gasoline and food. Just like in South Florida during hurricane season, I thought. Jody mentioned Homer Bigart, the well-known *New York Herald-Tribune* and *New York Times* foreign correspondent who used to live just up the hill. The late Donald Hall, the renowned poet who at the time had recently been named the nation's poet laureate, also lived in the New Hampshire woods, but by this time he bunked well over several country miles away. Jody gave me a copy of *Stop Time*, a Frank Conroy book. I promised to bring him Jim Tully's *Beggars of Life: A Hobo Autobiography*, and Fitzroy MacLean's fabulous *Eastern Approaches*, which I did the following day. Over time Jody and I exchanged other books, as I always looked forward to marching to Demmons, without trash in hand.

Digesting my ethnic-American hot dog, I forgot about my

abandoned trash bags shaking outside the front door. Before I could burp a second time, a customer aroused me and my luggage. Like a mild-mannered official of the Department of Homeland Security, a woman strolled in and asked, without accusation, "Whose bags are those out front?" Oh, shit, I shouted to no one but myself, here we go again. Surrendering quickly, I claimed ownership so I wouldn't be forced to explain the contents or circumstances.

Woodlands refuse in hand, but without blushing, I muttered to Jody, "Do you have a bin outside where I can throw this trash?" "Give them to me, I'll toss them here," Jody answered. I handed off my linguine boxes, newspapers and eggshells. Without breaking stride, Jody stuffed my trash into a plastic container under the counter. Touchdown! Game over! After hours of suspense, the disposition of my trash ended with a whimper, not a war. Until now I never explained the story to Jody. He never asked why I was carrying trash over the river and through the woods, although he may have wondered whether he would have to collect my trash every time I visited.

Given its history and location, I wasn't surprised to hear that Demmons echoes with sounds of the Declaration of Independence being read at 9 a.m. each July 4. When I bivouacked at Lucas Pond, that tradition was almost ten years old. More than a decade after that, it rolled on, as strong as ever.

A couple of days after my trash-walking excursion, I spotted the ultimate answer to those who would violate the dumpster code that governs the people of the woods: two padlocks sealed the lids on the dumpster at the corner of Bigelow and Lower Deerfield roads, where I was ambushed. No key, no dump; no ignorant strangers, no worry. A short time later, I noticed that a wire cord was laced across the lids, replacing the padlocks. Don't tread on me is how I read that message, which is either consistent with or in contradiction of the state's motto, Live Free or Die.

I was lucky. The tribes in the New Hampshire woods treated me well. W. H. Auden was dead on when he said, "Those to whom evil is done do evil in return." That's called revenge, and you'll find it wherever you find people. No one sought revenge against me for dumping or trying to dump trash in another person's trash bin. Perhaps my transgressions weren't sufficiently damaging, or anti-tribal.

On that long May day, when I set out to leave my trash in someone else's dumpster but ended up handing it to a Good Samaritan in a country store, I learned much about the woods and its people. Chiefly, keep your trash to yourself. Every three or four weeks, when Pat drove me to Portsmouth to purchase another month of fresh supplies and future trash, I hauled my accumulated cabin trash home to toss in a dumpster that I paid for.

Walks through the woods and along country roads also stimulated my writing, which was the point of my cabin life. Even my days away from Lucas Pond refreshed my mind and allowed what I had written to simmer, like my unpatented spaghetti sauce. Every recess from the cabin enabled me to cast a more critical eye on what I was thinking and what I had written, and to approach new chapters with fresh ideas.

Sharpened by my daily journals, my memory is as trustworthy as my conscience is clear. In February 2007, when I returned to the cabin to begin a new writing effort, I packed a stash of large black plastic bags to hold the weighty evidence of one person's presence on the shores of Lucas Pond. Back to Portsmouth I hauled the evidence of my life in the woods. Never again have I thrown trash into another person's dumpster anywhere, or even given a thought to such a transgression.

THE EYES HAVE IT

My year at Lucas Pond keeps knocking at my door, another sure sign of the success of solitude and meeting strangers. More than ten years after my trash and I were bushwhacked, I stared at a woman and she stared back near the soup counter in a farm store some twenty miles east of Lucas Pond. Here at the farm store in Dover, New Hampshire, another chance encounter smacked me head-on. After a glance, the woman and I thought we recognized each other, but weren't sure. Silence ruled. When I walked into the greenhouse attached to the store to dive into a bowl of fresh chicken noodle soup that I had just bought, there stood the same woman. After we looked at each other again, the woman said, "Are you the man who was writing a book at Lucas Pond?" I answered by saying her name in what was a mixture of declaration and doubt, but mostly certainty. She answered by acknowledging that she was the person I thought she was. After I told her my name, I said, "You know that was more than ten years ago." "No, not that long, is it?" she replied, astonished.

We exchanged a few more words before she moved on. Our conversation more than a decade earlier when I was walking my trash past her house near Lucas Pond remained fresh in my mind. She might have known, or guessed, what happened after I trod up the road looking to dump my trash on that bright May day in 2004. But because I never raised the issue with her, my former neighbor probably didn't know that I suspected she had triggered the tribal early warning system ten years earlier. She couldn't have known about my trash-walking trek to Demmons on that same day. I didn't tell her any of this back in 2004, and I didn't bring up the subject at the farm store more than ten years later.

Several months after the guardian of the woods and I stared at each other in the farm store, chance knocked again, this time in my own back yard. A young man, learning how to install stone walkways, looked at me and asked whether I was the man who was writing a book at Lucas Pond. Yes, indeed, I replied. You know, I said to the man who was about twelve years old back then, that was more than ten years ago. The young man seemed shocked at the passage of time. I was just as shocked by his presence at my house a decade after we first spied each other on Big Buck Road.

He was a son of the woman I had recently met in the farm store, the woman whom, I suspect, warned a neighbor of my approaching trash-dumping intentions way back in 2004.

DEMMONS REDUX

My time in the woods keeps circling and landing in my lap or on my head. Each July Fourth, for more than twenty years, the Declaration of Independence has had top billing at Demmons Country Store. Demmons is known locally for its July 4 celebration. It's about as routinely famous as it would have been if the town crier read the Declaration when the store opened under another name almost two centuries ago.

July Fourth happens to be my wedding anniversary, which meant that on each Independence Day since 2004, I was traveling and missed seeing Thomas Jefferson in disguise at Demmons. July Fourth, 2016, our fifty-second anniversary, was different. Pat and I decided to stay home and fly later. Our decision also meant that I could rise early on that Fourth to reach Demmons in time for its special celebration. Finally, twelve years after Jody rescued my trash and after I first heard about the Declaration being read at the store, I showed up to see and hear for myself. The reports are correct; the gathering is homespun, as red, white and blue as it gets, as if copied from a tapestry woven in 1776, and where any king or queen would be banned.

Anyone can show up at Demmons on July Fourth to enjoy a free breakfast, hear freedom-inspired folk music and listen to the reading. It's all free, a morning to wonder at the meaning and extension of that critical moment in American history. I had an open invitation, as did everyone else in the neighborhood. When I finally was able to assemble with others at Demmons on that Independence Day in 2016, I felt it a strange privilege, as if I were allowed a peek into a secret ceremony, which was in no sense true.

This was, I thought, the secular American version of religious experiences I witnessed elsewhere. The emotional effect of Jefferson's words reminded me of watching the Samaritans, an ancient but tiny Judaic sect, celebrate their 3,646th Passover on Mount Gerizim near Nablus in the Palestinian West Bank back in 1990. I also thought of the privilege I had in the early spring of 1992, enjoying a breakfast with men and women, Yazidis, who practice a pre-Roman Mithraic/Zoroastrian religion in Northern Iraq. There are many and deep differences in these events, of course, but it is the simplicity, smallness and tradition that make them so much alike.

From six to nine on the morning of July 4, 2016, about one-hundred-and-fifty Americans drifted in on foot, bicycle and motorcycle, in cars and trucks, as if they were gathering to raise a neighbor's barn. All they raised were their voices and their emotions in support of the independence and freedom expressed in the Declaration, as people had been doing at Demmons for two decades. Revolutionary Lane is only a couple of miles from the store. Maybe it's no accident that the Declaration of Independence is read aloud at Demmons. The surprise may be that the store had not hosted a reading each year throughout its nearly two-hundred-year existence.

Assorted musicians gathered in a circle playing guitars, fiddles, a mandolin, a tin whistle, and singing songs of liberty, whatever came to mind, it seemed. When I heard the tin whistle I thought of Tommy Makem, the wonderful Irish troubadour who lived much of his life in Dover less than twenty miles east of Demmons. This was a backyard party, not a symphony or Tommy Makem rollicking with the Clancy Brothers. Chris Vaughan, a Scot from Kittery, Maine, sang his own song of freedom: "There are plenty of men who would do it again, who would fight for the right to be free, because freedom does not dilute through the years and neither does liberty." A bagpiper in full regalia who lives on the shores of Lucas Pond waited to close the day's event by playing *Amazing Grace*. Some twenty teenagers from Camp Yavneh at Lucas Pond brought the energy of youth. Gathering near the circle of musicians, the teenagers sang Woody Guthrie's, *This Land Is Your Land*, and followed that with *Hava Nagila*, after which one of the guitar players said, "We tried to play that but we couldn't figure it out."

Declaring Independence at Demmons (circa 2009).
Photo courtesy of Demmons Country Store.

A police officer was there, too, with his official car, more for support than crowd control. No gathering of this sort would be complete without food, a free breakfast for all. Suzette, Jody's wife, led the way, frying eggs to order, with bacon, and serving home fries, along with red, white and blue desserts until the clock struck nine when Chris Reagan, a self-described "recovering musician," stepped to the store's small porch to read the Declaration. The crowd leaned toward the asphalt where gas pumps used to be to hear Reagan. A moment of silence was observed to honor those who died serving the nation. A woman from upstate played a bugle softly to the *Star Spangled Banner* and *You're A Grand Old Flag*. The crowd sang and a bugler played *God Bless America*.

When Reagan closed the Declaration with its powerful promise "...we mutually pledge to each other our Lives, our Fortunes, and our sacred Honor," nods of agreement bobbed through the crowd. There were no holdouts that I could see. Then, as always, the question is how long the deal would last, Fortunes being the pledge most difficult for most Americans to keep for anyone but themselves.

Demmons's Independence Day moment came as close to 1776 that I could imagine. It is more deeply felt, less artificial, than the usual Independence Day parades, barbecues and celebrations that I have witnessed anywhere, including at American embassies in other lands. "It's the real America," said Reagan, who has been reading the Declaration since 2010. "It's as homespun as it gets. It's an honor to do it. The words ring true now more than ever." Reagan succeeded the late Dave Behm who launched the oratorical tradition, almost on a whim, before nine or ten people. Since that moment, the crowds have grown—"It's taken on a life of its own," Jody said—but the event remains small and the aim is to keep it that way. The power of the reading flows from its simplicity: one person reading the Declaration while everyone else listens, and thinks. If the stage were larger than the small wood porch of a New Hampshire country store that's been standing for almost two centuries, the effect would surely be diluted.

Before I saw and heard 1776 come alive at Demmons, Jody described the reading this way: "It's different when someone reads it out loud. Many people never heard someone read it—ever. People get very emotional." If you can't walk, cyle or drive to Demmons on July Fourth, read the Declaration of Independence aloud in a room, and you'll understand what Jody means. In its own small way, a simple reading is at least a dollop of glue that binds people to history and continuously educates the community, at least for a few minutes a year.

Dave Behm was a local musician and craftsman who made Shaker chairs before he launched the tradition of reading the Declaration at Demmons about a decade before I moved to Lucas Pond. With that single stroke, he became an orator and a local hero, each July 4. Dave was gone when I showed up in 2016, but his widow Bunny Behm proudly carried on her late husband's mission. Breakfast, the music, singing and oratory are free, but contributions can be slipped into a jar to honor Dave Behm's memory and provide scholarship money for worthy music students at the local high school. In that way, Demmons further celebrates its role of making people better-informed citizens.

The reading and the singing that followed lasted about twenty minutes. Twenty minutes after that, Jody said, you wouldn't even know the gathering was held. He was right.

But change shadows tradition. If only for the moment, the July 4 celebration was cancelled in 2019. Aging, oddly it seems, had caught up to history and Demmons Country Store. My best guess, however, is that Thomas Jefferson, in the person of Chris Reagan or a neighbor, will soon return to the vicinity of Demmons and Revolutionary Lane.

The Late Dave Behm (circa 2009).
Photo courtesy of Demmons Country Store.

Yesterday was a bad writing day, maybe the worst so far. But overnight I figured out the best way to proceed on Afghanistan was to start with the two-day trip through the mountain tunnel from Kabul to Mazar. In the hazy light of half sleep, I gave myself a pep talk.—March 24, 2004

From the Ayatollah to Jesus

Living in the New Hampshire woods was similar to wandering in remote spaces in far away places. Here, I was a foreign correspondent again. What was supposed to be familiar wasn't, and I had changed too. The scale and risks were different for sure, as different as skirting a beaver pond in small woods is from disappearing in the Sahara's vast sands under a sprawling blanket of blinking stars. But roaming far and wide or close by expands horizons and opens the mind. Besides, what better way for a roving reporter to meet helpful strangers.

Not dictated by reporting assignments, breaking news or interest in ancients, the choice of time and place in my new world was mine alone. My isolation this time was deliberate. In and around my cabin, I read, dreamed, played cribbage, walked, thought and wrote, using every device I could command to spur the process. My writing cocoon was just that, small. But it was nothing like the dusky hotel room in Tehran where I wrote stories about the then recently deceased Ayatollah Khomeini, or the safe house in Mogadishu, Somalia, where I borrowed a United Nations satellite phone to file stories before I knew how a satellite phone worked. Still, the cabin and the trees enclosed me just as surely as did the frigid cinder-block box that shielded me from a raging snow in the mountains of southeastern Afghanistan.

Although foreign to me, the cabin was a five-star hotel compared with the tiny room in Bamiyan, central Afghanistan, where I slept with my rump in a chair and my feet on a desk to avoid scorpions, the neighborhood's deadly nighttime visitors. Absent any danger, roaming was again my calling along New Hampshire's roads and trails where I jotted notes for the book I was writing in the cabin, kept daily journals for this book, and sometimes talked with strangers. Leisurely walks to Susty's vegan restaurant, Demmons Country Store, Irving's convenience store, Hannaford's Supermarket and along Lucas Pond Road weren't exactly like flying northwest from Tel Aviv to Amsterdam and Frankfurt to jet back east to Tehran before the Ayatollah was buried, but I was roaming all the same.

Roving and reporting opened the doors to writing, wherever the continent. After I met Soviet Jews in Moscow's Central Synagogue, I wrote about them in semi-darkness at the Hotel Ukraine. On a wide hotel veranda at the port of Jounieh, north of Beirut, with shells whistling overhead moments before they plunged into the Mediterranean, midnight caught me writing about the Lebanese domestic and foreign war after spending days reporting in the mountains on the eastern front. Often it seemed as if I were in a bad movie, or maybe a good one because I survived without a nick. On one journey, my cabin was the rock-hard rear seat of an old Land Cruiser where I bounced from vinyl to roof and wrote while grinding in my teeth a small flashlight aimed at my Tandy 200 computer on the long drive to Amman from the Jordanian-Iraqi border. After I talked to the trees and a few strangers in the New Hampshire woods, where deer eluded me, I retreated to write in my little house on Big Buck Road. As much as I needed roaming to gather information, dark caves, hotel rooms of varying beauty and ugliness, and a cabin in the woods were essential to give life to what I had learned talking with strangers.

A boundless variety of welcoming strangers met me on wilderness trails and in unsafe houses. Sometimes roaming left me awe struck staring at Roman splendors in Baalbek, Lebanon and Plovdiv,

Bulgaria, or stupefied at modern atrocities in Algeria and too many other countries. Left unrecorded, my encounters with the bad and the beautiful would have been lost in the mists of memory as surely as if I had again stumbled through a blinding winter fog in northern Bosnia. If I learned anything from traveling, talking and listening, it's that people are much the same everywhere. They want respect, understanding, and a reasonably peaceful life with enough food, clothing and shelter to see tomorrow, and the day after. Many make it. Many do not. Limitations hover everywhere; the boundaries of time and history, place, culture, family and the larger constraints of tribe, low expectations and hostile, greedy neighbors, near and far.

As a newspaperman trailing donkeys to remote mountain villages, veering into ancient imperial capitals to collect memories or merging with the masses in the subways of European capitals, I often hoofed into terrain I never intended to touch. Grand mistakes those were. The more unplanned the journeys and destinations, the more I learned. Tashkent, the capital of Uzbekistan in Central Asia, was a good place to search for Jews packed and ready to run as the Soviet Union was becoming Russia again. Samarkand, south of Tashkent, beckoned. The fourteenth and fifteenth century capital of Timur the Lame's empire, with its beautiful mosques and Islamic schools still standing, wasn't on my reporter's map but it had been on my mind for years. History called, so I went to see more of the past in a few days than most people see in a lifetime, or after a reincarnation or two.

Plagues wrought by humans found me counting the daily dead and searching for the killers in Somalia and Algeria. When the chance came to take a United Nations flight to the northern Somali city of Hargeisa, I leaped behind the cockpit as one of two passengers in a huge cargo plane. Long a garrison in the Cold War struggle to control Somalia and its strategic location at the Horn of Africa, enough weapons planted by East and West lay scattered in Hargeisa to wage several wars. I hadn't planned it that way, but before long I was crawling on my hands and knees behind local men who were hired by a British firm to pluck anti-personnel mines from an abandoned airfield. Trying to sneak up on what could easily have been a deadly explosion wasn't one of my brightest decisions. Yet there I was—one, two, three—tallying buried but soon exhumed button mines and only later wondering what the hell that was all about. It was related, I decided, to doing my job. Trying to sneak up on an explosion was only part of my job; writing a story completed the circle.

Hardship overwhelmed me at times and in the oddest places. I watched *Giselle* from a center aisle seat in the seventh row at the Bolshoi Theater in Moscow. That was truly risky and punitive, I recalled with a chuckle. As the Soviet Union was collapsing, I looked on in amusement at a grand Russian circus and at a rollicking performance of the *Odd Couple* in a small Moscow theater where the language barrier was never an obstacle. No such luck greeted me in the New Hampshire woods, but Kismet awaited me later as I searched for a publisher.

Trudging along lightly trodden paths among oaks, birches, pines and hemlocks was not even remotely like snacking anxiously at the well-stocked home of an Afghan tribal boss who broke his luncheon date but left screeching peacocks as a reminder of his ethereal presence. My search for kidnapped westerners in Lebanon, by interviewing their captors, was slightly more risky than searching for the source of Lucas Pond and stumbling upon a man who handed me a magical walking stick.

A decade before I moved to Lucas Pond, I found New Hampshire in France. While reporting on the Fiftieth Anniversary of D-Day, I pulled into a small restaurant in Avranches, Normandy, France, near the boundary with Brittany. The maître d', or someone like him, told me that crepes were first created in Avranches. Who was I to argue with the creators? Besides, what did it matter; I love crepes, no matter their parentage. What happened next was remarkable. Hearing my American tongue, a husband and wife from New Hampshire introduced themselves, although they didn't reveal their hometown and I didn't think to ask. But they did reveal more telling information. French-Canadians by birth, they were in Normandy seeking their ancestral roots. I'll be damned, I thought; Jefferson, Lafayette, New Hampshire, France and O Canada! All in one place.

Restlessness lived on in the woods while the more medieval adventures lay behind me in Sarajevo, Algiers's Casbah, and the hog-tied Gaza Strip. This urge to talk to and learn from people helped me to think and write. Making notes, I figured, was a genetic necessity as well as an occupational requirement wherever I stepped. Never more than when I met the ancient Samaritans who held their Passover Feast on a mountaintop near Nablus in the Palestinian West Bank, or the Yazidis who, when they weren't being murdered by larger tribes, practiced their ancient Mithraic/Zoroastrian religion in northern Iraq.

Chatting on Big Buck Road with a puzzled high school senior wasn't quite as intriguing as watching a local woman negotiate a gold deal in a Damascus market or working in Israel with a fresh émigré from Russia. Chatting about Jesus and doughnuts in a line at a convenience store in New Hampshire was less exciting than being briefed by one of Mother Theresa's minions about Serbian oppression in Albanian Kosovo. The urge to push in doors is rooted in my nature, an urge to satisfy curiosity. There's an art and a science to it as well. Curiosity and natural instincts ruled my world. The more difficult the journey, the more motivated I became.

After almost a year of living, writing and hiking in the woods, I remained a stranger at Lucas Pond. My neighbors were foreigners to me, a shared and voluntary choice. One neighbor told me that even people who had lived in the orbit of Lucas Pond for years talked little to others like them. Perhaps that's a condition of living stranger-to-stranger in the woods, further deepened by living in the woods of New England, where personal reserve usually trumps a wagging tongue. Only time, much time, softens the edges of that behavior.

* * *

The news shook world capitals like a counter-revolution, although it was not. On June 3, 1989, the Grand Ayatollah Sayyid Ruhollah Mousavi Khomeini left this world, cut down in the prime of life at eighty-six. The real news, from my view, was that Iran would open its shuttered doors, if only to reveal a filtered view of religious populism, also known as religious fanaticism and demagoguery, wherever it isn't practiced. Khomeini's successors, Iran's mullahs, wanted people from pole to pole to witness the forced love that Iranians had for Khomeini and his religious revolution; eager; quizzical news hawks the world over were invited to be the couriers.

Pat and I moved to Jerusalem about a month before Khomeini's death gave outsiders a peek, if only for a week or so, at a land once called Persia. Our personal possessions were still in transit from the United States. My bank account had yet to be swelled by enough company cash to get me into and out of hostile embraces across three continents. But there I was, scrambling to find a magic carpet that would take me from Tel Aviv to Tehran in a breeze, under normal conditions a one-carpet flight of less than three hours. But conditions were far below normal: my journey would require three carpets and too many hours despite the proximity of the two cities.

The Jewish state and the Ayatollah's Shiite Islamic state were like two icebergs floating far apart in a frozen sea where nothing melted. If the Iranians had known that my journey east had started in Tel Aviv, they would have buried the Ayatollah without me. But national borders, religious barriers, territorial conflicts and flying far to the northwest in order to swerve sharply to the nearby east couldn't be allowed to stop me. My first long range assignment as Middle East correspondent for the Atlanta-based Cox Newspapers was to reach Tehran in time to report on the funeral of a religious leader whose revolution had flipped Iran upside down and rocked more than one world capital, most notably Washington. This was no minor story. It was a major test. A decade earlier, hundreds of Iranian students surged into the U.S. embassy in Tehran, taking sixty-six American hostages, fifty-two of whom were held for four-hundred and forty-four days, ultimately sending President Jimmy Carter into political retirement. Khomeini's revolution didn't sweep out of the desert like a sudden sandstorm. His rise came twenty-five years after the United States, buying Iranians as if they were chips in a casino, had engineered the ouster of Prime Minister Mohammad Mosaddeqh, a popular leader, and the return of Mohammed Reza Shah Pahlavi, the Iranian king who ruled with monarchical fervor and an overzealous secret police force for a quarter century. Iranians didn't forget that the United States engineered Mosaddeqh's ouster in 1953, and the subsequent quarter century of the shah's oppressive rule. Those volcanic events, however, were unknown to, or forgotten by, most Americans when Khomeini seized power and when he died, and they remain so today.

My personal American Express card, plus a few hundred dollars in company cash, would have to get me to and from Tehran. What money I gathered would also feed me while I interviewed mourners who one minute welcomed me and a minute later were shouting, as if on cue, death to America. Along the way, I had to shed all evidence that my new abode was in Jerusalem. My credit card represented cash to airlines that flew first from Tel Aviv northwest to Amsterdam in The Netherlands, then a short distance southeast to Frankfurt, Germany, which was my only ready flight path back east to Tehran and Khomeini's funeral.

Flying from Frankfurt to Tehran on Iran's national airline, the only carrier that was going the remaining distance, would be more expensive still, and more complicated. Cash-starved Iran wanted American dollars immediately, not a credit card, for a plane ticket from Frankfurt to Tehran and back to Rome on my return. By American dollars, the Iranians meant $2,100, an outrageous charge. But, as I learned later when peering through the everlasting dusk in a Tehran hotel room with the lame aid of twenty-five-watt light bulbs, American dollars were plasma to Iran after a decade of being frozen out of international financial affairs. Although not by design, it can be said that the Ayatollah died in a timely fashion because Iran was desperate for hard currency. With only a few hours to spare before flight time, the American Express office in Frankfurt came through for me. I was able to withdraw $3,000 on my personal card, all but $900 of which went straight to Iran's national airline. Where that cash ended up was a mystery, but I knew it wasn't all going to pay salaries for flight attendants or to buy brighter light bulbs.

Khomeini's funeral was delayed for a few days to give journalists from around the world time to reach Tehran and watch mourners mourn. A sensational burial without worldwide coverage would have been much less sensational, melting into a local event and hardening into a propaganda failure. I reached the capital in time to see hundreds of thousands of men, women and children filling the streets on the way to the funeral and later flowing like lemmings to the cemetery compound where Khomeini would be buried. Hundreds of people, following unspoken but clearly understood commands, shouted "death to America" at me and at two tall, light-skinned Norwegian journalists, who were obviously misidentified. I didn't take the threats personally, although my feet were smart enough to move quickly out of danger range when the breathing became as hot as the words. Shortly after that greeting, I flew with one leg and its accompanying hip hanging from an overcrowded helicopter to the jammed cemetery where I watched Khomeini's body fall from its litter, provoking a reaction of riotous proportions.

From the very beginning, good luck tracked me in Iran, as it did in every country where I courted and dodged trouble. Part of that stemmed from alliances I made with helpful strangers in difficult situations, people I would never meet again, but wished I would. At my hotel in Tehran, a young Iranian showed me how to file a story by pounding on a worn and weary Teletype machine and opening a line to the Cox Washington Bureau without the near-extortionist fee coming from my own shallow pocket, which had grown shallower quickly. If my office sent me a message via Teletype as I requested, I could then file my story on the line opened by Washington. That way, Washington would be charged and I would be spared the cost of sending my story. This sleight of hand allowed me to file my final Khomeini story, have enough cash to pay for a taxi ride to the airport at midnight, and tip my new Iranian teletype wizard with all the Iranian Rials I could spare, which totaled about one-hundred-twenty-five American dollars. I also promised to find a way to send the young Iranian more money as payment for his assistance, which I later did. All of those gratuities, by the way, totaled several hundred dollars less than I would have been charged had I paid out of my own pocket to file my final story about Khomeini's funeral. If I had exhausted my cash before begging for a taxi ride to the airport, I would probably have missed my flight, violated the terms of my visa, and maybe been forced to hang around praying for leniency from Khomeini's successors. Additional good news was that my story actually reached Washington, and did not go directly to a Hezbollah office in Lebanon or to an Iranian compound in Damascus.

When I strolled in after midnight, drained of cash, the Tehran airport was a ghost building. Iran's secret police were snoozing. A skeleton crew pretended to sweep the already clean floors; one worker danced with a broom while a colleague lodged his under an armpit. My visa was about to expire and my flight to Rome was almost six hours away. Before long I met another loner, an Iranian physician bound for a medical conference in Los Angeles. Wearing a shirt, tie and suit, the doctor looked prepped to wow colleagues in a Los Angeles hotel ballroom. My traveling uniform—baggy pants, rumpled shirt and no-wrinkle jacket—made it appear I hadn't changed clothes in more than a week. True enough. No matter. My eyes widened. Here was a conversation with a stranger that couldn't, and shouldn't, be missed.

Eager to put space between himself and Khomeini's Iran, for a few weeks at least, the doctor was also headed first to Rome. For almost four hours, and with no one around to hear or even watch our foreign exchange, the doctor and I talked comfortably about Iranian life and world affairs and of his pending trip to Los Angeles, whose Iranian community had swelled after the ouster of the shah and Khomeini's rise a decade earlier. "How is life in Iran?" I asked. "I'm fine," the doctor answered in excellent English, "but if you're not a doctor, a lawyer, a teacher or from the circle of religious believers and their supporters, you have a very big problem." Most people keep quiet to avoid problems, he said, or shout anti-American slogans when they're expected to. "If you can leave, you leave," he said. "If you can hide, you hide. If you can't hide, you go into the street to shout so no one can accuse you of being against the government." The doctor didn't ask any questions, not one. He was too excited about his temporary parole and his visit with friends and associates in Los Angeles to ask about life in America, or what I learned about Khomeini's Iran.

More passengers drifted into the hall as departure time neared. Abruptly and with only a slight movement of his right hand as if to wave goodbye, but without a word, the doctor strolled off. He no longer felt comfortable talking to a foreigner, let alone a foreign newspaperman, in the presence of other eyes and ears. As dawn approached and more passengers shared space in the hall, it was as if the doctor and I had never talked. We passed each other in the terminal, walking to and from the men's room, several times before takeoff, but the doctor and I never made eye contact again.

A security official asked about the funeral as I inched casually toward boarding. My occupation was no secret because I was compelled to reveal my purpose when I entered Iran. And I did not lie, except when I believed lying would save my life. The officer's inquisition was my first on the road, and it remains the most unusual. All he wanted was something other than the official view. He seemed to distrust the local versions so he turned to an outsider, a target of the Death-to-America shouts, for variety. What happened to Khomeini's body at the cemetery compound? he asked. I had nothing worth hiding and had been at the scene when Khomeini's body fell from its litter next to its burial plot. So I told the man what I saw, and the panic that followed. Nodding and smiling, the man thanked me. I boarded the plane without incident. My lips are sealed, I said to myself. But this was one security guard who had fresh intelligence, information he might share with friends, but probably not with his bosses.

Flying northwest to reach the so-near-yet-so-far east in order to watch the burial of an old man was my introduction to a decade of hurdling endless obstacles to report a story. It also shaped a life of traveling that became inseparable from reporting and writing, and of making friends with strangers in wildly different cultural climates. I was thrown into the game under difficult circumstances, the best way to learn how to get the story, survive and become smarter.

* * *

No old man died when the woods called one balmy May day in 2004. But lessons awaited me there, too, one about Native Americans that is older than the United States. Worlds away from the exotic East, my world at Lucas Pond was small, tethered as I was to cabin, woods, country roads and more incidental strangers. Seclusion alone pushes the mind and the pen to unpredictable places. Not only did I learn the creative power of quiet isolation, one day I heard it on the radio. A teacher in a one-room schoolhouse in a tiny

Nevada town put it this way: "I really believe the mind blossoms in a quiet place."

The time had come to seek the source of the stream that feeds Lucas Pond. This was a voluntary mission, not an editorial assignment. Exploring the small New Hampshire woods helped me write about other, larger, worlds as I had seen them, introduced me to more strangers and surprising places, and provided the grist for this book.

Old Man Winter had delayed my search plans. But with the Old Man's ice blanket restored to an earlier state, spring stood sprightly in its place, urging me into the woods to find Lucas Pond's holy grail. My companion on that day was a reedy branch I wielded lightly to scare off imaginary snakes as I trudged through the sodden woods.

My boots slid over and through autumn's dead leaves and pine needles, some drying but most soaked from spring rains as I skidded along trails the Indians once called their own. Rocks girdling the brook have probably been static for hundreds of years, guarding the water source itself until the stream fell into the pond. Bright young leaves on oaks and maples competed for sunlight with various evergreens, their needles growing invisibly longer and slowly changing their greenness so other needles could fall to the earth five or six months later. Evergreen toddlers, with short sticklike trunks, rose from the woodland floor in spaces too small for adult trees. Two or three feet from the ground, the pre-teen trees branched out in umbrella fashion as if screaming for help from the light above and pleading for space from surrounding brethren. Squirrels and chipmunks squeaked and fled from my path.

Green as I was, even I knew my search for the stream's source would be successful. Instead of following the money, which I had done often while tracking political corruption, I had only to follow the water. The source of the artery that feeds Lucas Pond is hidden in plain view, once you know where it is. Still, this was one time when I needed no coaching, no secret hand-written notes telling me, simply, to follow the stream.

My little adventure became a grand one as I pretended the source was hidden in a cave, like a lost gold mine or a prehistoric religious sanctuary. It wasn't, of course, but a little fictional mystery added interest. So I slogged quietly, slowly, through the greening woods. When I walk in the woods, any woods anywhere, I always slog or trudge. If there's another way to walk in the woods, I missed the hiking class where that method was taught. In my own mind, I always walk quietly, too, although trudging and quietly seem like they should hang out alone but never together. To my ears, whistling is the only noise I make in the woods. Whistling as I trudged was a treat because whistling in newsrooms is a taboo. If you whistled in a newsroom long ago, you might have had to duck from a glue pot that whizzed by your ear or cringe under a barrage of curses.

Observing and learning are inseparable when trolling among the trees. This day would be no different. After an hour or so of winding through brambles and bushes, I stumbled out of a thicket on to a driveway off the top of Lower Deerfield Road not far from Woodman Marsh in Northwood. At that moment, the driveway and lawn beyond spelled drooling hound, as in Rottweiler or Doberman. When I touched the turf near the driveway, the game was up. It was too late to flee.

The image of a large animal leaping from its den set my eyes frantically searching for a dog-proof cudgel. But all I could grasp was my reedy switch, useless now for sure. To my happy surprise, a friendly two-legged soul emerged to greet me, palms up. His broad smile reached across the gap between strangers, one comfortably at home, the other uncomfortable in unfamiliar territory. Comfortable in his home away from too many neighbors, the man wasn't fleeing a theocracy and he knew more about the woods than I.

My introduction was brief: name, hideout, purpose. Wherever engaged I always introduce myself by giving my full name. That's a small but helpful gambit I learned while traipsing on really foreign turf. The idea is to show that I have nothing to hide. It's also disarming, creating instant trust. Most Americans tell strangers only their first name, fearful of identity theft, I guess, or somehow losing their life savings to a thieving stranger who will later track them down.

Home From A Hike. Photo by Patricia Brothers Salome.

The stranger who greeted me didn't need to explain anything; I was in his territory. "You need a better walking stick," the man said, taking pity on my reedy pose. "A serious woodsman needs a serious walking stick," he said, "and I have just the one for you."

Near his house a short distance away, a splendid red birch walking stick awaited him and me. "Here, take this," the man said, holding the stick for me to take in my right hand while I shifted the switch to my left. This was a gift, from one stranger to another, with no bark attached. Cracked both at the top and at the tapered bottom, snapped from a tree rather than bought at retail, the wizened walker is thick and sturdy, its rough-hewn curved knob on top proof of its purpose. It reminded me of a shillelagh. Right then the walking stick became mine. Thanks to a stranger I met by chance in the woods, I'll never trudge alone again. My red birch walking stick will forever be evidence that I expanded my scant knowledge of the woods from elm, oak, pine, white birch and hemlock, to beautiful red birch.

Before I set off again, the husband and father of three told me about moose and deer that live in the woods, and hawks and grosbeaks that hovered above. The best time to spot deer, the man said, is at dusk. When it came to spotting deer, not dawn, noon or dusk worked for me. Along with this information about life in the woods, and his gift of a red birch walking stick, the man passed on a bit of woodland wisdom: keep an eye out for trees with branches that the Indians long ago bent at right angles low to the ground, leaving the branches looking like seats. Those bent branches were used long ago to mark trails, the man said. Searching for those branches seemed like an interesting way to tour and map the woods, until I started to think about it. If the Indians marked trails that way, those bent branches by now would be about a hundred feet above ground; a little difficult to spot, in other words, without acquiring a very stiff neck. They would be even more difficult for my derriere to find useful. As the deer were invisible to me, so were those bent trees and old Indian trails. I never saw trees bent to look like seats, and by mid-summer I was no longer looking.

A few years later, thanks to a friend who read an early draft of this book, I learned that the donor of my walking stick was correct all along. It is indeed still possible to spot a tree branch that was bent low to the ground generations or centuries earlier to mark trails and form seats in the forest. I had been barking up the wrong trees, tramping along the wrong trails. A bend in a tree branch will remain at its original height from the trunk as time passes. The branch will continue to grow upward, but from above, not below, where the limb was bent. Doubters should discuss this matter with the New Hampshire Forest Service, not with a townie whose knowledge of the greenery is mainly that some leaves appear in spring and leave in autumn.

Whenever I slogged along the paths and pavements of Northwood, looking for strangers to meet and learn from, I thought of all the strangers I met in the wilds of other worlds. Strangers here and there are matched by the fact that strangers everywhere have more in common than any of them know.

* * *

Men, women and children of the battered Yazidi tribe weren't expecting me when I tramped through a freezing rain into their northern Iraqi village of Ribebi. By my calendar, they should have been expecting something unusual; it was, after all, April Fool's Day, 1992. But they weren't fools, and neither was I. They were expecting two professors from the University of London tailed by two of their doctoral students. The Yazidis weren't disappointed. Both students from the university's School of Oriental and African Studies were women. Worthy of pursuit, a doctorate can require difficult on-the-ground research. Under the circumstances, however, I thought the research of both students was well beyond the call of duty. One of the women planned to live for several months with the Yazidis. The other talked of staying for only a month. The village wasn't next door to Greenwich or Hyde Park. It wasn't even near Haworth or any other moor. A chance to meet a tribe with at least 3,000-year-old roots didn't cross my path every day, but this time I was lucky enough to tag along with the academy.

Yazidis are a Kurdish people who practice an ancient, eclectic religion that contains elements of Zoroastrianism, the religion of ancient Persia. Practitioners of a pre-Roman-era faith called Mithraism, the Yazidis also have adaptive links to Judaism, Christianity and Islam. For Yazidis, as with most minorities, adaptation was essential to survival, often barely. They took from the old and gave to the new; patched the new to the old in order to keep on going. Many believers, however, prefer all or nothing, which can be a huge problem for anyone, especially minorities.

Living with the Yazidis, a minority within a Kurdish minority that is within an Arabic majority, would be difficult for anyone, let alone two young women from another culture and continent. The Yazidis were few, their living conditions just a bit unlike life in York or Yarmouth, and they face constant persecution from larger tribes in the neighborhood because they are neither Arabs nor Muslims. Saddam Hussein, the late long-time dictator of Iraq and a Sunni Arab, did his best to wipe the Yazidis from the Iraqi map in the 1980s. The Islamic State of Iraq and Syria, or ISIS/ISIL, picked up the cudgel and the rampage after Hussein's ouster and the national upheaval that followed.

In the Iraqi city of Duhok, the day before April Fool's Day, I had convinced the professors and their students to let me join them on their trek through a monsoon to meet the Yazidis. Reluctant to bring along a snoopy newspaperman who asked too many questions, the professors finally agreed after we struck a deal. My new friends from England agreed to let me walk in their midst after I promised only to look and listen, to remain silent and introduce no question marks. This was to be their mission, theirs alone. My role would be to remain nearly invisible, to hover, watch and listen. The accommodation worked. The Yazidis ignored me. I didn't ignore them. But we reached no agreement about dining protocol, however, so I joined everyone at a long table sheltered by a tent soon after our arrival in the village. A splendid meal of bread and olives, cheese, hard-boiled eggs and boiling tea was enjoyed by hosts and their guests. Everything the Yazidis had to offer they shared with us, all strangers. They proved another example of the many people I met along the trail who had the least but shared the most.

Women play a major role in Yazidi religion and society. For those who have been dozing, overt matriarchal power doesn't play well in the patriarchal Middle East. In that context, it wasn't surprising to watch Yazidi women warmly welcome the two women students as if they were members of the same tribe, which in the largest tribal sense of all they were. This embracing greeting among strangers was the strongest expression of sisterhood that I saw along all the roads I have travelled on four continents. One of the students, Christine Allison, went on to receive her doctorate and to teach Kurdish studies at the University of Exeter in England. The Yazidi women, along with Yazidi men and children, continue to fight for their lives.

* * *

Chance encounters were more frequent and more interesting than planned conversations in the quiet New Hampshire woods. Similar serendipity prevailed in other lands, although excitement and tension were added surprises. Scuffling along Big Buck Road on a late April day in 2004, kicking stones while admiring the buds of an infant spring and chilled water bubbling over rocks and gravel from brook to pond, I looked up and spotted a young woman. I didn't ask her name and she didn't offer. For simplicity purposes, I'll call her Sarah. She admitted, however, to being eighteen; oh, "I wish I was eighteen again," I thought, thanking George Burns for his words, lyrics trumping his grammar.

With a cigarette dangling from her mouth, the young woman lingered outside her family home near Lucas Pond. A sign of boredom and anxiety, I thought, the cigarette was an early misstep in what could easily become a dull and unhealthy journey through life. To an eighteen-year-old, however, cigarettes probably were a tangible sign of independence, social acceptance and relief. A few weeks from graduation, this jittery high school senior crouched at a pivotal point in her life. But the importance of the crossroad seemed like a complete mystery to this stranger. She was focused on saplings—the senior prom, graduation and a little job—that blocked her long view. "I'm happy I passed," she said.

Both forks in her road pointed to craters. Her choices were dismal; great challenges nearby or in far-off lands were not in Sarah's line of sight. She was torn between studying car mechanics in Illinois after graduation or sticking to her roots and living with her boyfriend while working for $7.50 an hour cleaning recreational vehicles. This deprivation of choice depressed me more than the grayest November day. Her decision might trail her for a lifetime; gray days in the woods would pass. Worse still, she was leaning toward cleaning recreational vehicles because the pay was better than the $5.50 per hour she could earn selling coffee and doughnuts at a local shop while living with her boyfriend. All she was doing, I thought, was fleeing her family's home to live with her man. Her urge to bolt from the tribal circle I understood. Going off to study car mechanics in Illinois would have been a better flight pattern, I thought, although hormones probably steered her from that direction. I kept my counsel, however, although I probably shouldn't have.

As Sarah talked, I said little but made a few mental notes. It's true; youth is indeed wasted on those with tight skin and thick hair, I thought from a distance of almost fifty years. Sure, but wisdom can slip past geezers before they remember how or when to use it. Even if wisdom could be employed earlier, would a younger person understand what would seem like a dead language? Probably not, I thought, because the young want to make their own mistakes: you had your chances, old fella, now leave us alone to make the most of ours. Separately, we all stumble over many of the same stones, but collectively we do enough right to move the boulder up the hill a little each hundred years or so. That's called making progress, something that Americans like to think they do better than anyone, while others prefer their own empires, and their own mistakes.

My ruminations remained mine as Sarah talked on. While I asked a few questions, mostly I turned into an ear, my habit of preaching and trying to teach quelled by the young woman's predicament. Even my more practical thoughts remained mine: whatever you do, make sure your lover boy wears a condom, all the time; save enough coins to see life through a long lens before you settle for cleaning RVs, selling doughnuts or having babies; consider traveling the world before you become convinced that swilling beer in a sports bar offers the clearest view of life; think hard about whether new immigrants should be greeted by walls rather than by Lady Liberty.

In more than a decade since our brief exchange, I have thought of this young woman often, hoping that she found a wider, brighter path. Did she rescue herself? Did others rescue her? Did the unexpected happen, so she avoided the mistakes of her tribe? I also think of my reaction to her, scolding myself for not preaching a little, for not trying to explain that her choices might have been more promising than she had imagined. Sometimes listening isn't the only, or even the better, answer.

Sarah was no Amira, a young woman I met at the gold market in Damascus. Amira, the name she gave me, acted as a mediator in bargaining disputes. If a buyer and seller were quibbling over price, Amira was called in as an "objective" mediator to identify the truth. Her job was to help consummate the deal for the seller and herself, while leaving the buyer happy too. At the time, I didn't judge Amira as I had later judged Sarah. Conditions and culture, I thought, determined that Amira was locked into her role; she had few, if any, choices. My attitude toward Sarah was totally different; I judged her because I thought I knew her culture. An American, Sarah had many choices, or should have had, because choices are supposed to abound in America. On reflection, maybe Sarah had few choices; perhaps her life was dictated by the conditions and culture that surrounded her, just as Amira's was in her own time and space.

* * *

Tens of thousands of people were straining to leave the Soviet Union in 1990, as the Communist state stumbled through its dying days; Masha was trying to help them. Reaching back into the mists of their ancestral, pre-Communist lives, many of the flight risks claimed to be Jews. They were eager to find another tribal homeland and Israel was their only open door. Fear and uncertainty stalked them in what soon would become old Russia and a host of new nations ready to blossom throughout the former Soviet empire. The Soviet economy had fallen through the cellar. Bare shelves greeted the sad eyes and long chins that fell on sinking chests in state markets. Local citizens were barred from the few foreign currency outlets that served foreigners. Taxi drivers screeched to a curb for pedestrians waving packages of Lucky Strikes, Winston, Marlboro or other American cigarette brands. No other currencies need apply.

A student and teacher of English and Hebrew, Masha was barely out of her teens. Cheerful and confident of her ability and prospects, she was teaching as many people as she could for the princely sum of less than seven American dollars per student for three hours of instruction. Actors, doctors, writers, engineers, mothers and fathers, daughters and sons were her students. All of them wanted to learn Hebrew so they could hit Tel Aviv with more than hello on their tongues and a smile and handshake in their quivers of respect. Masha was teaching twenty-one adults when I met her in Moscow in May of 1990. She taught them any place they and she could gather—in apartments, theaters, on streets and in the rooms of the Union of Teachers of Hebrew in Moscow.

Masha's parents were divorced. Her mother, who worked for

Aeroflot, the Soviet airline, was Russian. As she introduced me to some of her students, Masha told me that her Jewish connection was through her father. Because her mother wasn't Jewish, Masha knew that her Jewishness would be questioned under Israeli religious and legal definitions. She was willing, however, to take her chances in Israel rather than remain mired in the fear and uncertainty that, she believed, would mark Russia's future. With a wink and a blink, Israel would surely welcome a smart young woman, another warm body.

Masha, whose real name will remain in my notebook, was young, but she wasn't a kid. She had ambition, a red-hot desire to improve her life, and visions of easier years ahead. With a talent for languages, she had learned English and Hebrew, and even picked up some Mandarin Chinese. Her timing was perfect: Masha was a university language student when the end of the Soviet system lay dying on her doorstep and people with a hint of Jewishness were hungering to flee. With her knowledge of Hebrew, Masha had a nervous finger on the pulse of uncertainty and felt the popular tremors. She rolled the dice. Masha left one side of the desk for the other, choosing to teach students much older than she. "I don't want to teach Hebrew and English all my life. Teaching Hebrew is not a profession," Masha told me in one of our long conversations about life in the Soviet Union, its imminent demise, the looming rebirth of Russia, and her prospects in Israel. "I want to study linguistics and Chinese. I have no chance at all to do this in Russia. I have to earn a living and can't only study."

Two months before we met, Masha had applied for an exit visa. Without that official document, she couldn't leave the Soviet Union. As with so many before and after her, Masha expected to wait months, maybe a year, before she could squeeze that ticket out of the authorities in Moscow. She felt confident of her prospects, however, because her best friend was already in Tel Aviv, as were seven of her former Hebrew students.

Soviet citizens with Jewish lineage that ranged from gauzy to certain lined up to leave for Israel from throughout the Soviet lands. Other doors were closed. The flow outward would turn into a population flood for Israel. But that would be another huge obstacle to statehood for Palestinians because Israel's government encouraged the new immigrants to settle in the Palestinian West Bank, taking more land and water from Palestinians there and squeezing them into smaller spaces. From 1990 through 2000, more than 800,000 Jews from the former Soviet Union settled in Israel. From 1990 through 1994 alone, the number was 400,000.

During the course of many days, Masha proudly introduced me to her students from Moscow and its urbs. My interest was to locate people who planned to sell all they had, buy a new car and drive to Israel. I wanted to ride with them and write that story. No help to me, the exit process took months too long for me to coordinate my departure from the Soviet Union with those more eager to leave than I was. As a result, I wasn't able to find anyone who was cleared to leave during the thirty days I was searching in Moscow, Leningrad/St. Petersburg and L'vov, in western Ukraine. History was on Masha's side, however, although I have been unable to learn whether history delivered. If ambition, intelligence and fearlessness were the tickets out, Masha made it. "I think that Israel is the country where I will have the opportunity to work and to do what I want," Masha told me just before I left for what was then Leningrad (now St. Petersburg again) to continue my search for citizens with exit visas in their pockets, an auto at the curb, and Tel Aviv in their eyes.

* * *

Fourteen years after I met Masha in Moscow, a near-religious experience awaited me in the form of a pleasant and earnest young woman on another continent. This would be my only such encounter in the New Hampshire woods. The young woman, who was about Masha's age, surprised me at Irving gas station's convenience store on Route 4 in Northwood, New Hampshire. Irving's is more than three miles from my cabin at Lucas Pond, but it was within my orbit. It was early afternoon on April 22, 2004, Day 80 in the cabin, when I strolled into Irving's from Hannaford's supermarket on the other side of Route 4. To welcome spring to the cabin, I had bought anti-ant cups and room deodorizers, which had nothing to do with lunch at a convenience store or the near-religious experience that lay ahead. The bubbly, zealous young woman wore a red and blue baseball cap and sunglasses pushed up on her forehead. She was standing in line eating a doughnut and drinking coffee, waiting to pay her fair share. Waiting to order a small vegetarian pizza, I stood directly behind her.

Joking, the woman said she would only have to pay for three-quarters of the doughnut because she had already eaten a quarter of it. Also joking, I said, "Eat it all quickly and you won't have to pay for any of it." "Oh, no, I couldn't do that," the woman replied, seriously, "Jesus wouldn't approve. The Bible says you'll go to hell if you don't find fellowship with Jesus." Uh-oh! I said to myself. Still thinking about the doughnut jokes, I arched my eyebrows and answered that a merciful and just God, man or woman, wouldn't pitch such a nice young woman into the fires of hell for eating, stealing, a doughnut. She would have to commit a much more serious crime, I told her. The young woman laughed in a nervous way, without seeming to know whether or why to believe me. I quit there.

Then the woman asked whether I was Italian, a question with which I am most familiar. When I said that I wasn't, she followed up: "What are you then?" firing that old "Where you from, what's your blood?" question at me as if I were again in Macedonia, where a decade earlier my Albanian translator, trying to divine whether I was a friend or foe, asked me the "blood" question. "My ancestry is Syrian," I told the woman. "Oh," she said, "You have Italian eyes." "You have that wrong," I said with a broad smile and eyes twinkling, "Italians have Syrian eyes." The young woman blinked at that Mediterranean mystery. Still puzzled, even more than before, she paid her small bill, waved and said, "Have a good one" as she skipped out the door. I thought immediately of comedian George Carlin's response to that parting phrase, but I didn't say it. Mixed company. Instead, I answered, "And you have a long and happy life," a remark that drew only silence. The full version of my remark is "May God grant you a long and happy life." I usually omit the "God" part, because I don't want to confuse anyone, not even myself. I usually utter that Arabic saying when I hear, as I often do, "Have a good one" or "Have a good day," the latter sayings being too narrowly American for my taste. A few Americans understand the gap between "have a good day" or "have a good one" and "have a long and happy life," but most do not.

* * *

Often you spot them immediately; sometimes it takes longer. If you miss the signs entirely, you could be in for a long and painful night, or worse. They are always present—the secret police checking on foreigners, especially snooping journalists, in major hotels of most Middle Eastern and South Asian capitals. For a few moments, I didn't sniff out the man whose mission was to send me packing from Pakistan, pronto. Soon, however, the signals were too bright and loud to miss. Before long I was crawling around my hotel room, hoping not to die in Islamabad.

My last supper in Pakistan's capital began innocently, alone and with a standard tossed salad. A short time later, before I could digest my olives and tomatoes, it ended with a body-wracking illness that I thought would bury me in my hotel bathroom.

A very good Thai restaurant beckoned in the same hotel, but I had become bored by the sinuous dancers and their swirling, lacy skirts. So I decided to eat late and alone in the nearly empty main dining room of my Western-style hotel. Soon I was no longer alone.

A man casually left his table nearby and invited me to join him. Sure, I said, finishing my salad and figuring that solitude wouldn't expand my knowledge of Pakistan. Time wasn't a factor. A few hours later, in the early morning, I planned to leave for the airport and the long flights through the United Arab Emirates, London and back to Washington.

Looking like any Pakistani next door, my dining companion said he was visiting family, but lived mostly in England where he and his brother ran a real estate business. That was my first clue; a Pakistani man visiting his family and staying, not with his family but in an expensive Western-owned hotel in his nation's capital. Here, I thought, is a man who is lying to me or is so seriously alienated from his family that he has returned home to nick his share of the family's wealth. Or perhaps no family members wanted him anywhere near them. I smiled to myself as all that nonsense scudded through my mind. Before long, the man knew that I knew who he really was, and I knew that he knew. But that didn't matter. Our little game continued.

For three months, I had been in and out of Pakistan, staying many days in Islamabad, Karachi and even flitting to Rawalpindi for a long and wasted night seeking information about the fate of Daniel Pearl, the *Wall Street Journal* reporter who had been kidnapped in Karachi on January 23, 2002. On the night of February 21 of that same year, I was in Karachi when a video of Daniel Pearl's execution was dropped into the hands of investigators there. At 5 a.m. on February 22, I quickly rewrote a story about the investigation into Pearl's kidnapping that I had filed only a few hours before I learned of Pearl's murder. Trouble had yet to tail me in Pakistan, although it isn't a place where a Western journalist should hang out on a corner or around a hotel for too long. Weeks after my first stop in Islamabad, I finally wrangled a flight to Kabul. Two months after that, three Afghan men drove me from Kabul to the border with Pakistan. From the border I was driven alone in a not-so-mini minibus, switching armed guards along the route, all the way to Islamabad. The Khyber Pass, which links Pakistan and Afghanistan, never looked so dramatic, especially as my driver wheeled through hairpin curves on the wrong side of the narrow road where doom awaited but didn't arrive. So there I was, dining in Islamabad, finally ready to bid Pakistan goodbye.

As my new companion and I talked and chomped in the hotel dining room, the pleasantries couldn't mask my new friend's message: my Pakistani hospitality visa had expired. I had been in Pakistan long enough. It was time to leave. My new pal probably knew how many times I had been in and out of Islamabad, about my lengthy stay in Karachi, my short visit to Rawalpindi and my trip to Kabul. We had a pleasant conversation about London, Pakistan and Afghanistan, but I learned nothing new except a few more lies. Before paying our separate checks, we exchanged telephone numbers. My cell phone was useful only in Pakistan, so I wasn't worried about being tracked in the United States, Dubai, London or anywhere else.

A few minutes after I returned to my room to finish packing for my departure, the faux Pakistani real estate mogul from London called with an invitation. Would I like to meet a few beautiful Russian women in his room for a good time? For further enticement he offered good whisky. I didn't ask for names or descriptions or whether the whisky was single malt or a blend. Thanks, I said, but no thanks. I continued packing. It wasn't long before I realized that my friend had called to check whether I was still standing. At that moment, however, I was fine and eager to leave Pakistan just ahead of a trail of jet fumes.

A few minutes after the call, I became violently ill. Diarrhea erupted first. Vomiting followed fast. To the bathroom I tried to dash before I crawled. There, I stretched from the toilet to the sink. Locked in pain, I retched and heaved and stayed too long in the bathroom to remember how long. After I cleaned the bathroom tile, a long, warm shower came begging. Drowning in a Pakistani hotel room shower would be an embarrassing end, I thought, but I had to take the risk in order to catch a plane. How, I wondered, could I ever leave the hotel if I couldn't leave the bathroom? Eventually, I stumbled from the bathroom to dress and finish packing. A plane beckoned and I was desperate to leave, fast. Wracked with chills, hot sweats, and tremors, I called for help with my bags, which I had never done at any time, anywhere. My exit was free of further complications because I had pre-paid the bill.

Hugging my luggage, I was a passenger, stretched out, on a baggage carrier headed to an elevator, through the lobby and to a taxi. With more assistance, I was whisked through the airport to the boarding area. Seeing my condition, flight attendants found an empty row in the rear of the plane, two steps from a toilet, which was a relief. Every now and then, the attendants, who were Bulgarian, brought me orange juice and water, which were hard to swallow. I yearned for an intravenous drip. The flights from Islamabad to the United Arab Emirates and on to London went by quickly because I slept, when I wasn't visiting the toilet. Ill but harmless, all I remember is that I kept using the toilet, drank a little orange juice and water, shivered and slept under several blankets. More of the same accompanied me on the flight from London to Washington, where I recuperated for several days. I recovered well enough to eat again, ready to dine once more, although not in Islamabad.

Only after I recovered did I try to decipher what had happened. Had I been stricken with a virus that whizzed through me with no warning or symptoms? Was my dining companion, the security fuzz without a badge, the culprit? Did he slip a pill in my glass of filtered water? Nah, he couldn't have. I'm too smart for that.

* * *

Spies in the New Hampshire woods had a lighter touch than those in Pakistan. The secret police there weren't secret and they weren't even police. They were good neighbors, self-appointed wardens of the woods. Three months before I was ambushed trying to dump my cabin trash into someone else's dumpster, I ran into Clouseau, a young man who cracked open the door to this protect-thy-neighbor policy. Clouseau was long-forgotten, until I was tripped up heading to a trash bin.

On January 25, a Sunday and only Day 17 in the cabin, with the pond's expanding ice roaring like an angry Norse god, I walked more than three miles to Hannaford's Supermarket. On my way back to the cabin, I stopped nearby at Susty's vegan restaurant for tomato and vegetable soup with okra, carrots and quinoa, California rolls and hummous. As I prepared to leave the restaurant, a young man offered me a lift. All I knew about the man was that he and his girlfriend were regulars at Susty's. I didn't agonize over my decision to ride rather than walk. Winter's early darkness was descending, deep cold was locked in and several steep hills weren't going to become the Rockies, if not the Pamirs, had I walked. A ride without having to hitch was an offer I leaped at. A string was attached to the offer, however, like a tin can being pulled noisily by an auto, although I missed the sign at first. Quickly, I assembled my groceries for the short journey—two cans of chicken and rotini soup, a dozen large free-range eggs, a package of Arabic bread, ketchup, gherkin pickles, lettuce, tomatoes and cucumbers, two oranges, sixteen slices of American cheese, a pound of whole wheat bread, balsamic salad dressing and four triple A batteries.

The young man, whom I'll call Clouseau as I did then, said he was off to buy ice for the restaurant. Ice? You want ice, I said, trying not to shout. I know a pond so full of ice you could become an ice farmer on the spot, and it's free, I told the lad. Nah, he answered, I don't want to chop ice from a pond; I'll buy it at a store. The American way, I thought. Clouseau's real objective was to check me out, see where I was living and whether I was telling the truth about my digs, learn more about me, and maybe warn others about the mad old stranger living on Big Buck Road. With nothing to hide and hoping to deflect wayward speculation, Clouseau got the full story: I'm renting the cabin from Paul Dale and writing a book, I told him. A loner serving as a volunteer spy for the woodland community, Clouseau insisted on driving all the way to my cabin, although I tried to convince him that icy and bumpy Big Buck Road with its rickety wood bridge was better left to walkers.

Alert and still standing, I answered the telephone at seven that evening, long after dark. I recognized the voice, but didn't let on: it was Clouseau asking for Paul Dale, the cabin's owner. When I repeated my story, explaining that Paul Dale wasn't in and that I was renting the cabin from him, Clouseau promised to call another time and hung up. He never called again. The next time I saw the young man at Susty's, I smiled and addressed him as Inspector Clouseau, a reference to Peter Sellers and his Inspector Jacques Clouseau character in the *Pink Panther* movies. Northwood's Clouseau smiled back, stiffly, as if his mouth were crammed with ice. Whether or not he knew of Peter Sellers, Inspector Jacques Clouseau and the *Pink Panther* movies, he understood my meaning.

My Clouseau was drifting then, trying to figure out life, his life, but he didn't seem to be a serious, long-term drifter. Curiosity, I figured, would save Clouseau in the long run.

* * *

War ages even the youngest minds and bodies overnight, but youth had left this Bosnian man years earlier. At 74, Salih Reykovic felt only the anger, sadness, frustration and losses that lie in the wake of war. Post-war, to him, meant its detritus. Reykovic was just one of thousands of scarred casualties of the Bosnian wars of the 1990s, a vicious three-way struggle rooted in tribe and its usual companions—religion, history, language, land and culture, all instruments wielded to gain and hold power.

A teacher and writer of local history, art and guidebooks for tourists, Reykovic spent a lifetime building bridges among the peoples of Mostar, a beautiful small city in the Herzegovina region of Bosnia-Herzegovina, near the border with Croatia. Because he was breathing, Reykovic knew the air was still his. But the city he once knew was his no longer.

In the local Serbo-Croatian language, Mostar means bridge-keeper. But the bridge—called Stari Most, which means Old Bridge in Serbo-Croatian—had been reduced to river rubble by October 1996, when Reykovic and I met by chance in the divided city. With remnants of the bridge lodged in the muddy bottom of the Neretva River and war's passions still bubbling on Mostar's streets, Reykovic's talent for conciliation was withering. Ethnic-Croatians, who are Roman Catholics, hunkered down on the west side of the Neretva River and Bosnian Muslims, called Bosniacs, glared from the east side. Ethnic Serbs, who are Orthodox Christians and were smaller in number in Mostar were one more fragment.

Reykovic and his ethnic rivals were like the bewildered victims of tribal wars elsewhere: one day they dined together, the next day they shot to kill each other, and the third day they swore never again to speak to their old friends. Aided by power-mad leaders in Croatia and Serbia who ignited the wars that brought ethnic cleansing back into the lexicon of war, Mostar's people were living in ghettoes of their own making. With the Old Bridge a busted link to the past, local bridge-keepers of each ethnicity lost a symbol of their former unity and their duties to the city's monument. Reykovic didn't lose his life, but he lost a reason for living. In his splintered city, he was no longer able to write, teach or live a near-normal life. Whatever came next for Mostar would not last long for the aging Reykovic.

Balancing a small two-wheel bicycle between his legs, anger drove the elderly man. He could not afford to ride with pride, could barely live with any either. As we talked, the old man snatched a homeless chunk of stale bread from the top of a wall near the river and the dead bridge. Reykovic pretended to take a bite of the rock-hard bread, but didn't. He did not because he could not. Instead, he would take the bread home, he said, where a hammer and chisel would ease the dining process. The bridge I crossed to meet Reykovic was a sad, swaying suspension affair that inspired no confidence and on which a bicycle was useless.

His bicycle gave Reykovic a small measure of freedom, as long as he stayed on the Muslim side of the city. Bitter about how the war, inspired by ethnic-Croats and aided by the masterminds in Zagreb and Belgrade, had destroyed so many bodies and minds, Reykovic insisted that the city and its people weren't free even after the fighting stopped. With a mixture of anger and sadness, he pointed to the ethnic-Croatian enclave of the city and said, "The other side is fascist." No one was present to dispute the charge.

A few teenagers and elderly people gathered as Reykovic and I talked. "My father died fighting on the first front line," said Kenan, a fourteen-year-old. Asim, thirteen, said, "We were forced from the other side of the city because we're Muslim." Sanela, a fifteen-year-old girl, agreed. An older woman, also a Muslim, said, "We are not able to go to our homes. I can look at my home, but I can't go there."

On the Croatian side, Marjan, twenty, said, "I'm afraid to go to the Muslim side." Darija, a twenty-three-old Croat, said she has no reason to visit the Muslim sector. "So, I just look after myself. I used to follow all the news on the radio and in newspapers, and then I just turned it all off."

In his worn and tattered clothing, Salih Reykovic would never have been mistaken for a serious cyclist. He looked nothing like Ed, the eighty-year-old cyclist I met at Irving's convenience story in New Hampshire. Besides, Reykovic's wobbly bicycle, which he pushed as much as he rode, was suited more to a youngster than an adult. He looked more like a refugee in his own town than a teacher, a writer and cultural historian.

Three years of fighting left behind new cemeteries, people

sore with themselves and distrustful of their neighbors and former friends. Each of the tribes could have raised its religious beliefs to a higher calling. Instead, they bowed to the exploitation of religious differences by cheap political thieves seeking more land and power. This moral failure isn't peculiar to Bosnia-Herzegovina. It is a common feature of war zones, where warring parties are content to blame and kill "the other."

Sharp ethnic divisions remain in Mostar. Despite all of its human debris, Mostar became better known to the outside world for the destruction of its old stone bridge than for its obituaries and angry survivors. Occupying Ottoman Turks built the Old Bridge in the middle of the sixteenth century. Croatian fighters deliberately destroyed it on November 9, 1993. Its destruction was punitive rather than strategic or tactical, an ethnic, religious and political statement against history and culture as much as against contemporary conditions and new enmities. Such a testament to the warped aspect of human memory is not restricted to Mostar, elsewhere in Bosnia-Herzegovina, or singular outposts anywhere. That flawed fraternity resides in all war zones. Because monuments are signposts of history, culture and heritage, their destruction carves deep gashes among the living and their communities. Some monuments can be rebuilt, even if they are never quite the same. Resurrection and reincarnation, however, rest on faith.

With the help of the United Nations and the World Bank, recovered white limestone blocks from the river below were used to rebuild the Old Bridge; it reopened on July 23, 2004. Heralded as a symbol of reconciliation, coexistence and international cooperation, it is a United Nations Educational, Scientific and Cultural Organization World Heritage site. The cemeteries in Mostar are, well, more of the same, just like all cemeteries. Their tombstones tilt a little more each year and erode in the wind and rain. Their dead remain so and, unlike bridges, they can't, as far as I know, be given new life.

* * *

Jake, a neighbor at Lucas Pond, would have had a great conversation with Salih Reykovic. Separated by decades in age, a few thousand miles, and two continents, the two men never had such luck. If time and place had been different, their conversation surely would have centered on war, its futility, uncontrollable bloodletting and unpredictable consequences. War would have been the bridge that linked both men intellectually and existentially. He wasn't a soldier, but Salih Reykovic was an eyewitness to tribal war at his front door in Bosnia. Jake was an American soldier who had been shipped to wage tribal war in the land of others.

Both men were strangers to me when I met them. Jake, not his real name, lived with his family near Lucas Pond in weather fair and frigid when we met in 2004, eight years after I had met Reykovic in Bosnia. They lived worlds apart. When I met them, I was living in my own world, a different world in Bosnia and another world at Lucas Pond. My work freed me to travel into their worlds with impunity and immunity.

Talking with Jake reminded me of what I had learned long ago: the questions are what really matter. Perhaps I had prejudged my New Hampshire neighbors, or at least one of them, before Jake and I talked. Until we had our one and only conversation, I would never have surmised Jake's sentiments. If anything, I might have guessed they were the opposite of what they were. By speaking with Jake, I gathered further evidence of the value of talking as well as observing, and the value of separating individuals from the crowd.

Jake was friendly enough to leave me alone when he could have reached out without intruding. He was concerned for months, I learned a few weeks before I kissed my cabin goodbye, about how I had fared during the mean winter of 2004. One late October day, during the unmistakable changing of the guard when the varied colors of autumn were succumbing to winter's ubiquitous gray, I went looking for help after one of my heaters decided it couldn't take another year of the ice follies. When Jake returned from shopping, he heard of my plea for advice and came knocking. He became the only person to visit me at Lucas Pond excluding my wife, sister-in-law and brother-in-law. After a quick look under the hood of my dead heater, Jake diagnosed the problem: the coil had died in my made-in-Turkey electric radiator. Later, Jake brought over a heater of his own, which I didn't need because I had a spare. His gesture was more than generous; it was friendly.

After Jake crossed the transom, he never sat down, never relaxed in what Thoreau had called his seats for friendship or society. None of the chairs in my cabin had such names, but Jake would have been welcome in any of my seats that were reserved for reading, writing or coddling notebooks and tomes like *Don Quixote*. Jake stood, but he didn't just stand and wait. He talked, and he had served, too, which gave him standing. With gentle prodding, Jake surprised me and talked a little politics and war, one of the few times I dipped into those tempestuous realms during my year of living, a little, like Thoreau. Jake was a man in transition. Uncomfortable as more cabins and more people filled the woods, he and his family had Big Sky horizons in their sights. Not Western New England or the Great Western Reserve in Ohio, but the Great American West, as in Indian country. A hunter of deer and wild turkey, Jake no longer cared whether he bagged his prey. The solitude of the hunt and the woods was sufficient. Employed by a company that manufactured computer parts, Jake had worked in Mexico training workers who would snatch his job. As a thank-you gift, Jake said, his company dissolved its employee profit-sharing plan while giving its chief executive officer a million-dollar raise. It was the million-dollar raise and the profit-sharing implosion that stuck in Jake's throat. Greed and capitalism in the extreme weren't Jake's friends, and too many American strangers were creeping in to steal the woods.

With the 2003 invasion of Iraq fresh in his and the American mind, Jake compared deer-hunters with American soldiers operating in unfriendly Iraq. Jake was lucky; he still had two legs to stand on. Jake was, he said, a former Special Forces soldier. "In Iraq," he recalled from his own experience, "We go in there and it's like a hunter in the woods on the deer's land. The hunter carries human smells—coffee, food, and so forth. The deer watches the hunter and hides and the hunter can't see the deer. The hunter has to be lucky to see or kill a deer. American troops are in the same situation in Iraq; they are at a disadvantage in a foreign country."

Jake didn't intend to soothe my feelings, but he did. He didn't know that, despite intense vigilance during all four seasons, I never spotted a deer in the woods around Lucas Pond in the Great North Woods of Northwood, New Hampshire. That part of our conversation was just another reminder that I was a stranger in the woods.

Jake's comments brought to mind my criticism of the invasion of Iraq at a large community gathering in West Palm Beach, Florida, a little more than a year before Jake and I talked. Invited to speak at the civic meeting, I criticized the 2003 invasion as a major blunder that anyone who knew Iraq or the Middle East would grasp without a second thought. Widespread turmoil would follow, in Iraq and in neighboring countries, I said. The judgment of the audience was swift: I was nearly booed from the podium. The West Palm Beach clan of the American tribe brooked no criticism of American invasions, in Iraq or anywhere else. Asked if there was anything good that I could say about the invasion, I answered that Americans should express their opinions regardless of what criticism awaited them. Judging by the dead silence of the audience, my answer wasn't good enough. The invasion was a mistake when it happened; it remained a glaring mistake when Jake talked to me, and it remains an even bigger mistake today. Sectarian and tribal fighting in Iraq, twinned with the internal uprising and foreign meddling in Syria, prove that point. Criticism of the American invasion of Iraq was viewed in 2003 as treasonous or nearly so, but less now. The broad public memory, however, remains forever short.

On immigration and the silly proposal to build a wall along the U.S-Mexican border, which even in 2004 was a throbbing political, tribal and demagogic topic, Jake was as decisive as most soldiers would be at any time. "You can't seal a border," he said, "especially a very long one." When I mentioned a news story about the Great Plains emptying out and Native Americans moving back in, Jake was critical about the Indians being driven from the land in the first place.

Salih Reykovic knew all about ethnic cleansing. The Bosnian wars were all about Croatian and Serbian efforts to clear Muslims from most of Bosnia-Herzegovina, leaving the bulk of that former province of Yugoslavia in the hands of Serbs and Croats. Cleansing is an oppressor's filthy euphemism for starvation, expulsion, and genocide.

* * *

For twenty-three years, during a decade of war with the Soviet Union that stretched from 1979 to 1989, followed by a vicious civil conflict from which emerged the wildly theocratic Taliban (Students of Islam), Afghanistan was a country where people could join the oppressors, hide out underground and hope no one found them, fight back and live a shortened life, or flee. By the end of 2001, about two million Afghans, mostly Sunni Muslims of the Pashtun tribes, had crossed the fluid eastern border and settled with brotherly tribes in Pakistan. Almost one and a half million more fled westward to Iran, a Shiite Islamic theocracy unto itself. Several thousand more scooted north to Central Asia, where Islam is more loosely practiced, or southeast to rival India, which claims the world's third largest Muslim population after Indonesia and Pakistan. Those destinations were chosen because they were handy, and because they were free of war. The refugee figures quoted here are from the Washington-based Middle East Research and Information Project.

Other organizations say the numbers of Afghan refugees were much higher.

That lost generation of Afghan refugees was beginning to drift home in early 2002. Entrance doors opened to them in all directions after the American invasion drove the Taliban into Afghanistan's deserts and mountains and into temporary denial as they, too, melted facelessly but only briefly into Afghan society.

A teacher, Sidiqa Nawrozin, was one of those refugees who had returned from Iran a month before we met in Kabul on March 23, 2002. The date marked the reopening of schools in Afghanistan after almost six years of fearful and bloody recess under Taliban rule. Surrounded by girls and boys and other teachers, all eager to resume their lives in peace, Nawrozin was another stranger whose life and times once more became entwined with the lives of other Afghans, and with strangers like me whom she will never meet again.

When schools reopened in Kabul, in late March 2002, the scene was of unbridled joy, a ceremony worthy of a national holiday, which it was, at least in Kabul. Money from throughout the world poured into the country so boys and girls could wear new clothes to school, write in unstained notebooks and read books that many hadn't seen in half their lives, others not at all. In their native language, Pashtu, girls sang, "The education of the human being gives dignity to the human being. We were in jail for many years. Through the mercy of God we got out of jail."

Eight years earlier, Sidiqa Nawrozin had fled, bidding goodbye to civil war and the accompanying collapse of civil society. She could see the fanatical Taliban rising, with their cruel and stifling rule and the ban on schools other than of the sanctified religious variety. Under the Taliban whip, the only women who could work at all were doctors and nurses, and that was because men weren't allowed to care for women in Afghan society. Under the Taliban, women could not teach, although a few lived dangerously by operating underground schools. Girls were barred from openly attending school. Their only option was to attend an illegal, underground, school. If they went to classes at all, boys attended religious schools where they learned Islam as the Taliban taught it, which was strict, unbending and with military-like discipline. Upon her return to Kabul, Nawrozin resumed teaching Afghan children, this time boys and girls with six years of schooling missing from their resumes. In many cases, that meant most twelve-year-old children would be back in the first grade. Like an educational missionary, Nawrozin was ready.

With the Taliban out of power, women had a choice: they could cover themselves with a *burqa* in public or stuff it in the closet and take their chances. The choice wasn't as easy as it might seem because the Taliban's frightening influence still hung over Afghanistan like a dark and seemingly impenetrable veil. Wearing a black headscarf, but no veil, and a long green gown over black pants, Nawrozin left her burqa in hiding when she walked to school. Before she fled to Iran, Nawrozin said, she had been the head teacher at Zarghuna School in Kabul. With the Taliban banished, Nawrozin would resume her leading role at the same school. She wasn't rusty, at least not as far as her teaching technique was concerned. During her self-imposed exile in Iran, she taught at the Islamic Center in Mashhad. Nawrozin didn't reveal whether she taught only religious studies in Iran or whether reading, writing and arithmetic also filled her notebooks and those of her students. My mistake was to remain silent on that question. But Nawrozin wasn't silent about her desire to resume teaching normal classes to boys and girls in Kabul. She felt secure enough in Kabul to hustle back west to Mashhad and convince other Afghanis to return home, and to her school.

* * *

In Thoreau's time, it was still possible to come across an Indian, a real American, in the New England woods. And he did. That seemed impossible in 2004, at least in Northwood. But luck was my companion, in mid-June of 2004, when I met a member of the Lakota tribe, not a native New Hampshire species, who also happened to be a teacher. Her name was Mary, and she lived with her husband and their four large dogs on Lower Camp Road, some two hundred yards from my cabin. Mary hadn't fled to another country from a war zone to stay alive and to teach. But she had traveled to a very far away part of the United States to teach other real Americans. From where I stood, that was both natural and exceptional.

During our conversation along the dirt road in front of her home, which was festooned with flowers and rock gardens, I told Mary about Long Wolf, a Lakota sub-chief whose remains I met a few years earlier in London. What was left of Long Wolf was exhumed from a cemetery in central London in 1997, and shipped for reburial to a small piece of his tribal homeland, now called the Pine Ridge Reservation in South Dakota. Long Wolf died in London of pneumonia in 1892, while performing with Buffalo Bill Cody's Wild West Show. A few days after our first conversation, I brought Mary a copy of the story that I had written about Long Wolf's life and return to his tribal womb one hundred and five years after his death. With Long Wolf in common, Mary wasn't afraid to talk with me, a stranger. Besides, she was soft-spoken and we were both strangers at Lucas Pond. Neither did her dogs fear me; they confronted me loudly each time our paths crossed. Before long Mary told me her story.

Because she had been a teacher, Mary reminded me of Sidiqa Nawrozin, in far-off Afghanistan. Chance meetings usually are the best, and this was further evidence. For three of the six years she lived in Alaska during the mid-nineties, Mary said, she taught Inuits on an island ninety miles from Russia. Because she was a Native American, Mary said, the Inuit families welcomed her warmly, another example of trusting tribal behavior. "The Inuits welcomed me as a teacher," Mary said, "because of my own tribal background." Unfortunately, when Mary and I met, it was four years too soon to mock Sarah Palin and her day-visions of Russia as seen from a front porch in Alaska.

* * *

My journey from Jerusalem to the Soviet Union, back to Jerusalem and then to London, to Florida and then to the New Hampshire woods took a mere fifteen years. Walking wasn't my only mode of transportation, and I missed few welcome mats along the way. The stops were many as I reported from Europe, the Middle East, Central Asia, North and East Africa. One long trail began with an artist in Ukraine, Eastern Europe, when Ukraine was still part of the Soviet Union, and ended two continents later with an antiques dealer in Northwood, New Hampshire, North America.

As I scoured the city of L'vov, in the western Ukraine, searching for Jews eager to leave the Soviet Union for Israel, my best pal, Mr. Good Luck, steered me to the home of Peter and Stella Fleet, their son and daughter. It was June 4, 1990, the same day KGB agents had freed me after a few hours of questioning, when I met the Fleets at Peter's impressive art studio next to the family's large home. The Soviet secret police had held me for questioning because, without permission, I had taken photos inside the local train depot of luggage bound for Tel Aviv and Jerusalem. But that's an entirely different story, which might have turned out badly, but did not.

The Fleet family and I were strangers for sure, but any remoteness the family may have felt toward me fell away when they learned that I was based in Jerusalem. The Fleets were as warm and nice a family as I had encountered anywhere. Peter's face and manner gave away the sensitivity I expect to see in an artist.

An accomplished sculptor, Peter Fleet lives at the heart of this story. About fifty-five years old when we met, Peter had studied Monumental Sculpture at L'vov's High Institute of Art, and took part in various exhibitions in Kiev and Moscow as well as in L'vov. Later, I learned, some of his work was on permanent exhibition throughout what was then the Soviet Union, and that his thirty-foot high monument honoring the Jews of Vilna who were killed during the Holocaust had been erected in Ukraine.

Peter Fleet and his family were heading to Israel, hoping it would be a stop on the way to the United States where Peter had a brother living in Los Angeles. Peter also had a sister living in Israel. The family's Israeli entrance papers were in order and Peter expected to receive the family's Soviet exit visas "in a day or two." Their confidence in being able to fly to Tel Aviv before peace broke out in the Middle East seemed well placed, peace there being more remote than unity on the island of Ireland. As with most others leaving the Soviet Union then, the Fleets weren't allowed to go directly to the United States, unless they waited for three years. But neither the Fleets nor anyone else wanted to sit idly and wait for three years in L'vov, where things seemed unpredictable and the risks too great. They could go immediately to Israel, however, where they could stay until enough time passed for them to aim for the United States, if they wished.

"We'll leave all our things, but our family, and go to Israel. I want to go to America after we go to Israel for three years, but we'll see Israel first," Peter said. By Soviet standards of that era, the Fleets were very well off. They owned a car, a nice house and Peter's art studio to go with surrounding land. Their life, like Peter's art, bore all the trappings of success. Peter spoke through an interpreter, the same man who had guided me to the train depot—where I shook hands with the KGB—and elsewhere around L'vov. Peter seemed to understand more English than he spoke, which was very little. His wife Stella, however, had a greater command of English.

After I shook hands with the Fleet family and wished them my kind of luck, I gave Peter my address and telephone number in Jerusalem. "Call me when you reach Israel," I said, "so we can talk again." "Yes. Thank you," he replied.

In return for my business card, Peter offered me a beautiful bust of an African woman with a long, slender neck and stately head. His offer was genuine, more than just a way of saying, "Thank you. See you in Jerusalem." Peter Fleet wanted me to have a piece of his creativity, his genius, which I have never forgotten. Such generosity I couldn't accept, of course. Professional ethics prohibited me from accepting a gift from anyone I encountered while reporting or whom I might encounter again. Unsure of whether Peter understood my reasoning and not wanting him to feel insulted, I added that I couldn't very well carry around a ceramic sculpture in my small piece of luggage as I dodged the KGB.

More than a year passed. I continued to report along roads well worn and others less travelled. In 1991, dialing the telephone number on the business card that I had given them back in L'vov, Peter and Stella Fleet, their son and daughter in tow, tracked me down, in Jerusalem, their new home. Peter Fleet was now Pesach Flit, his Hebrew name. At my house in Jerusalem, Stella (I didn't learn her Hebrew name) explained that they were becoming Israelis, though slowly. Peter planned to set up his own art studio again while he and the family were working hard to learn Hebrew and become part of Israeli society.

During his visit to my house, Peter spotted a beautiful high school graduation photo of my younger daughter Mary. With Stella's linguistic help, Peter asked permission to make an etching of the photo. I agreed. No conflict there, I thought, because I would be leaving Jerusalem for another posting in London and wouldn't have any more to do with the Fleets professionally. Peter took the photo of Mary and we parted. The Fleets were busy learning a new language and way of life, and I was busy meeting more strangers in strange lands. For months all was quiet on the Fleet front. They didn't call and I didn't intrude in their lives.

Many months later, 1993 came around and I was bound for London to become the European correspondent for Cox Newspapers. I invited Peter and his family for another visit. Peter had not even started to do an etching of Mary's photo, and wouldn't get to it soon. Because I was leaving for London, Peter returned the photo of Mary. He felt very badly about failing to keep his promise. Again, he offered me the beautiful ceramic sculpture of the African woman, the same piece he had offered at his home in L'vov. As I was leaving for London and probably would have nothing further to do with Peter and Stella Fleet and their family, I accepted the sculpture as the wonderful personal gift that Peter meant it to be.

From Jerusalem to London to West Palm Beach, Juno Beach and Palm Beach Gardens in Florida and on to New Hampshire, the sculpture traveled with Pat and me. Prominently displayed, the sculpture sits on a wood plinth in our dining room in Dover, New Hampshire. But that's hardly the whole story. The plinth itself is a chapter in a story that might be titled, "Things you see when you're not looking." An accident, a stroke of luck, the plinth reached me through a stranger I met at Demmons Country Store in Nottingham, New Hampshire, more than a country mile from L'vov and Jerusalem.

One fine day after the snow and ice had melted, I was eating a hot dog and talking with Jody at Demmons Country Store in Nottingham, a little more than a mile from my cabin. A woman, a stranger to me, walked in and changed the subject. I kept eating my hot dog, burped silently, asked a few questions and listened. What I heard was mostly local news and gossip, something about a fight against outsiders who wanted to drill for local water and sell it. That wasn't important to me, although I chipped in with wisdom garnered from far away places. What was important was that I had met another person I could wave to if we met on a country road or in the local market. Not until after the woman left did I garner any useful intelligence about the neighborhood. Jody told me the name of the antiques store the woman operated along what is known as Antique Alley on Route 4 in Northwood. I tucked that information under my Irish cap. On one of my longer walks, I promised to gawk at the antiques, an activity that would fall far behind playing solitary cribbage and dreaming as productive ways to seemingly waste time, and stimulate my subconscious.

My antiques-tour promise I kept to myself until the moment arrived. This wasn't to be quite like meeting Peter Fleet and his family in L'vov, but it qualifies as meeting another stranger, this time a tall, sleek, inanimate, curved, four-legged wood plinth. My eye for good art has grown over the years, but I'm not an antiques connoisseur. In this case, however, that didn't matter. I was smart enough and lucky enough to see that L'vov, Jerusalem and Northwood belonged together. Instantly, I saw the beautiful sculpture that Peter Fleet gave me sitting majestically atop that plinth. A long and slender bust preening upon a long and slender plinth is how I envisioned the pairing.

A short time after that sighting, when Pat was taking me from the cabin to resupply, drop off my laundry and leave my trash in Portsmouth, we stopped by the antiques store for a second opinion, Pat's. Without the slightest hesitation, we agreed. She bought the plinth, took it home and introduced it to Peter Fleet's sculpture. The two have been together since, proving again that sometimes strangers are meant for each other.

A final note to artist Peter Fleet, originally from L'vov, Ukraine, Eastern Europe and to Pesach Flit lately from Jerusalem, Israel/ Palestine, Southwestern Asia: Your beautiful sculpture is alive and well in Dover, New Hampshire, the United States, North America.

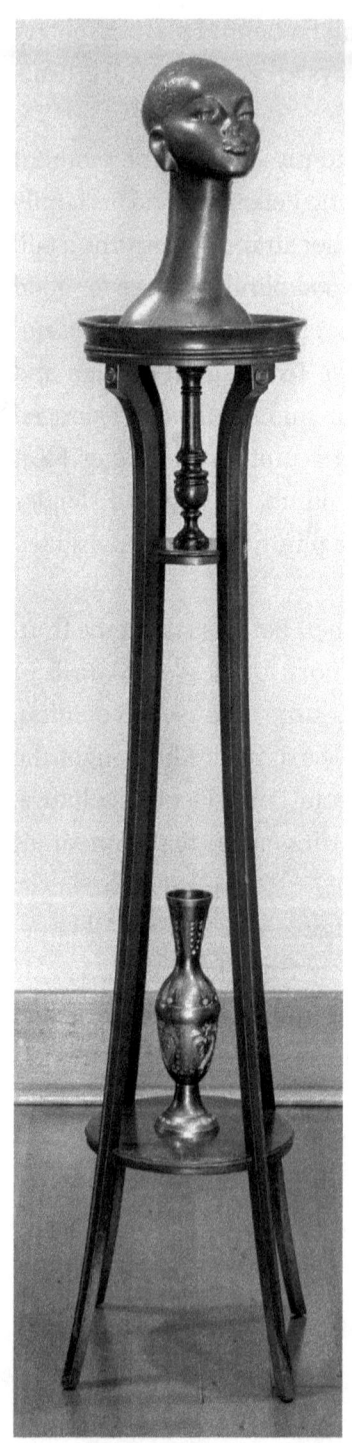

A Ukrainian sculpture paired with a New Hampshire antique.
Photo by Grace Peirce

From the Ayatollah to Jesus 151

* * *

After a month poking around Islamabad, Karachi and Rawalpindi in Pakistan, I finagled a seat on a United Nations flight from Islamabad to Kabul, Afghanistan's capital. Good luck greeted me at the airport there on the first of March 2002, and hung out with me for seven weeks, until I was driven from Kabul to the border with Pakistan, through the serpentine Khyber Pass and all the way back to Islamabad, Pakistan's capital. Two reporters, both strangers to me, whom I was replacing but didn't know, introduced me to Eymal, Assaf and Abdullah. After high recommendations from my colleagues, I kept my three new Afghan friends on the job, a decision that worked as well for them as they worked for me.

Eymal, the youngest, was my translator, and a good one. Assaf, the toughest, was my fast driver and essential mechanic who nursed his car and his passengers through dangerous mountain tunnels and fierce blizzards. Abdullah, the fixer, arranged meetings with real strangers who promised big deals and bigger news, and sometimes delivered. Abdullah had military and political connections good enough to arrange a meeting with a drug control czar who offered a nugget of opium that, he said, when eaten, would induce a twenty-four hour sleep. Abdullah also introduced me to a former soldier who wanted a $15,000 down payment toward the $150,000 purchase of a U.S.-made ground-to-air Stinger missile. For the record, one of my assistants accepted an agate-sized ball of opium, maybe enough for a solid eight hours of sleep, while I mined the arms merchant for information but gave him not one penny for it.

Finding helpers in strange places is often difficult. Honest and capable assistants can be even more difficult, often impossible, to find. Wherever I traveled in Afghanistan, Eymal, Assaf and Abdullah led the way. Wherever I bunked and ate—whether in a hostel, a private home or an apparent hotel—they stayed and ate with me. We were equals and I treated them that way. We learned from each other, too, about language and cultural differences, and the need to respect each other. They were like part of my family, and I treated them as such. I kept my promises, notably those involving cash for services, and they delivered on their promises to go where I wanted and meet people they knew and others they did not.

Every week I paid them as promised, one hundred dollars each. I increased the amounts if their assignments were especially difficult, which many were. On some trips, we drove countless miles across parched emptiness. On others, we drove slowly through mountain tunnels that were so poorly ventilated they killed the unwary. Scores of cars were marooned in small ponds in those tunnels, forcing Assaf and Abdullah to help push the stalled, flooded cars ahead of us through deep water so we and other cars could pass. Asphyxiation was a constant danger in those tunnels outside of which blizzards brought whiteout conditions so severe that I couldn't see my hand in front of my nose or the mountainside a few yards ahead. On the steppes in northern Afghanistan, near the border with Uzbekistan and under black skies, Assaf walked and hitchhiked for hours to find a fan belt so our van could move again. While Assaf headed to Mazar es Sharif, the nearest large city, Abdullah, Eymal and I practiced our English and Dari, the Afghan dialect of Farsi, with two twelve-year-old boys who had bunked school that day and joined us for Meals Ready to Eat, courtesy of American taxpayers, inside our disabled van.

In all the days we spent together, Abdullah, Assaf, Eymal and I never had a disagreement that I knew of. Not one. When they said my travel plans were based on a landscape that didn't exist, and explained why, I took their advice and followed their directions. Arrogance was not in my shoulder bag. When in the desert, is the way I've always looked at it, do as the Bedouins do. If my helpers said Wednesday was a better day than Tuesday to head south into the desert, we went on Wednesday.

When the time came for me to leave Afghanistan in late April, we made a deal. With hands on our hearts, we agreed that I would pay each of them a certain amount of money if they drove me to the border with Pakistan and found me a safe ride to Islamabad. My friends knew that I carried a lot of cash because I was paying them weekly and I had paid all our expenses for about two months. They didn't know where I stashed the cash or exactly how much I carried—$25,000 when I entered the region; about $15,000 when I packed to leave for Pakistan—but they knew I had more money than they might see before the next invasion or before American troops left to invade Iraq. American dollars were stashed all over my body and my bags, everywhere except in my ears, which would have been a bit obvious. Finding the money in my bags or on my limp body wouldn't have been difficult. When the day came to kiss Kabul goodbye, my friends asked for more money than we had agreed to for the journey to Pakistan. Ah-hah, a holdup, I thought. But I refused to pay more, although I could have done so without pinching my wallet. I told them that I planned to pay them a nice bonus, a tip, when we arrived at the border. That was the truth. But we had all agreed on a deal, I told each of them, looking them straight in the eye, and I expected them to honor—an important word in Afghanistan—that deal. They huddled briefly and agreed to honor the original agreement.

    My friends could have killed me anywhere along the winding, cratered and desolate road to the border with Pakistan. No one would have noticed, at least not until vultures had picked their way from my eyeballs to my toenails. My pals could have robbed me and left me with a few hundred dollars to reach Islamabad, while they would have vanished. What could I have done? Call 911? But only peace ruled as we traveled through the wilderness, a peace affirmed by mutual self-respect.

    Highway 7, the road from Kabul to the border, was a highway in name only. It was a slow, slow path. Our van bounced and swerved so much along the rugged road that it was impossible for us to hear one another well enough to carry on a conversation. The air was so filled with dust along some curves that large rocks in the road were almost invisible. My notes look as if a second-grader scribbled them. Along one precarious twist in the road, when I wrote, "Don't get stuck here," children were selling Pepsis and yoghurt. When we spotted a child—perhaps two years old—sitting almost naked near the road, Eymal said, "He grows here. His parents aren't around and he becomes a Taliban." Eymal's comments were telling and universal: poverty and ignorance make easy prey for manipulators everywhere. Few other words uttered by Eymal, Assaf or Abdullah made it into my notebook on that trip.

During the seven-hour drive to the border, some of it through prime bandit country, my friends asked if I wanted to see where four journalists were killed during the American invasion a few months earlier. I smiled, laughed lightly, and said they need not bother, that I could pay my respects from a great distance. Their offer was both a tease and a belief that maybe I did want to pay my respects to fellow reporters. Assaf was driving so we stopped by the roadside anyway, to see the piles of stones and a few wilting flowers that marked where the journalists had been shot. After a nod or two, we moved on, quickly, at my request. To linger might have been an invitation to others in the neighborhood who weren't named Eymal, Abdullah or Assaf.

At the border crossing in Torkham, my friends arranged for transport to Islamabad. I paid them what we had agreed to, plus a twenty percent tip. They were happy; I was happier. The next time I travel on vacation to Afghanistan, the first people I'll look up will be my friends, strangers no more, Abdullah, Assaf and Eymal, in any order.

From the Afghan-Pakistani border, the road was better but the journey was dreadful. Armed guards accompanied me in our four-hour auto flight to Islamabad. And a flight it was. In a van built for thirteen, I, the driver and a gunman riding shotgun whizzed through mountains and the twisting Khyber Pass into the teeming bedlam called Peshawar. My driver was skilled and my armed guards vigilant. They were all strangers in whom trust was my only coin, proving again that faith takes many forms. Speeding through the Khyber Pass on the Afghanistan side of the border, we passed cars on hairpin curves on the wrong side of the road. If a car headed straight at us, we veered hard to the right, creating space where none was visible. On occasions like this I learned long ago to look up, down or sideways, to say nothing, to pretend that all was normal, and not to appear frightened. It worked again. More than four hours later, after twice switching gunmen and after both the road and the journey actually improved, my guardians and I reached my hotel destination in Islamabad, the same hotel where earlier I had bought an elusive set of exercise springs and where later I would become violently ill in my room after dining with the secret police. Happily, with hand on my heart, I tipped the driver and the last gunman and wished that God would grant them each a long and happy life. We all smiled.

* * *

Without the help of translators, drivers and fixers, a fog of uncertainty would have blurred my view and understanding of other lands and peoples. My reporting would have been severely, and maybe dangerously, hindered without local guides I learned to trust. No matter how much I had studied about places and people, I would have been hobbled and in danger without strangers to advise me about what trails to follow or avoid.

Arzim, my ethnic-Albanian translator and guide from Macedonia, was one of many strangers I relied on to get me into and out of trouble. Without his help, I probably would never have found my way into oppressed Kosovo; no roaming, ergo, no stories. When I found myself in a tight spot, so did Arzim. It was as much, maybe more, in his interest as in mine for both of us to escape harm. This axiom bore no limits of year or geography.

A decade before I retreated to the New Hampshire woods, Arzim talked our way across the border from Macedonia into Kosovo, which was almost one hundred percent Albanian but which was controlled and oppressed by Serbia. On this occasion, Arzim and I proved that sometimes the direct approach is the slickest trick. Unable to obtain a visa from any embassy on any continent to enter Kosovo or any Serbian territory, I decided to walk with Arzim straight from Macedonia into Kosovo. We had nothing to hide except that Serbia didn't want me or any other Western journalist mucking around. At the Blacé border post, Arzim did all the talking while I stood mute, looking and acting like his helpless, harmless grandfather. Arzim swears that he didn't lie. After the guards handed me a visa, they waved us right through. No tough questions asked. The entire procedure took less than fifteen minutes while hundreds of locals in countless trucks and cars waited in a serpentine line for hours. Mute remained my middle name until after we hitched a ride from the countryside and later walked confidently into Pristina, Kosovo's capital. We were hunting for the Serbian killer, Zeljko Raznatovic, who went by the name of Arkan, and his army of fighters called Tigers. As an ethnic-Albanian guiding an American newspaperman into hostile territory, Arzim was at greater risk than I. He might as well have been wearing a shirt emblazoned in scarlet neon with the letter "A" for Albanian when we checked into the hotel that Arkan had ransacked and controlled. For safety, Arzim and I shared a room, the only room that was habitable.

A marauding mobster, Arkan took no prisoners. He used the killing grounds among Eastern Orthodox Serbs, Bosnian Muslims and Catholic Croatians, along with Serbia's oppression of the Albanians, to become filthy rich. Indicted by the United Nations War Crimes Tribunal in The Hague in 1997, Arkan escaped one form of justice because he was never tried in court. Another form of justice, his kind, found Arkan in the year 2000, when he was murdered, silenced, in Belgrade, Serbia, proving again that there is no honor among thieves, or killers.

Arzim and I found much evidence of Arkan's destruction, but we never found him. To be honest, I spent no sleepless nights fretting about our failure to corner the killer. We talked with saner folks, more interesting Albanians, including the supremely courageous Adem Demaçi—the polar opposite of Arkan—who had spent almost half of his fifty-eight years shackled in Serbian prisons solely because he advocated independence for Kosovo.

Help of Arzim's kind was routine as I stepped into and out of danger. But thousands of people take greater risks all over the world every day. Sometimes, the dangers aren't risks at all, just astounding acts of courage and the will to survive, such as starving mothers in Somalia eating rawhide so they can try to nourish their babies with milk from dry breasts. At other times, doctors and aid workers scattered throughout zones of war and deprivation struggle hourly to give life to the dying. So common are such brave people that they remain faceless and nameless even in their own domains.

In my New Hampshire woods, protection and foreign aid were unnecessary because the dangers were nonexistent. Strangers in the neighborhood were nonthreatening, as was I. From my cabin on unpaved Big Buck Road, I walked paved roads, worn paths and unmarked trails. No journalists had been killed in those woods; no clusters of stones and bouquets of dying flowers marked the site of an ambush, and death.

A car and driver, in fact, would have defeated my search for isolation. What meetings I had did not require a fixer to arrange. Those meetings were few and most were the gift of chance. But a cultural dictionary, if not a cultural translator, would have helped steer me through arcane woodland customs and mores. For sure I would have benefitted from someone with the unerring ability to spot a deer. At the same time, with proper guidance, my trash-dumping adventure, and the fun that went with it, would have been nonexistent. As it was, I learned on my own, slowly and maybe incompletely, but I did learn some ways of rural life.

Born in Woonsocket, Rhode Island, I grew up nearby in tiny Millville, Massachusetts, on the state line. I knew about towns and small cities in Southeastern Massachusetts and Northern Rhode Island, and later learned about exotic places thousands of miles from that territory. But I knew zero about the New Hampshire woods and their people. The population of Millville in my youth was about 1,600 souls. Barney the Blacksmith was the entertainment in Millville, especially when an ornery equine contemplating the glue factory kicked wiry old Barney half way across his tumbledown barn and Barney cursed the animal in language only the two of them understood. Millville and the city of Woonsocket, dots on the map of southern New England, aren't exactly London, Lahore, L'vov or the Sahara, but, believe it or not, they are different from towns and cities in Maine, Vermont and New Hampshire, which comprise northern New England.

Language is part of culture, probably its core. Speak to a foreigner in the local language and you will get a broad smile, good will and good deeds—a special meal perhaps—in return. Experience, however, tells me that language is only part of culture. In their totality, other aspects of culture may be considered as much a language as the spoken and written language itself. Food, clothing, music, dance, behavior among men and women, work habits, religion, history, territorial possessions, and the relationship of children to their parents and parents to their antecedents are also vital parts of a culture. The better a stranger understands a culture, the more success that stranger will have dealing with people who call that culture their own.

While secluded in the woods, no one asked my blood or my tribe, my religion or ancestral language, culture or land as had so many people elsewhere, where locals called me "Mr. Lou." This was their way of honoring me with a title, without being too familiar.

In the woods, I was just another American, and that was usually enough. But, without asking for their ID cards, I discovered that people of the woodland tribes share a desire to live far from others who don't appear to realize the simple tribal nature of their own lives. To the denizens of the woods, I wasn't one of them. To a few, I was Lou, but I was never "Mr. Lou." No one ever, as many did in Europe, reminded me that Lou Salome was Nietzsche's female lover. I was the stranger, the writer, the geezer from Portsmouth on what locals call the Seacoast, who lived alone in the cabin at Lucas Pond. That's how my own tribal affiliation was perceived in New Hampshire's woods, or at least how I perceived the perception. It's worth remembering that in the woods the state's eighteen-mile-long Seacoast is considered something like the New Hampshire Riviera; things being relative, maybe the label is apt.

I have felt at home nearly everywhere I've worked and traveled. At the same time, I have never felt truly at home anywhere, which might explain why I have been able to move easily from land to land, culture to culture. I have always felt like a stranger in my own shoes. My life in the woods didn't change any of that. Though a stranger there, an outsider, I felt comfortable. But I never felt at home there either.

A few strangers I met in the woods around Lucas Pond became—like Eymal, Abdullah and Assaf, my Afghan aides— friendly, people I came to trust. But I never became a member of the woodland tribes any more than I became an Afghan or a Parisian.

Around Lucas Pond, the closest I came to meeting anyone even remotely like Arzim in Kosovo were the strangers who gave me a lift as I hitchhiked to the market and back to Lucas Pond, thus testing, on days fair and foul, the charity of the good Christians of New Hampshire. Hell, I thought, if I could hitchhike from a battlefield in northern Iraq and into a conflict in Kosovo, where I was more of a stranger than I was in these United States, I should be able to hitch a ride in rural New Hampshire. But on most of those random excursions I ended up walking the seven miles or so to the local agora, Hannaford's Supermarket, and back to my cabin. A few motorists were charitable, and for that I remain grateful, especially on return trips when I was carrying lettuce, tomatoes, cucumbers, bread, cans of baked beans, vegetables and garbanzo beans, or when darkness was closing in. People are afraid to pick up hitchhikers, one pleasant motorist remarked, because these days they never know whom they're picking up. As a hitchhiker, I replied, I didn't know who might pick me up, and we both laughed at the value of perspective.

The landscape surely changes when the leaves are dead and
    gone.
Squirrels store acorns for the frigid time ahead.
The forest floor is already cold and dry
Awaiting winter's snow.
The robins yield to the crows,
And the deer hide from the hunters
Till the thaw comes in spring.

Seasoned

The description of nature's changing seasons on the previous page is my last journal entry, dated November 19, 2004, Day 193 in the cabin. The mood fit the spirit of my cabin life as the door closed behind me and the last brittle leaves floated to the cold earth like featherless birds, dead. My journal is silent about the source of those words, although I probably read the passage rather than heard it. I thank the author for capturing my thoughts, although I have been unable to discover his or her name. But I include those lines because they reflect my seasons of seclusion with the squirrels, birds, fish, pond and trees that I saw daily, and the deer I never spotted. They are also examples of words and ideas I would have ignored had I not been living and writing alone in the woods, a stranger in a world strange to me that for a time became my own.

My solitary life began when persistence and luck merged with an intense desire to write about tribal behavior and war in Europe, Asia and Africa. To delay would have been to dull my drive, perhaps enough to talk myself out of the project. Otherwise, there was no grand strategy. From that opening day in January, I could see all four seasons as if through a large telescope that could penetrate time as well as distance. In the beginning, no single season beckoned like a lover that couldn't be ignored. In the end, however, winter proved the charm, the best time to hide out, narrow the eyes and broaden the mind. Winter in the woods made me feel as if I were alone again in the French Riviera stalking and finding Jean Claude Duvalier, the former Haitian dictator, or in Uzbekistan zooming—siren blaring, emergency light flashing and live grenade lolling under the front seat—with a retired but still toting former Soviet army officer from Tashkent to the old imperial city of Samarkand.

Until those first frigid moments in the leafless woods, my idea of observing and embracing nature was framed more than fifty years earlier when I dashed home through the woods, enveloped in darkness and fear, after ice-skating at Kimieck's Pond in Millville, Massachusetts. In the vernacular of that era, I was scared shitless. Twelve years old at the time, skates slung over my left shoulder and hockey stick in my right hand for defense against ghosts and wood nymphs, I had two goals in mind: first, to survive the fright; second, to beat the dinner curfew so I would be allowed to go skating again after school. Twisting and turning as I ran to spy attacks by the invisible forest gnomes that were forcing frozen trees to snap, crack and go boom in the wind, I stumbled over rocks, fallen branches and stone walls as I raced through this terrible shortcut in the wicked darkness. If the noise and forest creatures didn't create fear enough, I recalled the town lore about the little girl who died years earlier while running down a nearby road as she was being consumed by flames. In those days, fear filled what spaces were left in the gray matter often called a brain. When my feet finally landed on asphalt back then, it was as if I had escaped from a carnival echo chamber lined with loud, laughing skulls.

As an adult more than fifty years later, I found the woods in winter spectacular in their simplicity. More gray than brown though sprinkled with green holiday conifers, the woods are lifeless-looking and noiseless except when deep silence speaks through harsh winds, frozen branches chatting or the ice spewing echoes as it expands and deepens in the glacial pond. It's true what they say about silence making noise. Sometimes silence shrieks. When concentration allows, silence can even be seen, like a ripple in the air, as well as heard. I heard it many times, and saw it, too. It's the kind of weird quiet that rattles the stomach and makes the ears ring. It's deep and seems limitless, like darkness in a mountain cave where no light penetrates. Stillness is different from silence; it is easier to see and hear and is more transient. Embraced by a thick blanket of ice and snow, Lucas Pond offered the widest horizon in the woods in winter. It glares, especially at night, like a giant searchlight in bright contrast to its encircling hem of bare gray maples and oaks.

Steady below zero cold brought the expanding ice to life with a low, throaty sound, something like the trombone section of an orchestra, sometimes like the brasher sound of stereos rimming the pond. In the coldest days of January, with the distant sun briefly at their backs, tall and sturdy pine trees cast long shadows on the pond, the shadows of shorter trees being obscured by the shadows of larger ones. In the woods, where the competition is stiff and always growing, the biggest guys do cast the longest shadows.

With the cabin, the pond, the woods and very few people, the seasons framed my writing life during 2004. In the beginning, at 4:15 p.m. on January 12, my fifth day alone, depression brought on by too-early darkness filled the cabin. Outside, on Lucas Pond, life was noisier, happier. Five kids, a black lab trailing in their wake, skated on the pond while two other kids pushed shovels to clear patches of snow from the ice. Two older boys drove a small tractor on the pond to dispatch the snow in a comparative blur. On this day of small contrasts, I saw my first bird, a blue jay. This was notable because even birds are scarce in winter's woods.

Sometimes falling snow obliterated the pond, but never blinded me. Snowstorms on Lucas Pond were nothing like the total whiteout I experienced in the late winter of 2002 more than 12,000 feet up in the Hindu Kush Mountains of Afghanistan. At my left elbow stood an Afghan man, wearing plastic sandals, a short cotton shirt and a traditional longer garment called a *shalwar kamez*. No hat, socks, coat or gloves decorated the man, named Hamid, who was puzzled by my gloves, scarf, hat, and heavy, hooded coat. Hamid swore he wasn't cold. In New Hampshire's winter woods, I dressed as if I were back in Afghanistan, although I was never struck sightless by a blizzard in Lucas Pond's time zone.

Not far from the main stream that feeds Lucas Pond, directly opposite from where high water flowed from the pond in summer, my cabin rested a few feet from the edge of water and ice. From the outside, my cabin looks like a small house. Inside, however, the cabin has the look and feel of a, well, a cabin, a place of adventure. With its piney walls and thick wood beams that crisscrossed the ceiling of the main room, and the many effects of family and children whose summer home this was, the cabin was friendly in a human way. It was very much lived in. Cabin and trees blended as they should have, although even cabins seem like intruders in a land where nature builds nests in trees. A teepee would have been more natural, but much less accommodating to me.

Between the shore and the cabin's deck rose a small, lovely pine tree, posing almost in the center of the bay window. Thin and with a naturally sculpted top, the tree was imperfect in shape yet its imperfection created its beauty. To the left of this eager next generation of forest was an ailing predecessor, the high stump of another evergreen that, to my untrained eye and mind, seemed to have been withered by lightning. A little hope remained in that crippled tree, a sprig that continued to reach for light and life. Nearby was a spindly cousin, naked and shivering in winter's grasp. To the right of the deck were large evergreens, tall, straight and stately as Swiss Guards, and ringing the pond as they saluted the sun, moon, stars and air that seemed as frozen as the ice below. On winter's sunny days those majestic trees shaded the ice, seeming to protect it. In summer, those same trees cooled the water. Beyond those trees and the thin shoreline lay Lucas Pond, in winter the emperor of the woods.

Lucas Pond, Wrapped In Fog At Dusk.

After my debut day, the cabin was deathly quiet until the propane heated the pine as I exercised, cooked and ate. On the wall near my day bed, rock-climbers' grips provided steps to the loft above the three small bedrooms behind the main room. My soles never left an imprint in the loft. An American flag and several fishing rods stood at attention in a corner near the radio. This was a place where a family had fun, in summer. But for now, this was one man's home and writing den. Though basically a summer outpost, the building wasn't drafty except for the cold air that whistled up from the basement through spaces in the wide boards that marked the floor above. On January 19, Day 11 in the cabin, propane heat raised a summer fly back to life for an afternoon. Darkness, and cold, returned it to sleep. Flies, I decided, held the secret to life and not-quite death, to hibernation and revival. More than a month later, a tiny, translucent winged green insect fluttered and faltered inside the bay window, staring not at me but at bits of moisture dripping on the deck outside. The fly was content to drift daily from full life to dormancy and near death. The green insect wanted nothing to do with a cap full of water I left near the corner where the insect lay half-awake, happy to gawk instead at the water that dripped outdoors and beyond its reach.

Besides stuffing pillows at the bottom of the doors leading to the three small freezer-like bedrooms behind my living space, a small braided rug pushed against the bottom of the front door, protecting me from wind propelled over the pond. I preferred the warm drafts of book chapters to the frigid drafts that could sweep over the pond and into the cabin. In cracks where the bay window met the cabin frame I stuffed newspapers to further thwart nature. Pillows, blankets and a large braided rug as well as newspapers were useful for covering and filling the spaces between the wide floorboards to block cold air that flew north from the basement. But I let nothing disturb the families of baby spiders that hung out near the propane stove. Hang in there, I said, speaking to myself and laughing at my joke.

On January 18, I saw one small bird, and two fluffy squirrels playing in a fallen tree off the deck. Brave and bored souls, I thought. Powerboats aren't permitted on the water, but on the ice anything goes as SUVs, vans and tractors raced over the pond. It wasn't until February 12, Day 31 in the cabin, as I marched off to bring back lettuce and tomatoes, that I spotted a lone chipmunk, this one dashing under a building near a summer camp at the pond's far northern edge.

Winter's woods lack life, which surprised me and offered time to make small discoveries, or none at all. In six weeks, I saw only two squirrels, twice, two birds and one chipmunk. Well-trained by genetics and eons of experience gained by others, the animals know where to hide and keep warm. On a small farm just north of the pond, two shaggy Scottish Highland cattle stood daily like horizontal totems in stiff, ice-covered relief against the wind. Their thick coats meant they didn't have to know better. When I shouted, "Hello! Hello!" in English, they answered in a brogue so thick I understood nothing. Gazing toward the pond one day, I stood puzzled as a strong gust whipped past me, rattling one, only one, tree while its neighbors stared ahead motionless, a phenomenon that I still don't understand and don't expect to see again.

January 2004 was reported to be the second coldest month in the region since the last woolly mammoth shed its fur. Quoting the U.S. Weather Service, the *Boston Globe* put the time limit at 1888, when records were first kept. A small thermometer hooked to my belt with its neighbor, a compass, recorded an unofficial low of thirty degrees below zero while a neighbor said the ice on the pond was thick enough to support a large house. "Coldest day so far," I wrote on January 16. "Minus forty-five degrees atop Mount Washington. Almost three-hundred Massachusetts schools, south of the border, shut due to cold."

On late January afternoons, I could sense the cold marshaling its forces, ready to rush my cabin at darkness like a foreign army on the march. The army was a silly fiction, but the plunging temperatures were not.

Except for the intermittent roar of ice deepening in the pond and frozen branches crackling in the wind, the woods were more silent than audibly shrieking in pain from the cold. A dog barking at the wind broke the serenity of night, sounding like a gunshot echoing through a far-off valley. Smothered in ice, the pond appeared to freeze the surrounding woods. In a strange way, the more transient snow protected the solid ice although the ice could take care of itself, it seemed to me.

Walking on the pond, on the ice, gave me a powerful feeling of possession. As I was indeed walking on water, the feeling was much more enabling than trudging among the trees in any season. Walking on the ice made me feel as if I were in a painting, one with the horizon, the pond and the surrounding trees, which formed the frame. The sun, clouds and falling snow dictated the brightness and colors in the painting.

As much as I enjoyed trudging through the woods and along roads and trails, I never walked at night. Not until I left the cabin did I realize that walking and darkness didn't stroll hand-in-hand during my life in the woods. Even Lucas Pond, with its glacier-like ice and its spotlight effect in darkness, didn't lure me. It wasn't fear that imprisoned me at night either, at least not consciously. I never conjured up the vision of a crazy old man leaping at me in the deep, dark woods. Hell, I was that crazy old man, someone else would have thought. Did I fear that the deer I never spotted would mug me behind an old oak tree? Not even in my weirdest dreams. I'm not that loony. The answer is more simple and mundane. Most nights I wrote late to keep the promise I made to myself in the beginning, which was to write something, anything, every day. I wrote indoors at night, but not in darkness. If I hadn't written by midnight, I would have broken that promise to myself and perhaps concluded that promises were made to be broken at any time without consequence.

Wrapped in the seclusion of the woods in winter it was easy to fill my days with wasteful routine. Though short of daylight hours, winter days seemed long because I was living in my own timeless world. Beyond the routine necessities of existing, my life revolved around reading good books, writing something, anything, every day; playing cribbage, doing crossword puzzles of varying difficulty, exercising and walking on the pond or in the woods, during daylight. All those unrelated activities seemed to sidetrack me from confronting the hard job of sitting down to write. But those activities, I learned, were indirectly related to writing because they stimulated my subconscious to deliver the words and ideas I was searching for.

Throughout the harsh winter, I watched for signs of life in the woods, and raised my antennae to capture more writing help from my dreams. Deer, though supposedly hidden in plain sight, I never spotted while woolly mammoths and wood nymphs existed only in my imagination. The denizens of spring and summer were either in hibernation or had fled southward with the sun. It wasn't until the end of February that my eagle eye spotted three crows and one hawk along hilly Route 43, which was lined with dirty snow, and sand to cut the ice. Tomatoes, lettuce, cucumbers, multi-grain bread and garbanzo beans were the objects of my desire on many winter walks. My favorite, and only, supermarket housed those supplies. Except for the stranger in the cabin, the woods showed few signs of life. If a change of seasons was on the horizon, I couldn't see or feel it. Fortunately, my dreams never slipped into hibernation.

On February 29, the leap day of that Leap Year, I saw maple sap seeping during that unusually warm daytime. A woodpecker hammered on a tree near the cabin and two chipmunks chased each other, thrilled no doubt at the prospect of the coming of the green. Those chipmunks sensed something that I did not.

Come March 4, I noticed less snow in the woods, which exposed carpets of dead leaves, pine needles and, fittingly, dead branches made brittle by the deep cold and finally felled by the weight of snow. Without snow and before spring's greens arrived, the woods lost their ground-level brightness and became even more depressing than they had been. Snow brightened the forest floor like beams from powerful beacons flashing among trees. Yet with less snow on the ground or clinging to branches, more cabins emerged from hiding, looking like fresh wooden skeletons as sight lines opened.

Fog so dense it felt as if the sky itself were sitting on my head like a helmet created a northern Russia-like landscape when I jogged over the frozen water on March 5, Day 49 in the cabin. I couldn't see the opposite shore because the pond was trapped in fog, which grew even thicker the following day, limiting my vision to a few feet from the cabin's front door. The scene that day reminded me of being in Tuzla, northern Bosnia, one winter in the mid-nineteen nineties, when I groped through a fog trying to avoid plunging into small ponds in a bomb-cratered road. The heavy fog that engulfed me at Lucas Pond also brought to mind the North Sea on a bad day in just about any season.

Then came my sixty-third birthday, March 9, Day 53 in the cabin. That's called progress, of a sort, or at least aging. Two years earlier to the day, I was holed up in a one-room cinder block building in the mountains of southeastern Afghanistan toasting my sixty-first birthday with an American radio reporter. Don't leak this to the Taliban, but our toast was a shot each of smuggled single malt Scotch. Whisky, my friends in Kabul, whisky. Freezing inside, a blizzard raged outside at midnight back then as we celebrated my birthday. Winter didn't smile on me in 2004 either. But conditions at Lucas Pond were closer to partying in London than they were to sweeping the sky in search of the elusive Indian Ocean satellite so I could file a story as snowflakes, stinging my cheeks like rampaging bees, whipped through the remote Afghanistan mountains.

In my woods, as I came to call the woods around Lucas Pond, a light snow had fallen overnight and I was another day older. Water from the main brook flowed through the woods under ice to the frozen pond. This also happened to be another of my trash-walking days, as I hadn't yet been nabbed trying to dump trash into someone else's dumpster. Because my reporter's notes from the roads of Europe, Asia and Africa were moldy, I had celebrated my birthday by dusting off notebook pages and dodging a few falling flakes on the deck outside the cabin door.

Pat arrived merrily at 11:20 in the morning with many surprises, the topper being the Dobecks—Pat's sister Joanne and Joanne's husband Bill. We drove to the town of Meredith at Lake Winnipesaukee for a lavish turkey dinner, one of my favorites. My salivary glands kick in when I even think of a turkey dinner. No description of an actual turkey dinner is complete without the word lavish. To merit a blue ribbon, however, a turkey dinner must include a mess of mashed potatoes, stuffing made of ground lamb, rice and pine nuts seasoned with allspice; peas and pearl onions, gravy thick with giblets and a few fresh vegetables sprinkled in, meat from the thigh, drumstick and wings, plus cinnamon rolls. On my sixty-third birthday, only the ground lamb and rice stuffing failed to find the turkey. Thanksgiving lay eight months ahead.

Joanne and Bill Dobeck on March 9, 2004.

Birthday Boy, age 63, March 9, 2004.
Photos by Patricia Brothers Salome.

Dessert ambushed me back in the cabin. A deep-dish custard pie, which at that time topped my dessert list, bore only one candle to make the simple point that this was a birthday celebration. Champagne, a large balloon that clung to the cabin ceiling until I was two days older, and gifts, such as music CDs, books and a bush hat ringed the pie. Margaret, Mary and Andrew, our children then in Seattle, San Francisco and New Orleans respectively, called and sent cards and gifts. Lois and Mary Lou, my sisters, also called to find out how the hermit in the woods was holding up. With the arrival of dusk, my visitors fled in the deepening cold. With them went my dirty clothes, but no trash, as I had none, having earlier and unknowingly that day violated the woodlands' defining rules of trash-dumping.

Four days later, on a sunny but frigid March 13, Pat rescued me again. The cabin was far back in my rear view mirror until a week later, when I returned to Lucas Pond. In the intervening time, Pat and I went to Boston for three of those days to celebrate Pat's birthday, on March 18, by tickling our ears at the symphony, widening our eyes and minds at the Museum of Fine Arts, and walking the city. We met my younger sister, Mary Lou Etheredge, for lunch in Wellesley, Massachusetts, and saw friends at the Neiman House at Harvard. Even during those "off" days, my subconscious churned and chugged and I poured book thoughts into my ever-handy Reporter's Notebook.

Diversions, such as birthday celebrations and a trip to Boston, interrupted the solitude I enjoyed at Lucas Pond. But even they were as much a part of my writing year as waking at night to record my dreams and writing at midnight to meet my self-imposed deadline of writing something every day. Writing was the core of my life in 2004, and all my other activities fed that lust.

A lingering winter welcomed me back to the cabin on March 21. The calendar proclaimed in bold print something about that being the first day of spring. In reality, that was nothing but a typical Gregorian lie.

The following day, number Fifty-Nine in the cabin, was

brutally cold. Screw you spring, the ice-covered pond seemed to say, as winter's gray trees still dominated the woods and it seemed that winter would be everlasting. But the sun that inched higher each day would win the seasonal battle. Early spring rains followed. Those storms were like late winter monsoons that soon joined forces with the sun to thrash the ice. I could hear Old Man Ice cracking in reverse, moaning and dying, if that's how ice feels when it melts.

To a keen observer of nature, the coming spring would have been visible back in late January, as slightly longer daylight hours began to expose that secret. Never before had I noticed that around January 20 the lengthening daylight hours concealed spring hibernating in the cold, gray darkness of winter itself.

On many days and in all seasons I searched valiantly for deer in the woods. All I ever saw were signs the stealthy critters had left behind, leaving me to feel like some sort of weird spiritualist trying to interpret animal droppings and hoof prints among the leaves, in the snow and dirt. March 23 was typical of my searches, and of my futility. For hours I trod through the woods, stopping often to make book notes, and to search for deer. None. Nothing. Nada. Only more scat and trails.

Rain and more fog heralded the coming spring as temperatures rose in early April. A large, long-necked gray bird stood on the ice, appearing in the rain, haze and fog like a mini-Loch Ness Monster. This was the first sign of anything even slightly exotic that I had seen in the three months since I had become an iceman.

A higher sun brought still-rising temperatures and all-out war with the snow and ice that remained to shield the pond's watery essence. The ice melted a little each day. Caught in the jaws of vicious natural enemies, the ice was gnawed at from above by the external powers of rain, fog and sun; below, the enemy was water itself. For Lucas Pond in winter, there was no escape from spring. To me, it seemed that the pond itself was dying a slow death as its ice vanished. Everywhere else, however, the coming of warmth and green meant new life, not death. My world was changing, too. Whenever I walked on the ice, I felt as if I possessed the pond, that I, a weaker being, controlled a stronger natural force. This is different from rowing on the pond; in that case, I felt as if the pond possessed me.

Winter yields its grip grudgingly in the New Hampshire woods, but it yields. I had come to feel like one with the ice because it was steadfast, empowering. I thought of the frozen pond as a distinct entity, a personality, like the land because I could walk on it. As the ice melted and weakened, I missed it and felt a loss.

Winter at its harshest I could handle because the physical challenge matched the creative. So, too, with high summer. Because they were extreme and predictable, those conditions made it easier for me to live in the woods and focus on writing. October and April, being most unpredictable, were the most difficult times for me. Freezing when it wasn't supposed to be or too warm for the season made those days in the cabin and the woods the most difficult to manage.

The Vanishing Ice Spirit.

Thick, jagged edges of ice near the shore looked like the teeth of a menacing gator that was most dangerous because, even if it weren't thrashing about, it was dying. On April 4, I realized that winter was doomed. Daylight Savings Time, after all, would begin the following day. I saw that on the radio. What better notice did I need? April 7, a Wednesday, was mild, so it was fitting that I saw two fish jump in open water in a fit of primitive jubilation. Do fish bump their heads on the ice when they jump in winter? I asked no one but myself. No, they must be too smart for such stupidity, I answered. Strong gusts pushed waves from the shore in front of the cabin toward ice farther out, giving the appearance of thousands of lemmings perched atop the ice. A day later, the shoreline was entirely free of ice and the local version of a huge iceberg floated in the center of the pond. The largest remaining ice floe began floating toward my cabin, as if to salute me and say *adios*, see you next winter.

Despite the slow death of my friend, the ice-filled pond, the change of seasons was awesome. The shift from ice to warm, green buds was more striking as I watched alone in the woods than it would have been if seen in the more complex context of town or city life. Once seeming to be indestructible, by April 21, Day 79 in the cabin, my friend the icepack had vanished, now part of the air and the open water where once it lived impregnable and imperial. The shifting power of nature also exposed the fragility of the pond and everything around it. Nature's new face replaced the old. The facelift, however, would be temporary.

With the change of seasons came the birds. In a tree just to the left of the cabin deck I spied a tiny white-breasted bird, the smallest bird I had ever seen, smaller even than a hummingbird. Nearly invisible, this bird's back was black and gray, its head gray, white and black, almost too many colors for its size. My journal entry for April 23, Day 81 in the cabin, says that the tree was filled with specks of life. Awesome. Triumphant. No silent spring this year.

Anonymous and Quiet — Not The Kid And Jack Sharkey.

Open water introduced the fishing season. Fisher folk arrived with the ardor of kids playing baseball at the first sight of bare ground. The anglers, however, were countless. They glided as silently as the hawks that cruised above, crossing the green, blue and sometimes gray water that reflected the slow greening of the woods and the alternating celestial colors.

Unaware of the season's opening on that Saturday, April 24, I raised the blinds of the cabin's small bay window to witness a seasonal event that would have excited Ted Williams and Jack Sharkey, although those old pros would have boycotted the amateurish mob. Canoes and rowboats, filled with anglers rabidly seeking rainbow, brown, brook and tiger trout, stretched from shore to shore. It was early on that April day, but not that early, about eight I'd say, and I wasn't hung over. But still I blinked and rubbed my eyes for about five minutes before I realized what was happening a few feet away. I was stunned by the number of boats that covered the water almost as completely as did the ice in winter. As worms, flies, artificial lures and their masters ruled the water, not one goose would have been able to land on Lucas Pond without first tripping over a human head.

My first thought in the morning haziness was that the natives had returned to reclaim their waters and their land. About time, I thought, as I scanned my tight living quarters for a white flag. Soon, however, I realized the time wasn't quite right for a counter-revolution. Shortly after I stepped on the deck facing the pond I realized how off my timing was. One fisherman received a call on his cell phone while fighting a fish from his boat, and the conversation went exactly like this: "Hold on, I got a fish on. I'll call you back." After the fisherman hauled in his fish, and released it because it was too small, he put fresh bait on his hook, cast again and called his friend back. Water does indeed act like a megaphone.

A few days later, in May, the pond wore a new face. Looking like an eighth-grader daubed in streaky makeup while waiting for her first date, the pond reflected the oaks and maples turning from wintry grays to sprouts of Ireland greens. Skies of desert cobalt hues imbued the warming waters with the brush strokes of a prodigy.

Only a few boats floated outside my cabin on May 4, the day I took my trash for a walk and discovered one gigantic secret of woodland etiquette. Prized trout, I hoped, had noticed the shadows of the gliding boats and so could leap without fear of hitting their heads and feed without being lured to their death. Not all the casters of opening day had sheathed their weapons of the hunt and towed their canoes and rowboats to shore for use elsewhere. The gentle splashing of oars, of bait kissing the water and the silky sound of glistening rainbow trout rising in futile attempts to fling a hook made louder the otherwise prevailing silence.

As a lifelong townie from countless villages, towns and cities on four continents, my antennae strained to pick up most signals of the woods. Graceful geese, easy to notice because of their signal honks, soon became an exception. As spring and summer wore on, the woods and the people who lived there would teach me much more.

Spring filled the woods with emerald replacing winter's ashen grays and lifeless browns. Leaves made the trees balloon in size and seemed to shrink the pond. Blue skies and the open water itself made the woods shine in reflections over the pond. The shadow of a duck flying low over the flat water under a sunny sky made it appear that two ducks, rather than one, were seeking a landing location. Lucas Pond is stocked with trout several times a year, so the old fishing magnet yields a fine catch. Large trout and even larger bass that survive from year to year bring glee to the anonymous fishing descendants of Ted Williams and Jack Sharkey, even if those two fly-casting wizards never fished together at Lucas Pond.

Great blue herons, mallards, red tail hawks and honking Canada geese that sounded like barking seals flying in from San Francisco joined the local bird population in welcoming the warmth and sparkling water of spring and summer. On lawns far from the pond I spotted regal robins, which I decided on the spot were the eagles of the small fry.

Scribbling book notes while assembling mashed potatoes, peas, carrots, corn and sautéed slices of a turkey drumstick, I gazed out the small window above the sink at a great blue heron rising from near the shore in front of the cabin. The majestic bird skimmed low across the water, gliding like a lumbering cargo plane carrying the weapons of war into Bosnia or Afghanistan. The kitchen sink was a fine place, as was just about any place, to think about my book, but not as good a tool for me as it was for Agatha Christie. As quoted on the radio, Christie said, "The best time to plan a book is when you're doing the dishes." She was on to something universal in the abstract, but for me her details were off, nowhere near as sharp as my dreaming and playing one-man cribbage.

Well after dinner, I prodded myself to return to the story of Lebanon and its fifteen years of tribal and proxy wars, power grabs and religious fervor run amok. Far from Lebanon in years, miles and circumstances, happy woodpeckers hard at work in the New Hampshire woods welcomed spring like joyous kids whacking baseballs for the first time since October. The rhythmic pounding of the woodpeckers was more than matched by the staccato sound of hammers hitting nails and the wailing of saws that roared around the pond. Humans in the numbers of summer were returning to Lucas Pond. Seasonal cabin-dwellers began arriving on weekends, having shed their woolen garb and woolly minds while preparing their rustic quarters for the joys of sun and heat.

Local Olympians floated a diving platform from the main beach in an attempt to entice summer to a neighborhood where seventy-two degrees is considered jungle-like heat. The small diving platform, while a source of floating fun, was to me a poor replacement for winter's all-encompassing ice. I loved to walk on the ice, but never once touched a toe on the diving platform, not even so I could boast about walking on water in summer.

Writing the chapter about Lebanon bored, or maybe frightened, me on Sunday, April 25, so I used the pleasantness of the day to escape the cabin and walk to a small restaurant on Route 4. This was my version of taking a long drive to avoid writing. At the restaurant, Ed and I sat at the same table because there was no choice. What followed was another example of the benefits of hanging out alone and talking freely with another stranger, knowing that we would never talk again.

Ed was a cyclist, a real one wheeling a bike made for long hauls. At the age of eighty, Ed was trying to remain relevant no matter what anyone else thought or how the world changed around him. He reminded me of Salih Reykovic, the writer and local historian in the Bosnian city of Mostar, whom I met eight years earlier when he was seventy-four. Although they were contemporaries, age and bicycles were all that Ed and Salih Reykovic had in common. Ed's bike was slick. Reykovic's bike was old and wobbly, meant for short hauls, when the absence of war permitted. Ed could roam widely. War limited Reykovic's travels to his side of Mostar's Old Bridge; he couldn't even ride across town because the Ottoman-era bridge had been bombed into the river below.

Clad in full, colorful riding regalia after he had just cycled twenty-six miles, Ed's workout was the rough equivalent of the Boston Marathon run on wheels. Ed was enjoying a blueberry muffin and breakfast tea when we talked. I was waiting for two slices of pizza. He was, I must say, an inspiration, a strong-minded, independent and philosophical New Englander. Ed still worked, selling truck tops after owning a business selling recreational vehicles. His wife played bingo in Portsmouth regularly, he said, and she was younger than he, a mere 75. A wise man, Ed left me with this thought, "You must seek your point of contentment when things go wrong." Ed's point of contentment was, it seemed clear, cycling, alone, whether or not things had gone awry. But something had gone awry in Ed's life, it seemed. He never said what that was, leaving me to guess that going from owning a business to selling truck tops wasn't his idea of the most exciting way to face the days. Maybe Ed's problem was the relentless cudgel of aging, although I didn't believe that was the whole story. Reykovic's problem was war, which is almost as universal as aging, when friends become enemies in a battle for land and where religion is a main power source.

With late May came my personal Mosquito War. I held my own inside the cabin, but lost badly outside. This was a skirmish compared with the assault of biting black flies that swarmed in high summer. Black flies never lost a war.

The pond looked like a footprint stamped on the land by a local Paul Bunyan. Reading *Don Quixote* in the old rocker under a lamp near the front door, I looked up at the small octagonal window on the right side of the loft and saw only leaves outside, so many bright green leaves that branches were invisible. In winter, the branches alone, which looked like feeble gray sticks, were visible.

Thick with leaves, the woods in May began to resemble a rain forest. Spreading and reaching for more light, ferns encroached along dirt roads while trees flung artistic shadows on the water. The sands of winter, which earlier collected in mounds on the verges of Route 43, had disappeared, replaced by grass that embraced the asphalt. Where was I when that happened? I wondered. Inches deep in winter, the sand appeared to be part of the asphalt and would remain so forever. Now I could only guess where the sand was buried.

Rising from the rocker to track honking noises, I spotted six goslings—brown, furry and pet-like—and their parents. To get closer, I bent low and moved quietly out the door and from the deck down the stairs to the right of the cabin, toward a small beach on Lower Camp Road. It was no contest. Hearing my approach when I took my first step from the deck to the stairs, the family paddled in frantic silence for open water. I snapped photos of their beauty as they fled, on foot so to speak, across the wetness they preferred.

As summer sped toward me riding the rising sun, I noticed that the pond had lost its power to the encroaching and girdling woods. When bound by winter's ice, the pond was king, hard and immoveable, a constant color and form. Kids on skates and riding machines played on it, but nobody played with it. In summer, however, the pond was malleable, more like a serf than a king. People swam and fished in it, floated on it, watched it rise and fall with rain or drought and saw it shrink, vulnerable to the swelling and shadows of the woods and the changing colors of the sky. The open water also tricked the pond into behaving as a megaphone, which I first heard when a fisherman answered his phone. From the cabin I could hear voices, spoken not shouted, on boats far from shore. Summer brought its own beauty, but for me the stillness and simplicity of winter still stood stolid and supreme.

Much can be said about the call of the loon, the musical chirping of small birds, a frog's moan, mountainous clouds and deep blue skies over flat, glistening water that changed color with the sky. It's spectacular, I wrote in my journal, hoping not to betray winter's beauty or be accused of being fickle when it comes to appreciating nature and its vagaries. A sultry summer day can be eerily quiet, too, except for the splash of trout leaping, which highlights the prevailing silence of a brooding pond, quiet and flat. A fading afternoon sun that slices past pines, maples and oaks, and makes the pale arms and legs of white birch trees light up like elongated flash lights have their own allure. White birch trees are especially beautiful, the largest looking like canoes in waiting. Their silvery leaves swiveling in light breezes remind me of an airman using coded hand signals and waving signs to guide a jet fighter onto an aircraft carrier.

July was my vacation month. High summer would allow for sailing on wider waters to let what I had written about the tribes of the world simmer like my red sauce. Time away from the loons also helped my subconscious generate fresh material for my Reporter's Notebook. July 4, 2004, was also our 40th wedding anniversary. So, as promised, Pat and I sailed far from Lucas Pond. Thoreau often walked home to the center of his Concord, so we took a ten-country Baltic cruise to celebrate forty great years and three of the best children anywhere. We topped off the cruise with a week in our London, the town we knew so well from 1993 to 1998, when I was based there as the Cox Newspapers European correspondent.

Our vacation began when Pat steered her small Honda over the rocks and gravel of Big Buck Road on June 27, Day 126 in the cabin. An exercise roughly the reverse of January 8 followed. After we piled all of my clean and dirty clothes, fresh and frozen food and personal research and writing tools into Pat's hatchback, we cleaned the cabin so Paul and Karen Dale would recognize it and enjoy a month of summer there with their children. The cache of canned goods that remained I stored in the basement, which served as my personal market. There, the cans of baked beans, tuna, crushed, diced and whole tomatoes would await my return without knowing exactly when that might be, reading a calendar being beyond the ability of canned tomatoes and associates.

A cruise isn't my favorite mode of travel. Donkeys, camels, horses, planes with standing-room-only space and chortling chickens in the laps of passengers, and fifty-year-old cars that break down each time they brake for any reason are my preferred cruisers. But our Baltic cruise was nothing short of special. Before docking near the white cliffs of Dover, England, we saluted Sweden, Norway, Denmark, Finland, Germany, Poland, Estonia, Latvia and St. Petersburg, Russia. After a later trip, in 2008, to St. Petersburg via Helsinki and later from Severodvinsk and Arkangelisk in Russia's far north, I can say that I have entered St. Petersburg/Leningrad by ship, plane, train (twice) and car, each time so memorable that I'm eager to return again by any means. Herein lies a tip for travelers who are searching for hours and hours of silence on a train: through countless country miles of Russia's great northern forests, the train ride from Arkangelisk to St. Petersburg took twenty-five-and-a-half hours. If you're hungry, tired and your weak Russian falters further, ask the Azeri chef in the dining car to prepare a meal. Do so by flapping your arms out wide and making sounds like a chicken. Everyone around will laugh, including the chef, who will then point to his leg and chest, a universal way of asking whether I wanted a chicken leg or chicken breast. Two legs, I answered, holding up two fingers and pointing to my legs. The laughter will then grow louder. That story is another reminder that sign language works anywhere.

On August 1, I returned to Lucas Pond and its binding woods. By then, after more than four months of staring at knotty pine walls, the cabin had become my second home. Primed for the rest of summer and the coming autumn, which would be my fourth season in the woods, I resumed reading old notes and writing about the Israelis and Palestinians and their tribal war rooted in land, history, religion, culture and language. Before focusing on tribal wars elsewhere, I had to shake a lasting impression of the cruise and its passengers—the loud nasal whine of a stalwart faux sailor complaining about breakfast on the ship that failed the Kansas test: "Cream of wheat is not supposed to be lumpy." Not to be outdone, a couple agreed upon visiting St. Petersburg, formerly Leningrad, "This is just like Disney World."

Re-entry in August was much simpler than my arrival at Lucas Pond in the Arctic-like conditions of January 8. Cabin water, hot and cold, was up and running, and I didn't need to consult Paul Dale's notes to ignite the propane gas heater, artificial heat being unnecessary. In addition to my warm-weather clothing, computer, printer, notebooks and other materials needed for writing, I lugged in a dozen gallons of drinking water to supplement the cabin's shallow well and thwart any drought. Fresh food joined the canned goods that I hauled up from the cool basement to provide a full pantry. I was ready once more to dream, read notes about my reporting trips and classic books for stimulation, to walk in the woods and, critically, to battle my demons of doubt by writing something, anything, daily.

Long walks were vital to stirring my subconscious, although I usually didn't know that was happening until it happened. Each time the mystery was revealed, I reached for my omnipresent Reporter's Notebook in my right rear pocket to jot down what my inner mind had plumbed lest the wisdom be lost in the ether of failed memory. That done, the writing and rewriting would resume.

Woodman Marsh, an alluring name, was one of my favorite thinking corners during all seasons. Glistening like a large eyeball dropped on the larger land, Woodman Marsh pumped water that gurgled over a pocket dam into the stream that feeds Lucas Pond. The marsh reminded me of a secret fishing or swimming hole deep in the north woods that was known only to twelve-year-old boys. The soft, near-silent flow of water over the dam made the marsh seem even quieter, more remote and much less consequential than it is.

With a copy of Dante's *Inferno* in hand, and my notebook handy, I headed for the end of Lower Deerfield Road and Woodman Marsh on August 5, Day 131 in the woods. There, I sat for an hour reading on a boulder that jutted out like an elbow next to the dam. The marsh, the open water and the trees around them failed to cough up any form of life. Then I decided to close the cover on Dante to better serve the moment.

Woodman Marsh, Where A Reader Thrived.

To stimulate my subconscious mind, broaden my knowledge of the woods and their mysteries, and maybe even see a bounding deer, I set off on a path into a thicker tangle beyond the marsh.

After a time, not terribly long or disappointingly short, I reached a "T" on the trail. A left turn took me to Coffeetown Road, another alluring name. If there was a Coffeetown, I missed it or the passage of time made it miss me. After a long jaunt, my red birch walking stick in hand, I passed high tension electric wires before reaching a house, an actual lived-in building, unlike the abandoned and crumbling cabin that I had saluted a mile before and left behind leaving me to wonder about its past. Nearby, four kids were fishing in a pond that beavers made by blocking a stream with trees that had been felled by their teeth and artistic handiwork. Catching fish in a pond created by beavers seemed to me as improbable as trying to catch a whale in Lucas Pond. How would fish reach the beaver pond? I pondered. But I'm ignorant about beaver ponds and their contents so I said nothing to the kids. Anyway, I mused, must kids catch fish to enjoy fishing? I had learned the answer to that question long ago. Should the beaver dam eventually break, as they often did, the pond would morph back into a meadow, a fine and natural reversal. Then where would those invisible fish go? I wondered.

Farther down Coffeetown Road the path disappeared, having been flooded, washed out, creating a small pond that was the work of clouds, not beavers. Swimming isn't in my survival kit, so I kissed the small pond goodbye, made a U-turn and weaved my way back to Route 43. As rain began to fall, tapping like an indecipherable Morse code on my head and on the green leaves of summer, I stuck out my thumb and got lucky. A young man, with pity stitched on his cap and painted on the hood of his pickup, picked me up and drove to the top of Route 43 and the vegan restaurant on Route 4.

With a major storm minutes away, my hitching thumb and I were lucky again, reminding me of how important hitchhiking had been in my life in the late 1950s, when hitching rides had been my forte. I hitched to and from college classes, about 25 miles one-way, for two years. Daily, I thumbed the seven miles from Millville north to Uxbridge, where I met the brothers De Young, Danny and Bob, and their car. From Uxbridge we drove to Holy Cross College in Worcester. On some of my return trips, I hitched, often at night, all the way from Worcester to Millville. A small confession is in order. My morning rides from Millville to Uxbridge were almost as easy as taking a taxi. The walk from my house to Millville's single traffic light, then a blinker on Route 122, took fifteen minutes. If I reached the corner by 7:15 a.m., I could bank on a ride from either

Dickie McCrohan or Mr. Berkowitz, both of whom were headed to work, probably at Whitin Machine Works just north of Uxbridge. If I arrived after 7:15, I was left to hug the curb and hope for another friendly driver. Mr. Berkowitz, whose first name I don't recall and probably never knew, was always generous and New England reserved. If he said one word, maybe hmmm, I missed it. Dickie McCrohan, however, overflowed with chatter and quivered in the birthing stages of animal rights activism, once stopping to free dogs that were locked in what seemed like eternal copulation while I worried about missing my ride with the DeYoungs.

But that was a different era, as I am too-frequently reminded, although few mention that this new epoch is one that Americans have created and accepted.

Back on Route 43 in New Hampshire, in the hands of a Good Samaritan and his pickup, and with the rain gods hovering, time passed quickly before we reached Route 4. As the skies opened wide, I dashed to Susty's vegan restaurant a few steps from the trucker who sped away, rejecting a free lunch. The food at Susty's was good, although I'm no vegan. Susty's thrived in that neighborhood, which amazed me, and its success said more about the neighborhood than I knew. Susty's was a great place to learn about New Hampshire's rebellious side, the many rural corners and crevasses where government is deeply distrusted except when rebels need services that only government can provide. Here, for example, I heard stories about people who preferred jail time rather than be forced to take driving classes as punishment for driving without a license. The choice was theirs, and some made it without a whimper.

On this unplanned dining excursion, I fell into the Blue Plate Special—tomato and pasta soup, tofu pot pie and salad—and listened to a young man named Malachi recite his rap-like poetry. Those who worked and ate at Susty's were mostly young, trying without knowing it to divine the meaning of life and what to do with their slice of it. Many of those young adults looked as if they should be named Earth, Wind, Fire or Water. On this day at Susty's, Ben from Illinois and bearded Michael showed up in Ben's small camper. Their destination remained secret, but they didn't seem to be strangers at Susty's, which also catered to a surprising number of older people. Behind Michael and Ben came a man who said he taught English As a Second Language at a local university and in Thailand and Malaysia. Flee from your comfort zone, meet enough people, I thought, and you'll always be surprised. On second thought, do that often enough, and you'll never be surprised.

Susty's older patrons seemed to have made it. At least they seemed comfortable in their own clothes. Who among the young and the searching will make it? I asked myself. What does "make it" mean? What do I know anyway? I'm an observer, a stranger, a visitor living for a short time in the woods and trying to write a book.

No longer hungry, I strolled from Susty's and headed for my cabin. After another turn at hitching proved futile, I hoofed the three miles or so from Susty's back to the cabin, writing book notes as I went. My subconscious hadn't been sleeping. Along the way, I spotted several wild turkeys in the woods. Although they lack the long, lean grace of elusive deer, if you are lucky enough to spot one of those, I find wild turkeys beautiful because they are feral and free, sure of themselves, and bravely protective of their young. Wild turkeys, I realized, were the only forms of wildlife I saw in the woods, although I never stopped searching for others.

"It seems like I walked halfway around the world today," I wrote in my journal that night. Although that was a slight exaggeration, there was no doubt that I had earned the right to say it. My worn walking stick knew it had been around and we still hadn't seen Rudolph. Many of my walks were in a widening circle around the pond, up to Route 4 to eat lunch or buy groceries, over to Demmons Country Store to chat or exchange books with Jody, the owner, or along the loop from Lucas Pond Road to Route 153 and up along Antique Alley on Route 4 before I turned for home on Route 43.

Occasionally, as on this August day, I wandered far from the matted ground. Always, the purpose was to allow my inner mind to become the thinking and writing tool that my conscious mind required.

Besides feeding the vegan famished, Susty's serves another living purpose: it stands in silent vigilance over the dead, a cemetery I toured on several occasions when I walked, thought and wrote. Tipsy with age, the weary stone slabs leaned to all compass points as I slipped among them, careful not to rattle the bones below. Here I was exploring a slice of New Hampshire's past. Where better to wonder about the past than in a graveyard? This activity was a practiced one; I learned it on other continents. Alone, I gazed in ignorance at rows of stunning centuries-old sandstone tombs near Karachi, Pakistan, on my way to sit on a wall in an embracing sun and gaze at the Arabian Sea; standing, barely breathing but surely not alone, I stared into the sprawling, placid war cemeteries of Europe; in Bosnia, I leaned on a dying tree trying but unable to decipher the purpose that led to the mass graves; in Somalia and Algeria, I stopped counting the mounds of nameless dead; I took photos in a cemetery in Maarrat Saidnaya, Syria, while searching for the names of relatives.

* * *

In the ice and snow, the spring mud and the dryness of summer, on crisp dead-leaf autumn days, I ambled through Northwood's history in the cemetery behind Susty's trying to imagine the faces and lives of the town's past. The present was all around me, in three-dimensional life, yet I could fathom a mere fraction of that mysterious past. With only names and dates to go on, I was left to conjure the fortunes and times of the dead. But the imagination isn't to be shunned entirely, not in Northwood and certainly not in other places where the living vanished long ago and only the dead and their shards remain.

* * *

Death is like earthly gravity; it always fulfills its nature. There must be something to be learned from that alone, and where better to try than, once in a while, to read the names and dates in a cemetery. And to wonder.

* * *

No one stalked me in that Northwood graveyard, no church warden, cop, minister or bum bumming around. I was free to wonder and read the stones as if their etchings were an ancient language. But that wasn't true in Maarrat Saidnaya. There, I was a stranger in a small town walking with Randa, my guide, translator and friend. Three men followed us for two reasons: I was someone they didn't know and the young woman they knew was someone they thought shouldn't be walking about, anywhere in town, with a man they didn't know. They spoke in Arabic and I understood much, although I let my guide do the talking: "Who is that?" they asked. "His name is Lyos, he's American and he's from the Assaf family," she answered.

"He's looking for family members buried here." After that brief exchange, all was quiet on that cemetery front, even quieter later after I gave the men a photo of themselves on the steps of their local storefront.

* * *

In the cemetery behind Susty's I was free to wonder whether an undiscovered Emily Dickinson, Abigail Adams or Thoreau lay hidden there. Those are the names I wrote in my journal. I wasn't thinking of generals, ship captains or captains of industry. The oldest gravestone I found was dated 1802. Most of the people there had died in the mid-nineteenth century. Each of my self-guided tours brought me back to the Leighton family, a crusted name in these parts. I couldn't escape George W. and Nancy Leighton and their three children, each marked by small headstones: Anna J., Auretta and Amy M. Leighton. Martha J. Leighton, George W. Leighton's sister, joined them in the family circle. How had they lived just off the path that marked New Hampshire's first turnpike? It was easier to imagine how the family died, buried as they were in a cluster. An epidemic, a plague of some sort, I decided.

Lucas Pond's water level was down four or five feet on August 11, Day 137 in the cabin, when another walk seemed like a great idea. But the mean-looking sky warned me to lay anchor near the pond. The day was as hushed as high humidity could make it. Dense and darkening clouds choked the heavens. When clouds choke a summer sky, rain usually follows, drenching treetops and all things below. The trees never talked to me, and I didn't talk to them. But at moments like this, it seemed as if the trees talked to each other. Did maples talk only to maples, I wondered, and did oaks speak only to the heavens?

Guided by a painter's brush and ink high in the sky, the pond turned alternately black and dark blue; leaves around me flipped back to front and back again in the rising wind, a sure indication that the sky would soon fall. Four hours after noon came the deluge, or three. My journal doesn't reveal which came first, rain rampaging through the woods or thunder roaring high above and snapping below like a whip on wood. Sheets of rain streaked straight down like a hail of arrows striking the pond, the trees and the bare bed of the forest floor. The sounds and sights were deviations of excess that forced more appreciation of nature's shades and subtleties. August's storms were more violent that year than January's, when snow accumulated steadily in small amounts as the blizzards drifted away from Lucas Pond despite that winter's deep and enduring cold.

Religion doesn't animate me. Even deeply held spiritual beliefs aren't necessary for me to appreciate the awesome beauty and variety in nature. All that's necessary is to take what you see and hear at face value; that's enough to inspire awe. I do believe that all living things are connected, however. How they became so and what that means at its deepest level are puzzles I have yet to solve.

The audio version of that day was so striking that I opened the front windows of the cabin to better hear the hissing rain pound violently on the deck. The cabin remained desert-dry even with the windows wide open because the rain shot straight down from the hostile clouds and the wind camped elsewhere. Each time thunder roared anew, its companion, rain, thickened into a blinding flurry, creating a shield of solid gray water in front of the tree line at the far side of the pond. At times, wind joined the fray, but it blew outward from the cabin, across the pond all the way toward the far shore. Waves swept over the pond, a combination of rain, wind and the pond water churning as if being thrust by a powerful engine, which it was. Perhaps too fearful of engaging in this episode of nature's combat, lightning took a pass. One more thunderous roar sounded like a cannon blast around the corner from where the goslings and their parents had earlier paddled away from my gaze.

In twenty minutes, the storm moved to the east, southeast. Lightning finally paid a visit, after the main battle was over and only to dimly light the sky and trees. Thunder, now frail, kicked far off in the distance, as if to punch me goodbye. A light fog covered the pond as one person jumped into the now-smooth water from a canoe captained by a pal. Sounding like a soft symphony, maybe the string section, water dripped and drizzled from thousands of leaves to the forest floor; it was as if the rain continued. A second and third storm followed during the next hour and a half, but they were much less severe, less remarkable. Thin gray clouds covered the sky when mallards returned to reclaim their home on the water. Stimulated by nature's power and majesty, I read and wrote on and off until 11:30 that night. That's when I fell into the daybed hoping that overnight my subconscious, another of nature's puzzles, would open new paths into my book.

During the second week of September, I spotted autumn in the treetops, hints of yellow outlining the pond in one of nature's early warning systems. In the bright autumn days ahead the sun set the woods ablaze, targeting red, orange and yellow leaves and creating the effect of a swiveling strobe light dimmed only by darkness. With the changing colors came shorter daylight hours, a lower sun, and cooler mornings followed by frosts. The march of the seasons was gathering speed again. Even if daytime remained warm and pleasant enough, the woods, the pond and the sky knew that was fakery at its finest.

Autumn's Road To Winter.

After mid-September the future knocked in earnest. One electric heater was pressed into service to counter the early morning chill. As I neared the end of my manuscript, I felt very alone and frightened. Judgment time was near. All the writing demons that I faced in the cabin were rolled up into this last big one, when editors and publishers would decide whether my book was worthy.

Even the beautiful days depressed me because the painted woods and the cool nights told me that gray November was even closer than the calendar showed. Enticed perhaps by a single female mallard paddling on the pond, a lone sunbather took to the beach in a fleeting moment of self-deception. Lace-like white clouds in a pale blue sky and the low hum of fading crickets couldn't mask the approaching death of summer and the stronger whiff of autumn swelling in the woods.

The feeling of change was palpable, visible. A touch of winter dripped into the woods on a cool, rainy September 18, Day 150 in the cabin. Low and dense, the clouds appeared to be living in the treetops, if not on my head. "To see, hear and feel nature on its many levels, you have to sit quietly, watch and listen," I wrote in my journal, after I heard my footsteps echo on Lower Camp Road, like water rushing from a brook and dashing hard over jutting rocks. At midnight on September 19, I began reading *Sons and Lovers* before I fell into a restless sleep. Soon after, I woke with an idea about how to begin the chapter on Central Asia, an ageless story of hoary native tribes reemerging from the Soviet era and members of an even older tribe at the same time fleeing for safety. As asleep as I was awake, I told my thoughts to the computer, while thinking of the wily deer trying to dodge arrows in the woods. It was the hunting season for archers. Go deer, go, I thought.

A perfect blend of day and night, when light and darkness merge into reading and writing, arrived on October 2, Day 164 in the cabin. This smooth, seamless flow was what I had been seeking, but seldom found. More often the writing process seemed like riding in a Model T on a road filled with potholes. I woke at 5:30 a.m., angry because it was so early. When I couldn't fall back to sleep, I rose for good at 6:20, and decided to write until my mind was empty which, some might think, shouldn't have taken long. By 10:35 that morning, I wrote all I could at that moment about the tribes of Central Asia. My usual routine of exercise, breaking the fast, playing cribbage and doing crosswords to avoid writing was fractured, if for only one day. After reading for a couple of hours, I surrendered again to the cocoon. Still tired and now hungry, I rose again, for the third time within eight hours. After a light meal, a tuna sandwich, I wrote about Central Asia on and off for the rest of that day. Very sleepy, I dove into bed for the night at 10:40 p.m., pleased at what I had accomplished but doubtful that I would repeat that success.

The Cocoon.

My writing road veered toward research on October 5, when Pat drove to the rescue. Soon after we fled the cabin, I left to pan for nuggets of family history at the National Records and Archives office in Waltham, Massachusetts, and at public agencies in Woonsocket, Rhode Island, and Providence, Rhode Island's capital. Both sides of my very tribal family fled Syria a hundred years earlier when it was still part of the Ottoman Empire. All four of my grandparents settled in Woonsocket, a French-Canadian-American city in Northern Rhode Island. None of my grandparents ever spoke directly to me about their lives in the village of Maarrat Saidnaya, Syria, of their rough sail in steerage accommodations to France and on to New York, or of their early years in America. They probably thought there was no need to burden the second generation born here with such a dated and foreign past. Whatever my parents knew of their ancestral histories, they kept mostly to themselves. But I wasn't inert; I eavesdropped incessantly, inside and outside the immediate family, and even asked a few questions of my grandparents and parents, although the answers were far fewer.

But I learned much about my grandparents during several visits to Maarrat Saidnaya and from public records in this country. My mother's parents, John and Mary (Shaheen) Monsour, arrived together in 1905, along with a boy wrapped in a blanket and the boy's mother. John Monsour, however, first reached these shores on a scouting mission with his brother-in-law a couple of years earlier. Louis and Mary (Ghazale) Salome, who were much younger than the Monsours, landed here in 1908. Of my four grandparents, only Louis Salome became a U.S. citizen, and Salome wasn't his real family name; Assaf was. That and other aspects of my surprising tribal story are unveiled *In Syria, My Name is not My Name*, the last chapter in my first book, *Violence, Veils and Bloodlines—Reporting from War Zones*, the book I wrote at Lucas Pond.

As I researched my family's past in the national archives, the Boston Red Sox were about to end an inglorious eighty-six years of baseball futility. Two dozen figs would have meant more to John Monsour, my maternal grandfather, than the Red Sox putting a stake in the Curse of the Bambino—the long and dismal aftermath of when the Sox sold George Herman (Babe) Ruth to the New York Yankees in 1920. But to Abraham Louis Salome, my father, who died at age fifty-two in 1963, nothing would have been worth a longer, louder shout than the Red Sox rising from the cemetery of baseball's dead to win their first World Series in almost a century. When the Sox played on the road or at home in the 1940s and 1950s, my father would listen to games for hours on his car radio outside our house because the reception there was better than it was even when he grasped the ground wire on the radio inside the house. Those broadcasts were dramatic re-creations of Morse Code-like ticker-tape reports. When Ted Williams hit a homer, it seemed as if the ticker tape rapped as loud as the hysterical announcer, louder than any other hitter's grand slam. If there were a bigger fan of Ted Williams than my father, it would have been The Kid himself.

Sox fans swear their team's first championship in eighty-six years was another shot heard round the world. That series victory may not have echoed as loudly as the shots fired by farmers in Lexington and Concord more than two hundred years earlier, but in most of New England it was worthy of a twenty-one-gun salute. Without question, the 2004 championship buried the myth of the Bambino's Curse, a myth so strong it became legendary throughout New England. Ruth, later and forever known as the Sultan of Swat, was a Sox hero for five seasons, when he won eighty-seven games as a pitcher, helping the team win their last two world series until David Ortiz rose to power. After Ruth hit twenty-nine homers for the Sox in 1919, he was shipped to the Yankees for $100,000 in cash and a $300,000 loan. Harry Frazee, who owned the Sox at the time, produced Broadway shows thereby helping baseball, it seems to me, become as much theatre as sport. As a slugger, Ruth led the Yankees to seven series championships while the Sox spent eighty-six years losing games in every way possible—because of injuries, fielding and other lapses, bad managerial decisions, home runs by singles hitters and blowing huge leads late in seasons.

In the fall of 2004, my timing was flawed, not nearly as sharp as David Ortiz's, the Red Sox clutch slugger. I returned to the cabin in baseball darkness, just in time to miss the visuals of the New

England nine snatching the World Series trophy. If I had stayed in Portsmouth a few hours longer, I would have seen that magical moment for myself. But I was busy catching up to the end of my book, a happy and frightening prospect.

That night was both wildly jubilant and peaceful in New England: the Red Sox had finally buried the big gorilla in the region, The Curse. As noted in my cabin journal and in thousands of places throughout the area, the Sox swept the St. Louis Cardinals and won the World (United States) Series. Whoopee! I wrote. Cheating, I reached the cabin in time to hear the end of the last Series game, crackling with static, on the radio, my secret link to the old ball yard and the world. It was as if I were squeezing the ground wire on our radio fifty years earlier.

To wrap up research about my family, I spent most of January 2005 in Syria. Much of that time I passed with relatives, including first cousins on my mother's side and second cousins in my father's line, in Maarrat Saidnaya. My mother's parents had left a two-year-old daughter, their first-born child, in Syria because the little girl's grandmother wouldn't let her leave. Daughter and parents never saw each other again. The little girl, my aunt, married very young and had several children: hence, my first cousins in Syria. In that small town some twenty-two miles northeast of Damascus, Syria's capital, I peeled away more layers of the past to help understand the extended present.

Throughout October 27, 2004, Day 172 in the cabin, I read my notes about the vicious Algerian civil war in the 1990s. The tangle of killing in Algeria pitted Islamic fundamentalists against the power of the army and the state, although innocents suffered most from the excesses of both sides. In time, place and bloody ground, Algeria occupied my mind, but that conflict was light-years from Lucas Pond.

Those late October days heralded November and winter's arrival well ahead of the calendar's call. In the woods that I knew, cold weather came sooner than the calendar says it should have, but warm weather seldom came earlier than expected. Harbingers of the hard freeze to come, squirrels scurried across the dead leaves collecting nuts and new flooring for their nests. So many squirrels dashed over the land that at times it appeared that the earth itself was moving in small pieces.

Like an army, and perhaps more than most people, I travel on my stomach. Near the end of October, preparing for the sprint to Thanksgiving when I planned to finish my manuscript and kiss the woods goodbye, my horn of plenty overflowed with three loaves of multi-grain bread, six frozen tuna and swordfish steaks, six cans of chicken soup, lettuce, cucumbers and fresh tomatoes, six cans of whole and seasoned tomatoes, balsamic vinaigrette salad dressing, orange juice, powdered milk, croutons, garbanzo beans, four cans of cranberry sauce and a bonus, apple pie. I would survive until the end. Eating well, or at least eating plenty, would carry me to another turkey dinner. With that holiday in New England flowed memories of being in London, England, a decade earlier when Pat and I advised the new owners of the Mayflower Pub in southeast London about the intricacies of preparing pumpkin pie and a full Thanksgiving dinner for visiting Yanks.

After five days in a row when visibility was no higher than the treetops, I felt as if I were trapped back in London in any January but without a playhouse beckoning. Naked branches replaced the leafy trees of summer and the pond's warm-weather visitors had long since departed for their urban cabins. At the same time, my notes about the tribes that ran amok in Algeria came into focus.

When Daylight Savings Time ended on Oct. 31, it meant nothing to me. I had no schedule, no real time piece, no fixed hour to wake, sleep or write. "Today I took a shower and changed clothes. First time in eight days. The world rejoiced," I wrote in my journal on the last day before November. My mind wandered; oh, how much I will miss the cabin, the pond and the woods in winter. Creativity revived, I wrote until midnight about Dick Cheney's Halliburton and other United States oil-related businesses operating beyond the eyes and minds of the American public in the vast and truly isolated Algerian Sahara, hundreds of miles from Algiers on the Mediterranean coast.

My time in the cabin ticked closer to its end as November swept over me and the land. As one regular at Demmons Country Store said, the time between autumn and winter is called November. To me, November, as much a real state of mind as the low cloud cover and spindly trees standing like teepees without the animal hides, is more winter than autumn. Two days before Thanksgiving Day was to mark the end of my cabin life. That's when I planned to close the circle. By then I would have finished a good rough draft of my book. Revisions, vastly different from creating the draft, I could finish at my home in Portsmouth. Before I tackled refinements, I would make that trip to Syria in January to fill the holes in my family's story.

After a lunch of tuna steak, mashed potatoes, corn, peas and carrots, I walked to the end of Lower Deerfield Road and one of my favorite spots, Woodman Marsh. The date was November 5, which marked my sixth full month in the cabin. Wind walked with me, whistling and roaring across the treetops and sounding like a train climbing a long, steep grade or a jet revving on the tarmac. Gray, lifeless-looking trees could no longer hide houses that in summer were shielded by layers of green that filled the woods like spotted sheets of emerald. Waves whipped across Lucas Pond in all directions, sending the trout and bass deeper underground, so to speak. Amid those changes, the ice was only four days away, creeping toward me in small encroaching waves, first in a swamp along Big Buck Road and later along the shore of the pond itself. Fixed and unrelenting, Nature was having its way again, ahead of schedule.

This change in the world around me and in my mood clarified the moment: my time in the cabin was over, my work there finished.

The cabin knew it. I knew it. My ability to benefit from the cabin in a creative way was exhausted. I was merely living in the woods, which wasn't the reason I went there. The cabin, the pond and the woods had become too familiar, not challenging enough, for them to help me. After I finished writing about Algeria's sectarian war, the cabin and I would separate. It was probably no coincidence that my sense of being finished with the cabin and the reality that I was nearly finished with the draft came at the same moment. The cabin had served its purpose, which is all it could do.

My plan was to pack up and leave the cabin on Tuesday, November 23, two days before Thanksgiving. Technology had different plans. At 3 p.m. on Thursday, November 18, my computer, predictably given the season, froze. Day 192 turned out to be my last working day in the cabin, although I returned the following day to remove all traces of my presence there. Pat rushed over from Portsmouth so we could beat the 5 p.m. closing time of a computer store in Dover, about twenty miles from the cabin. We packed my notes and equipment, books and some clothes and sped to Dover. Sorry, pal, a technician said, you need a new logic board and screen. (Nothing logical about that, I thought.) Leave it with us, the technician said. My computer was a bit like the flies in the cabin in winter and spring: it would hibernate for a time, but would return to life.

Pat and I returned to the cabin at one o'clock the next afternoon. We did more than say goodbye. Most of the afternoon passed before I finished hauling all the heavy canned goods, frozen foods, personal and work materials to Pat's hatchback while Pat cleaned the fridge, swept the carpets and mopped the kitchen and bathroom floors. To protect the vacant cabin from winter's harshness, I followed the last page of my draft of Paul Dale's cabin bible: drain and shut down the water system, pour anti-freeze into the toilet, kitchen and bathroom sinks and shower drain. Before Pat took photos of me in front of the cabin and by the shore, I removed several bags of trash so I could dump them in our own trash bins in

Portsmouth. No one living in the woods around Lucas Pond would ever again have to worry about this stranger dumping trash in their personally paid-for dumpsters.

Red Sox won the World Series, first time since 1918. Whoopee! Derek Lowe pitched seven shutout innings. Damon homered in the first inning, and tripled. Nixon had three doubles in a 3-0 victory to sweep the Cards 4-0. Where were The Kid and Jack Sharkey?
—October 27, 2004

Touch 'Em All

A stranger writing alone in the woods, the Great American Pastime and book publishing are peculiar partners, rarely found in the same sentence, let alone the same life. Sprinkle Jerusalem into that mix and the oddity expands like winter's ice on Lucas Pond. Those odd connections are as real a part of my reporting life as bumping into a gadfly from Miami protesting at the gates of Auschwitz, and stumbling upon a bored American diplomat who left his assignment in the testy Middle East for a dreary new outpost in Central Asia.

It wasn't by accident that I stuffed into my shoulder bag The Seventh Edition/Revised, Updated and Expanded of *The Baseball Encyclopedia* when I moved to Jerusalem in 1989. Time in Jerusalem is seven hours ahead of American time, the East Coast version. That meant I would often work sixteen-hour days, eight during the workday in Jerusalem and eight more during the workday of the Cox Bureau in Washington. Late at night, I figured, *The Baseball Encyclopedia* would be a simple diversion if I were troubled by a story. Flip the pages and I could learn just how good Stuffy McInnis really was, or about Snuffy Stirnweiss, Warren Spahn, Van Lingle Mungo, and Pumpsie Green. The hefty baseball book would be my security blanket.

Moving ahead fifteen years—as Lucas Pond's ice blanket became liquid again —the green leaves and the Boys of Summer began sprouting in tandem. The sound of a wood bat whacking cowhide over stone walls and into sodden fields rang loudly in my imagination. Whether I saw it or not, baseball was spiking in New England, which was natural because that's what happens when melted snow leaves lawns and meadows bare enough for kids to play ball. The New England spring also brought flashbacks to Jerusalem, baseball in Jerusalem, no less. My dreams also created visions of Ted Williams, the Splendid Splinter of the diamond, casting, in legendary myth if not reality, for trout from the lip of Lucas Pond right outside my front door. In a weird but real way, baseball was a serendipitous ally during my writing life at Lucas Pond and for years after, until my book was published.

An early inning of this odd ball game occurred in Jerusalem back in 1991. Three baseball bats, two gloves and several unstained Major League baseballs from the mid-1950s were the tools I brought to the rocky patch at the front yard of a desert. A Palestinian family I met in Jerusalem was the training squad. My aim was to toss the parents and their children a bit of Americana, show them indirectly that America wasn't only about the CIA and military aid for Israel. Whether the family caught on to the game or my message was another matter.

After I explained the critical points—throw, hit, run, catch—the game didn't go well. Things could not have gone worse, and I should have been forced to shout, "Can't anybody here play this game?" as some wit—either Casey Stengel or Jimmy Breslin, or both—said of the stumbling New York Mets in their founding ineptitude. On a beautiful day in Jerusalem, well before the seventh inning stretch, it was I who didn't play the game so well.

This is how you play baseball, I proclaimed to the four children and two adults, each equally puzzled by my antics, in the gravelly front yard of the family's comfortable stone house. A moment later, while demonstrating the rudiments, I slapped a ball through the kitchen window, which wasn't open at the time. Disaster—1. Visiting coach—ZERO. "No, no, sorry, sorry," I explained, that's not part of the game. I could read the faces and minds of the kids who wondered about this absurd exercise and the man who was teaching it: "Who brought this man here to break our windows? We don't need a stranger, an American, to do that. The Israelis will do it." The instructional league had barely started when the game was over, called because of stupidity. If I was sure of anything in the Middle East, it was this: no one in that Palestinian family played baseball again. No one asked me about the game either. But I hung in there.

Under the driver's seat of my car, I stashed a baseball glove that I kept handy after the big game that went badly. My silly idea was to catch rocks thrown by Palestinians when I drove through the Palestinian West Bank sporting yellow Israeli license plates on my rental car. That plan didn't go so well either. Erring, I caught no rocks and missed the big one, a chunk of concrete thrown at me as I drove from Jerusalem toward Nablus and some four millennia into the past to attend a Passover Seder of the ancient Samaritan sect. Lucky for me, the block of concrete bounced off my windshield and spun off into foul territory. That was, I decided, truly a foul rock.

* * *

Baseball was out of play for more than a decade. My best sport was dashing to real and faux peace conferences in Belfast and Madrid, to battlefronts in Lebanon, and Iraq, and to caves carved in the mud in northern Azerbaijan, where old women lay dying in alien territory and pining for burial in their own land. But like a good pal you meet over and over in the strangest places, or like a worn Luke Appling glove (Go ahead, ask: Luke Appling, a shortstop, is in the Baseball Hall of Fame, and his model was my first glove.), baseball was back in play when I moved to the woods years later and more than a few country miles from Jerusalem. There, at Lucas Pond, I ran into Ted Williams, figuratively, of course. Even the thought of catching a whiff of Williams in the woods seemed as remote a notion as running, which I did in the mid-1990s in London, into basketball giants Jo Jo White, who died in January 2018, and the legendary

Kareem Abdul-Jabbar. Williams, I was told, may have fished at the pond in the early 1950s, during the off-seasons of his heyday with the Boston Red Sox. But even the person who heard this story in the late fifties admitted that he never saw The Kid actually fling a line into Lucas Pond. This may be a fish story, lying somewhere between legend and myth, leaning heavily toward myth. Yet it's dramatic enough to become a very tall tale around Lucas Pond.

By the early summer of 2002, Williams had died, but remained very much alive in memory and baseball statistics. What did his Red Sox do? They rose from the baseball cemetery to claim another championship in 2004. An event worthy of centennial status, that championship season bears repeating because it was Boston's first in eighty-six years, and my writing year in the woods. These are facts, not myths, factoids or alternative facts. Boston's long-awaited triumph was real; I heard it, and saw a little of it in my own way on a radio in my cabin on Big Buck Road. Was anyone in Jerusalem listening? I wondered. When I was trying to find a publisher for the book I wrote while alone at Lucas Pond, fate introduced me to another stranger, the wife of a former major leaguer who told me the name of the publisher of her baseball book. Kismet, tied to persistence and shoe leather, worked again for me; the woman's publisher ended up publishing my book. My entire book-writing exercise even brought me to the Red Sox Fantasy Camp in Florida, and later to play ball at Fenway Park for an entire day. So, you see, the ties between baseball, Jerusalem, Lucas Pond, writing and book publishing may not be as tight as the stitches on a baseball, but they are real. In baseball lingo, I hit a grand slam home run, and touched 'em all as I circled the bases of life. In strange ways, baseball has been very good to me.

* * *

In literature and other corners of American life, baseball is more than a game played on a field of green in, usually, weather warm and sunny. As a metaphor for more heraldic aspects of Americana, baseball has earned a metaphysical or mystical gloss. Like the founding fathers bathed in wisdom and glowing in the early days of their dreams to beat the imperial odds and drive the king's minions back across the big pond. Or like a national hero swatting a ball a country mile to win a game in the last of the ninth inning and giving new meaning to the national purpose, whether to kill or imprison people across a continent, defeat the Nazis, terrorists or opioids.

The mid-twentieth century was the perfect moment to be a kid loving baseball. We could look back fifty years or so and see the beginning of baseball time. Go forward another fifty years and a century of ball looked us square in the face. That's a lot of baseball, a lot of players. Baseball for me was the history of the game and the players who graced the diamond. Their statistics made the game intelligible. Baseball was also fun. It's all physical and mental, maybe even fantastic, but never metaphysical, except to dreamers in the outfield who pick their noses waiting for the next pitch. The field is an open space where individuals can thrive. Baseball is a team sport, where one team wins and another loses. At the same time, an individual is declared the winning pitcher, and another individual is tagged with the label of loser. Individual players win and lose all the time. They strike out or get a hit, maybe even clout a ball into a river or a bay, if not into a cornfield, and often commit errors. Sometimes batters take a walk, a deficiency for pitchers but as good as a hit for hitters.

Periodic bursts of speed and power interrupt dull moments of sublime quiet and calm on the diamond. That's part of baseball, sort of like the sex act following mental foreplay. The lulls in baseball are as much a part of the game as the excitement, moments when fans chat about what just happened, what might happen soon, and what happened long ago when they were young and better than anyone around. Television, which thrives on constant frenzy, in between commercials, is no friend of baseball. But the prying eye of the television camera makes outfielders think three times before poking at their crotches. The ballpark itself is and always will be baseball's biggest fan.

Playing ball is enabling, freeing, even when nothing seems to be happening. An outfielder waiting under a high sky for a pitcher to deliver may enter a day-dreaming zone, pluck a blade of grass next to his right cleat, if he's right-handed, think of the girl he never spoke to or his new squeeze in the next town on the schedule. Maybe he's even thinking, as he should be, of where he's going to throw the ball if it's hit his way. Smarter fielders may think about the hitter's tendencies or what pitches his own pitcher likes to throw in different situations.

Tension builds each time a pitcher toes the rubber and a batter digs in and flicks his bat like a hummingbird in heat. This duel concentrates the mind as the pitcher tries to outfox the batter and the batter tries to guess which pitch is coming his way. When a runner hunches at third, poised to steal home plate, that's the greatest tension of all, as all eyes focus on a small space—on the runner who may take the initiative, the catcher who sees the play developing in front of him and is ready for Armageddon, and lastly the pitcher who, if he's paying attention at all, must hurry and throw the ball to the catcher to complete the play. Then it's the umpire's turn. Safe or out? That's when Jackie Robinson dashes toward home. Whitey Ford throws a strike to Yogi Berra. And then it's the umpire's turn to shine; enter Bill Summers, the final arbiter, who calls Robinson safe. Yogi leaps and screams in anger and derision. But Summers was right; Robinson was safe then, and he still is. More about Bill Summers later.

Those baseball connections were always with me at Lucas Pond. They were as much present as they were past, and they stretched in the long line that led to the publication of my first book. Holing up and writing in the woods, I wouldn't know the rest of the story for more than five years. Yet baseball was as much a part of my life growing up in mid-twentieth century America as was hanging out at Ryan's Spa and Big Louie's pool room, and learning about Edmund Hillary and Tenzing Norgay's conquest of Mount Everest in Miss Harrington's seventh-grade class at Longfellow Elementary School in small-town Millville, little more than a hundred miles south of Lucas Pond.

The not-so-mighty Blackstone River, the American Industrial Revolution and big-time baseball played on small but brilliant stages and all flowed through southeastern Massachusetts and Little Rhody. The river valley—with its small towns and cities, canal and locks, farms and historic mills—is actually a national park. Tucked as it is into the Blackstone River Valley National Heritage Corridor, the park is a memorial to American mills and factory workers. Less than fifty miles long, the Blackstone River drained the region from the hills in Worcester, Massachusetts, to the Rhode Island coast. The river flows through two-dozen small cities and smaller towns, including Woonsocket, Rhode Island, and Millville, Blackstone and Uxbridge, Massachusetts.

A mother lode of major league baseball talent flowed through that region in the early part of the twentieth century and into the early 1950s. As the Industrial Revolution walked its way up river on the shoulders of workers in the late eighteenth century, throughout the nineteenth and into the twentieth centuries, baseball lately hitched a ride. My guess is that more young men leaped from the mills and town teams of the region to the big leagues than from any other similar area north of the Mason-Dixon Line, certainly more than from any other area that has only six sunny days in July, three in August and two-and-a-half in early September. Those big-league players and big-time umpires were not, as rival bench jockeys might have labeled others, ham-and-eggers.

It can be said, if you take the long view, that Samuel Slater founded the Blackstone Valley League. Born in England, Slater launched the factory system in America. In 1793, in Pawtucket,

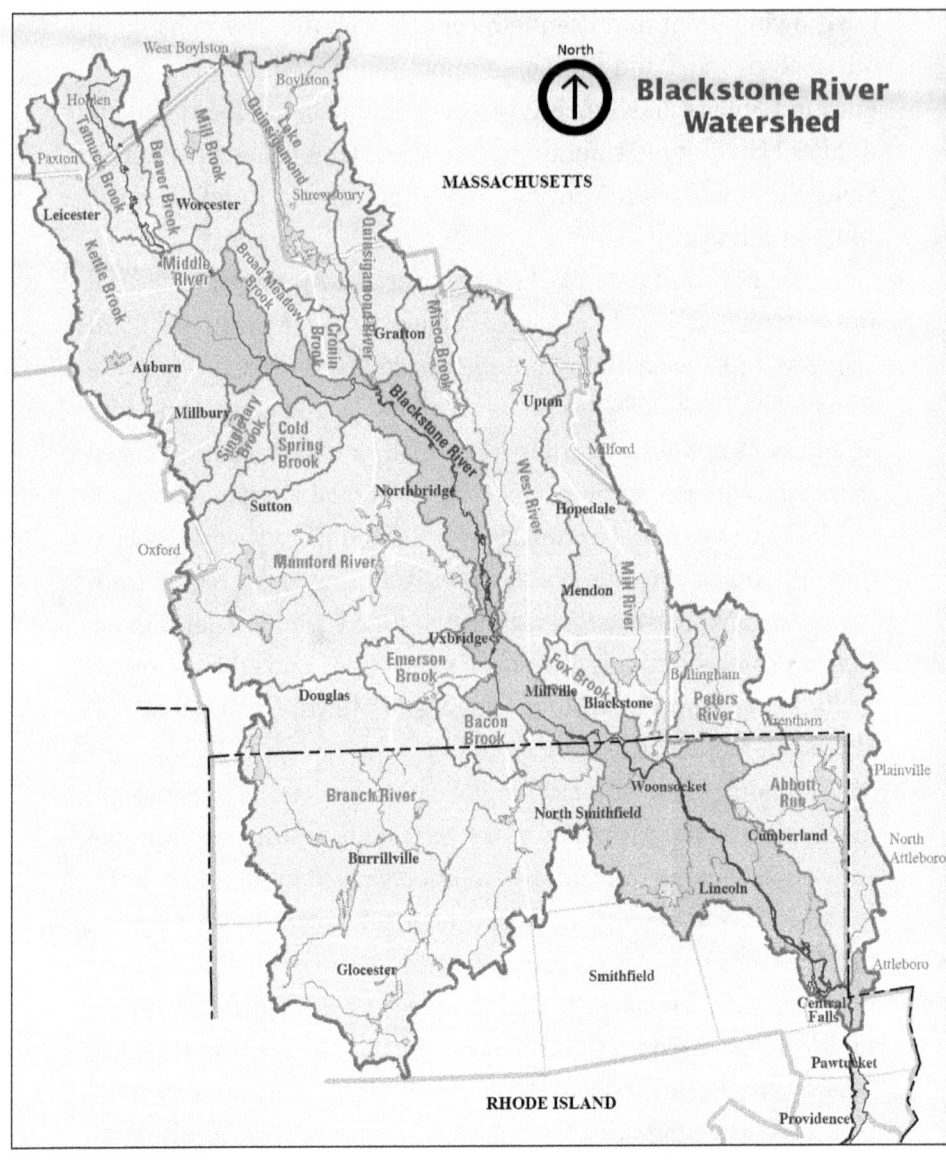

Map of the Blackstone River Watershed. Courtesy of U.S. Geological Survey and the Blackstone Heritage Corridor, Inc.

Rhode Island, Slater built the first successful cotton mill in these hallowed grounds. Mills—Slater's industrial offspring—sprouted in towns throughout the Blackstone River Valley and along smaller rivers in the region. In those mills and towns, a century later, semi-pro baseball eventually took off like a Ted Williams wallop into the right field seats. In the early twentieth century and as late as the early 1950s, the Blackstone Valley League (BVL) flourished. With his brother John, Samuel Slater founded in 1803 what is now the village of Slatersville, Rhode Island. Slatersville is right across the state line from Millville, in Massachusetts, Gabby Hartnett's town.

Baseball was king nationwide in the early twentieth century. It was imperial in the Blackstone Valley. Mills had their own ball clubs, as did many towns, some of which were virtually owned by the mills. The Blackstone Valley League was an incubator of great talent, homegrown and bused in; the magic couldn't have been in the water, which was polluted by the mills on the river's banks. As late as the early 1950s, we in the knothole gang where no fences kept us out knew that Dick Hall, all six-feet, six-inches of him, had leaped from the BVL to the majors where he hurled for nineteen years. Before Dick Hall, truly great players such as Hank Greenberg and Lefty Grove batted or hurled their way briefly through the BVL, to say nothing of their local teammates.

By far the biggest name in Millville was, and probably remains, Charles Leo "Gabby" Hartnett. A townie born in nearby Woonsocket, Hartnett grew up in Millville and will be forever known as Millville's own. A Hall of Fame catcher, Hartnett played all but one of his twenty years with the Chicago Cubs, and managed the Cubs for three of those years. How big is Gabby Hartnett in Millville? The main road through town, all of 1.6 miles long, is the Charles L. "Gabby" Hartnett Memorial Highway. That's not all: Gabby once watched me, his nephew Freddie Hartnett and several other kids play a snappy throw, hit and catch game of pepper in the small park across from Ryan's Spa. Talk about pressure!

Born in Woonsocket, Napoleon (Nap, Larry) Lajoie, was one of the top two or three second basemen ever, anywhere, including the Middle East, Canada and France. A Hall-of-Famer, Lajoie hit .339 lifetime and in 1901, batted a measly .422, the seventh-highest single-season average in the history of the game that Ted Williams didn't invent. Lajoie played for twenty-one years, and for a time before his team became known as the Indians, it was known as the Cleveland Naps.

Clement Walter (Clem) Labine, surely Woonsocket's own, although he was born in neighboring Lincoln, Rhode Island, pitched the second-best World Series game in history, in my opinion, after Don Larsen's perfect game in the 1956 World Series. Labine was a relief pitcher, a sinkerball specialist during his thirteen-year career. When his desperate Brooklyn Dodgers ran thin on starting pitchers in that same 1956 World Series against the mighty New York Yankees, Labine was summoned in a true emergency role, red lights flashing and sirens blowing. All he did was toss a 1-0, ten-inning victory in which the groveling Yanks swatted only seven hits. Labine finished third in the 1951 voting for National League rookie of the year honors, behind the winner, the wondrous Willie Mays, and Chet Nichols, the next man up.

Chester Raymond Nichols, Jr. was born in Providence, but his big-league-pitching father was born in Woonsocket. In his 1951 rookie year with the Boston Braves, the younger Nichols won eleven games and lost eight. He never again matched that, injuries being his nemesis, but he was good enough to last nine years in the majors. The slender southpaw went nine and eight in 1955, although by then the team had fled Boston for Milwaukee. Nichols had the honor of presenting me with the most valuable player award for my Woonsocket Babe Ruth League team in 1955. My pitching line that same year was seven wins and one loss, although Willie Mays played elsewhere.

Millville-born Timothy Aloysius McNamara pitched for five

years in the National League, four of them with the Boston Braves, in the 1920s. When Tim McNamara and Gabby Hartnett rose to the top, Millville had fewer than 1,600 people; many of them played baseball, and all, women and men, honored the game.

Louis Joseph Lucier was born in Northbridge, Massachusetts, adjacent to Uxbridge and a few miles up river from Millville. Lou Lucier hit the bigs just long enough to drink a few cups of coffee or tea with crumpets with the Red Sox and Philadelphia Phillies in the 1940s. But just before he died in October of 2014, Lucier was remembered as the oldest living former Red Sox player.

Few remember Max Surkont, but I do. Born in Central Falls, Rhode Island, Surkont pitched for nine years in the majors, three with the Boston Braves. I was eight years old during Surkont's first year in the majors, which made us contemporaries, of sorts.

Even smaller than Millville is Chepachet, a Rhode Island village that generously might be included in the Blackstone River watershed. Chepachet's own Phillips Steere Paine wasn't a phenom, but Phil pitched for parts of six seasons with three National League clubs during the 1950s. No one from Chepachet ever matched Phil Paine.

Baseball enthusiasts in the Blackstone Valley sixty or so years ago were as familiar with big league umpires as they were with the players. They had to be. Three of the seventeen American League umpires in 1958 lived in the Blackstone River Valley, a short river in a small valley. A remarkable statistic, it's nothing less than official, coming from the Baseball Hall of Fame in Cooperstown, New York.

Hank Soar, a former professional football player before he became an American League umpire, lived down the line in Pawtucket; he was the first-base umpire when Don Larsen threw his perfect game. Not given readily to objections, and with the muscle to back up his attitude, Soar practiced the fine umpiring art from 1950 through 1975, umped five World Series and supervised umpires into the mid-1980s.

Born in New Jersey, raised in Woonsocket and a resident up the line in Upton, Massachusetts when he died, Bill Summers called American League games from 1933 through 1959, umpired in eight World Series and seven All-Star Games. Summers was never better than when Jackie Robinson stole home in Game 1 of the 1955 World Series, a call that sent Yankee catcher Yogi Berra into his famous apoplectic pogo-stick-like rage. Summers made the correct call because Yogi touched Jackie's toe after Jackie's toe had touched home plate.

Bob Stewart was a perfect third leg of the Blackstone Valley umpiring triumvirate. Stewart was born in Blackstone, smack between Millville and Woonsocket, and died in Woonsocket. In 1950, Blackstone had fewer than 5,000 people, but it had a big league ballpark. Stewart was an American League umpire from 1958 through 1970, called two all-star games and three World Series. Roosevelt Park, its emeralds sprinkled on a hundred thousand blades of grass, sprawled behind the Blackstone Town Hall and well within a country mile of the Blackstone River. The diamond was the town's playground and home plate for Bob Stewart. Roosevelt Park had major league caliber lights, actual dugouts, a concession stand, toilets and a water bubbler tucked in the rear of a grand grandstand behind home plate. Playing night baseball at Roosevelt Park in 1955 seemed like playing at Fenway Park.

*　*　*

All of those baseball connections made it seem natural for Ted Williams, also a world-class angler, to show up in the New Hampshire woods. Lucas Pond lore has it that Ted Williams, the forever maestro of clocking a baseball and a concert-master of fly-casting, and Jack Sharkey, a heavyweight boxing champ in the 1930s, together tried to force Lucas Pond to cry lunker. Fishing as he did throughout the woods around his home in Epping, New Hampshire, Sharkey surely cast many a line into Lucas Pond, a most deserving target for any angler. Despite the rumors and my sleuthing into the deep and disappearing past, I never found evidence that The Kid and Sharkey lurked together at Lucas Pond. Neither the public library nor the historical society in Northwood turned up any information about a Williams-Sharkey fishing expedition at Lucas Pond. Neither did the public library nor the historical society in the nearby town of Epping, where Sharkey lived for decades after his retirement and was well known.

Sharkey's life is well documented in a muscular file at The Epping Historical Society. Most of the stories and photos concern his boxing exploits, with not a word about any fishing adventures at Lucas Pond with Williams or anyone else. My search for evidence that Williams and Sharkey actually fished together at Lucas Pond was like my search for deer in the woods. Nada. Nothing. In the case of Williams and Sharkey, not even the detritus of their presence at Lucas Pond caught my eye. The story seems mostly myth, part legend and entirely good drama. Personally, the story is just another weird way in which baseball seeped into my writing year in the woods, and beyond. Whatever it is, the "it" deserves scrutiny because Williams and Sharkey were crusty characters, alike in ways shared and strong enough to bring them together outside their official professions.

This much I learned from personal interviews and published accounts. Williams and Sharkey did lock casts in exhibitions during the 1950s, mostly in Boston, Williams's dugout and Sharkey's boxing corner. Sharkey, according to news reports of that time, was an excellent fly-caster. Williams was better, maybe as good a fly fisherman as he was a hitter. Statistics—records to be broken—fill the time lines that stock and shape the histories of both big-time fishing and big-league baseball. Test lines, the various species of fish, even the waters where big fish are caught, offer almost endless grist for the numbers game of serious anglers worldwide. When it comes to the diamond, statistics are the gems and arteries of the game.

Hunting and fishing excited Sharkey after the mighty Joe Louis knocked him into retirement in 1936. Who could blame Sharkey for shifting from the sweet science to more harmless vocations? Sharkey's adopted town of Epping is about twelve miles south and slightly east of Northwood and Lucas Pond. There is little doubt that Sharkey flung many a line into Lucas Pond, even in his day a magnet for fisher folk in the region. "It would surprise me if Jack and Ted didn't fish at Lucas Pond," said Bruce Dix, who said he knew both men. "I can tell you they fished throughout the area, and that they knew every pond and lake and river from here to Canada. But I don't know for sure that they fished at Lucas Pond."

One long-time resident of Epping recalled that Sharkey, his wife and Williams occasionally attended church on Sundays before the two men fled to fish. As much as that sounds like another fish story, Williams being more an earthy lover than a heavenly worshipper, men sometimes do strange things in search of absolution to cover obsessive behavior that reflects their true character.

Williams was a diamond god in New England where baseball was, and to many still is, a religion second only to Puritanical reserve, and where Boston's Fenway Park is the faithful's temple. He was also noted for hunting salmon in New Brunswick, tarpon and bonefish off the Florida Keys and other large game fish just about everywhere within the confines of Planet Earth. Although Nimrod-like in his younger days, Williams was more of a singles hitter as a hunter compared to his Homeric skill and zeal in the fishing game. The same driven personality that made him a fantastic hitter also made The Kid seem like a conductor, sort of Arthur Fiedler with a fly rod.

Williams and Sharkey shared a social and territorial bond that went beyond fishing. Sharkey moved to Boston as a young man, while Boston was Williams's baseball haven for his entire nineteen-year major league career that touched four decades. A native of San Diego, Williams broke into the major leagues in

1939, and retired after the 1960 season. Sixteen years older than Williams, Sharkey wasn't a Sharkey at all. Nearly every reference I've read says that Sharkey was born Joseph Paul Zukauskas in Binghamton, New York, a son of Lithuanian-born parents. In one newspaper story, however, Sharkey said his real surname was Cukoshay. Either way, it wasn't Sharkey. To crack the fight game in Boston, he took his Irish name from the first name of heavyweight champ Jack Dempsey, who ruled boxing's heavyweight division for years, and the last name of a local fighter named Tom Sharkey. The name Jack Sharkey sparkled in Boston's neon. Joseph Paul Zukauskas/Cukoshay never would have. A sailor before he became a professional fighter, the son of Binghamton climbed through the ropes as a Boston Gob.

Known also to sportswriters and Red Sox fans as Teddy Ball Game, the Splendid Splinter and the Thumper, The Kid didn't feel the need to alter his name, Williams being sufficiently American for the Great American Pastime. But The Kid's mother was of Mexican ancestry, a reality he did his best to conceal, figuring that Babe Ruth's America wasn't ready for a star whose parents were not all American. For him to be at the front and center of baseball lore, Williams needs no joke or trivia. He remains the last player to hit .400 or more in a season, batting .406 in 1941; his .344 lifetime batting average is sixth all-time, and his .634 career slugging average is second in big league history. The Kid's family background gives him a poetic niche in baseball trivia: who is the only player of Mexican ancestry in baseball's hall of fame? Ted Williams, of course.

A brawler who died at age ninety-one in 1994, Sharkey made a name for himself because of his failures as well as his successes. In that sense, he was no Ted Williams. But Sharkey was the heavyweight champion for one year and eight days in the 1930s. Even Sharkey's failures are tinged with distinction: he's best known in the history of the fight game for being the only boxer to have fought, and been knocked silly by, both Jack Dempsey and Joe

Louis, although Dempsey sucker-punched him while Sharkey was complaining to the referee of being hit below the belt. With his thirty-eight wins, fourteen losses and three draws, Sharkey resides in the International Boxing Hall of Fame. The Baseball Hall of Fame, Cooperstown, rocks for Williams. The Kid is also a member of the International Game Fish Association's Hall of Fame and the National Fresh Water Fishing Hall of Fame, making him one of only a handful of people to be inducted into the hall of fame of more than one sport.

The two men shared similar temperaments as well as fame, magnets strong enough to attract them. One New Hampshire outdoors writer told me he was never able to get within a home run or a cast of Williams and Sharkey on the hunt or anywhere else. "They were the two most miserable guys you'd ever be around," the writer said, although he was seldom allowed close enough to hear their cussing or feel their dragon-like breath.

Williams had a certain affinity for toughness, which might have attracted him to Sharkey in the first place. But The Kid would never allow anyone to share a gold medal podium with him. If he were involved, Teddy Ballgame ran the show—telling others to sit, watch and listen while he explained the rules and necessary skills—and won the top prize. A perfectionist who never tired of learning and practicing the art and science of hitting a baseball, Williams made himself into a great hitter. Intense in his pursuit of perfection, Williams had the superior vision and the other physical tools necessary to make him the hitter he became. But he wasn't the greatest all-around athlete; his fielding, throwing and base running were adequate, but in that regard he was no Willie Mays.

Sharkey, by comparison, seems to have made the most of what talent he had. Not the best of his era, he still won his fair share against good foes because he was tough, unafraid and determined to reach the top, a feat he accomplished for a short time. Williams would have admired Sharkey's work ethic as well as his success.

Before he aged, Sharkey was widely regarded locally for his hunting and fishing skills, a reputation he enhanced by claiming to know every tree and pond in a twenty-square-mile radius of Epping, his home. "I taught him (Williams) to fish, you know," Sharkey said in the June 18, 1972 edition of the *Boston Sunday Herald Traveler Magazine*. I would like to have seen Williams's face and heard his cussing and howls when he read Sharkey's words. However doubtful his claim, Sharkey didn't stop there. "I knew Ted better than anyone right from the time he first came to Boston and hired a house out on Beacon Street.... I used to take him out on Lake Waban. That's the place where the Wellesley girls go canoeing. Pretty soon someone would find out that Ted Williams was there and we'd see people on the shore and people coming out in boats and then Williams would start to swear." Maybe Sharkey and Williams fished at Lake Waban, but Sharkey said nothing about fishing with The Kid at Lucas Pond.

Sharkey had been a sailor well before Williams flew Marine fighters during World War II and again in the Korean conflict. But Williams was well known for having a sailor's talent for cussing that few gobs, or anyone else, could match. Of Williams's penchant for swearing, Sharkey said in that same article about hanging out at Lake Waban, "It was embarrassing. You can hear voices better across water, you know. Williams would start to swear and cuss and I'd say, 'For crissake, Ted, shut up, will you?' But he wouldn't."

If Jack Sharkey taught Ted Williams how to fish, then I taught Williams how to hit.

As for whether the sweet swinger and the old brawler actually fished at Lucas Pond, this is how I imagine the local trout population would have recalled such a competition.

Williams snapped off a cast that reached halfway across the pond, much too long for a fly cast, of course, but this is a trout's memory at work. No fish took Williams's bait. Counterpunching, Sharkey flung his line high and far, yet not close to where Williams's bait hit the moisture. But Sharkey hooked a rainbow trout so large that denizens of the nearby cabins rushed to watch the old fighter outfight the leaping fish as Williams swore at Sharkey and the rainbow. Then it was Williams's turn again because he just had to catch a fish, a big one, even if it took until spring training. After many more casts and one long fight, Williams brought in a huge brown trout. Large it was, but not nearly as big as Sharkey's trophy. Angry, hissing and swearing at the prospect of finishing second, Williams cast into the vanishing daylight as Sharkey laughed and mocked his friend, calling him a second-placer. Just before darkness would end their fishing day, Williams hooked the largest fish, a largemouth bass, that any trout or human in the neighborhood had ever seen rise from Lucas Pond. The Kid was in second place no longer, although Sharkey chided his mate for changing species. Sharkey would say they both won. But Williams would never say that; he would never surrender the blue ribbon.

Jack Sharkey is buried in the earth in Epping, New Hampshire, his home for decades. Separated after his death in 2002, Ted Williams's head and torso lie frozen in separate containers in Arizona, awaiting some sort of physical, if not spiritual, rebirth. The two men will not participate in fly-casting exhibitions again. Nor will they ever fish together at Lucas Pond, which they probably never did when each was in one piece.

With the passing of time and people, the legendary myth of Williams and Sharkey competing reel to reel at Lucas Pond is fading from the local woods. But the mere possibility that it happened makes the vision almost as real as certified reality and will not easily fade from my mind. What is real and not at all imagined is the sorcery between baseball and me. Baseball took many mighty swings during my writing time in the woods and beyond. Like Louis Armstrong's nighttime dance that scored his *Someday (You'll Be Sorry)* tune, baseball kept hittin' on me after I pulled out of the cabin.

* * *

On and off for several years after I left the cabin, I searched for evidence of a Williams-Sharkey fishing expedition at Lucas Pond. No luck. In 2004, near the end of my writing year, the Red Sox checked in with a secular miracle, their first world championship since, it seemed, Paul Revere rallied the farmers. As interesting and intrusive as those developments were during and after my writing year in the woods, they remained coolly distant. Baseball had not yet become personal again, remaining instead a country mile away from the publication of my book.

A little more than a year after I left the woods, but still four years before publication, baseball and the publication of my book inched ever closer. That's when I put on a uniform at a Red Sox Fantasy Camp for never-weres. Seven months after that week of fun, I slugged balls over the wall in Fenway Park for the first time in what was then my sixty-five years. Then came a game-winner. By chance I met other helpful strangers—a woman, her baseball book and her publisher who was to publish my book. Serendipity never hurled a more perfect game.

Those moments would not have occurred if I hadn't hauled a raft of my Reporter's Notebooks to meet fascinating strangers in Jerusalem and other zones of conflict and inspiration. My solitary life at Lucas Pond writing about those experiences added a domestic layer to my meetings with strangers in strange places. Serendipity's mystique walked with me along roads less traveled. In the end, it was baseball's magic that pushed me to touch 'em all. Although most familiar to me, baseball became just like any other stranger who helped me when I least expected it. Baseball behaved like the stranger who, against army orders, led me through the warrens of Algiers, and the woman in Hungary who guided me to the abandoned military base where American troops would be billeted on the way to keep a shaky peace in Bosnia.

After nine months of revising my manuscript at home in Portsmouth during 2005, I grew more confident as the end drew near. Rewriting, after all, is as different from a first draft as crafting fine furniture is from rough carpentry. When I find a publisher, I told Pat that autumn, I will sign up for the Red Sox Fantasy Camp. Pat didn't wait for a publisher. She booked me to play at the camp for dreamers in Fort Myers, Florida, from January 29 through February 4, 2006. Some surprises are better than can be imagined; this one almost equaled being rescued from Iraq by Turks riding a raft.

Playing Fantasy Ball for manager Ralph Treuel's Trolls was more fun than simply feeling the soft turf beneath my spikes and the warm Florida sun on my bare arms in mid-winter. Treuel was the Red Sox bullpen coach during the 2006 season and later the team's minor league pitching coordinator. He had the right touch for directing a collection of wished-they-weres who took the field for serious play but didn't want to die there. Ralph realized that this Fantasy Camp was our show, not his. Win or lose, he managed us so we all could play when we wanted to and in the positions of our choice. Our coaches, former centerfielder Amos Otis and former pitcher Dave Tomlin, caught the same spirit.

Fantasy Camp baseball was fantastic because it was both real and make believe. I ended up having two uniforms and two numbers; first Number 9, the retired number of The Kid, the Splendid Splinter. The Thumper, and Teddy Ballgame (all the same person, remember), and then Number 12, the one I requested because it was worn by Elijah Jerry (Pumpsie) Green when the Sox brought him up in 1959, my eighteenth year.

By giving me The Kid's Number 9, camp organizers may have thought they would silence my silent tribute to Pumpsie Green and my small statement against old time racism in baseball and in Red Sox history. But that gambit didn't work. Pumpsie Green was the first African-American to play for Boston, and the Red Sox were the last Major League team to field a black ballplayer, twelve years after Jackie Robinson and the Brooklyn Dodgers shattered and buried the color barrier. I wanted every player on the Fantasy Field to recall

Pumpsie and the history of the old Sox. After I complained loudly about being given Number 9 and insisted on wearing Number 12, I received a second jersey, this one with Number 12 on its back. With great pride, I wore Number 12 for an entire week and later for a day at Fenway. Threads reminiscent of both The Kid and Pumpsie still hang in my closet, two jerseys from a fantasy camp, if not from real spring training.

For me, wearing Number 12 sent two messages. First, it was Pumpsie's number, and I wanted to salute him and his role in Red Sox history. Second, twelve was the number of years it took for the Red Sox to put a black man on the field after Jackie Robinson set the new standard. Wearing the Number 12 at Fantasy Camp was a critical comment. When Green chose that number, he was making a very powerful statement. How Green came to wear Number 12 remains a mystery to me. Did Pumpsie choose that number? Did a clubhouse manager choose it? However it happened, the choice was brilliant: Twelve long years after Robinson crossed the line, the first black man to play on the last Major League team to sign a black player wore Number 12. The symbolism was more than symbolic; the connection was literal.

Owner Tom Yawkey's Sox had a chance to sign Robinson, but Yawkey and his team, like so many others at the time, were too white and too bigoted to make that leap. A few years later, the Sox had a shot at Willie Mays; the Boston team whiffed on the great Say Hey Kid, too, which is another pitiful chapter in the same old story. Pumpsie Green was not a great player, but the number on his uniform radiated brilliance. Green and his Number 12 say more about the old Red Sox than those Red Sox ever intended.

Delicious irony was woven into the baseball lives of Ted Williams and Pumpsie Green, although no one at the Fantasy Camp seemed aware of the connections and the contradictions. It wasn't until after we pitched camp that I realized how fully The Kid and Pumpsie were separated and linked.

Williams loved playing for Tom Yawkey, the longtime Red Sox owner who waived on Robinson and Mays. Yawkey paid Williams what then was a king's ransom during The Kid's entire career. When Williams was inducted into the Baseball Hall of Fame in 1966, he called Yawkey "the greatest owner in baseball." In that same speech, Williams, no barrier-busting liberal but fair-minded when it came to recognizing wrongs and rewarding talent, shook the staid baseball world by calling for the inclusion into Cooperstown of ballplayers from the old Negro Leagues. "I hope that some day," Williams said, "the names of Satchel Paige and Josh Gibson in some way could be added as a symbol to the great Negro players that are not here because they were not given a chance." Williams's Mexican ancestry was unknown to the public at that time. But he knew it, and he knew that his own struggles would have been enormously greater if baseball knew that part of him had originated in Mexico. Williams could conceal his Mexican ancestry, but Satchel Paige, Josh Gibson and countless other great but largely obscure black ballplayers couldn't hide the color of their skin.

Satchel Paige was inducted into the Baseball Hall of Fame in 1971. Josh Gibson and many others from the Negro Leagues followed. Eventually, the old ballplayers from the Negro Leagues who made it to Cooperstown entered as full-fledged hall-of-famers and not, as first proposed, as members admitted only to a special wing; they were not given seats at the back of the bus. Baseball, and American life, can thank the hard-assed Kid for that.

* * *

Ralph Trueul's fantasy camp Trolls had a so-so win and loss record, but we had our triumphs. In the Trolls 7-6 win over former big leaguer George Thomas's Tomahawks, the camp newsletter reported: "Trolls Jeff Crampton went a sparkling 3 for 3 with 3 singles. Sweet Lou Salome hit a rope to left field and later scored. He wound up with 2 hits, one of which was a double. Scott Young, Tom Urbanski

Jr. and Lou Salome combined at the mound for the victory." Only two lines were devoted to the sad losers. What story would you expect me to save, the one about our shut out loss when I whiffed three times?

Despite our mediocre record, the Trolls weren't a so-so team. All thirteen teammates were eager and talented to varying degrees and committed to having great fun together. Each of us bought into the spirit of being boys again, while trying hard to be as good, or even better, as some of us thought we once were. A mixed group of ballplayers who probably wouldn't have played together when young, we were exceptionally cohesive when the games didn't matter, although, of course, they did. Our lineup included two lawyers, two cops, a dentist, a naval lieutenant commander in the submarine service, a devoted Sox fan from Hawaii and another from Kansas, a financial consultant, an airline pilot, an about-to-be groom, and a serious event planner. Not one whiner among them.

Except for a father and son, who were Fantasy Camp regulars, we were all strangers to one another, which meant that we liked each other instantly. Maybe that's because we didn't know one another well enough to behave otherwise. This has been my experience all over the world, whether riding with five smugglers on a train from Bulgaria to Serbia, bunking with a host of aid workers in the bush country of Somalia or staying the night in a safe house with disparate travelers in northern Afghanistan. Strangers become like old friends in an instant when they share a common condition, feel free to talk openly and don't expect to see each other again.

As much fun as the Fantasy Camp was, the bonus was better. On August 22, 2006, along with all but one of my teammates on the Trolls, I played ball for seven full hours at Boston's Fenway Park, the oldest ballpark in the major leagues and home of the Red Sox since 1912. For a moment, it appeared that the Sox brass might back away from that Fantasy promise of a day on Fenway's hallowed turf, but they yielded after one of our clubhouse lawyers, a real lawyer, swung into action.

The Sox were playing away from home on August 22, so we fantasy-campers pinch hit. At nine that morning, Pat and I hurried, but not fast enough to be missed by fans willing to be deceived, from our hotel just across the city line in Brookline to Fenway. We arrived a half-hour later. Like a teenager heading to a big-league tryout, I wore my Sox uniform through the streets, with the name Salome, and Pumpsie Green's Number 12, radiating neon-like on the back of my uniform. Like a real ballplayer, I slung real spikes over my right shoulder, careful not to cover the name on my shirt. My day on the sparkling diamond ended at 4:30, when I walked from the sun back into the shadows, but still in uniform.

We used Fenway's locker rooms and dugouts. For a moment, the crowded field itself reminded me of the massive cricket pitch in the heart of Karachi where at least a dozen matches went on simultaneously and overlapped without damage to the shoeless players or concern about the outcomes. To warm up between the fantasy games at Fenway, I hit balls over the lofty left field wall from second base, warmed up in the bullpen, slid gingerly into third, fielded caroms off the wall, played pepper—that snappy game of throw, hit and catch—touched every part of the field and did everything I thought a player might do during a season at Fenway. To my great regret, however, I didn't topple over the low wall in right field and into the bullpen snagging a fly ball off The Kid's bat. Neither did I get yanked during hours of warm-ups, but that would come later when it counted, sort of.

Fenway was filled on that historic day. Standing room only—along the railings. Roughly sixty-five fans jammed into the old ball yard; a few were my family and friends who milled around the dugout where Treuel's Trolls limbered. During the Trolls's hour-long game at Fenway, I hit two singles and scored a run, had two assists playing a flawless second base, and made a putout at first base in our 5-2 victory over long-forgotten losers from the Fantasy Camp. Those statistics aren't in the *Baseball Encyclopedia*, but they are stone cold true and accurate. And I have plenty of witnesses, all unimpeachable, although they might not recall the details as I do. I also pitched, but was yanked (a word one utters softly in any context at Fenway) after two batters because of control problems. After toeing the rubber gracefully and shaking off the catcher twice without embarrassing him, I twisted a little like Luis Tiant before I uncorked a wicked curve. That's when I could hear the crowd moan and begin to question Manager Treuel's decision to let me make my pitching debut at Fenway in such an important game. My curve didn't curve and my fastball wavered with all the zip of a dying swallow. I was high and wide, slow and ugly with everything. Sadly, I never had a chance to settle down before Ralph took the ball from me, patted me on the shoulder and sent me back to play second base, my other natural position. Luis Tiant, my locker mate at the Fantasy Camp, I was not.

The day before we played our real game in the same park where The Kid slammed balls into the right field grandstand from 1939 through 1960, with five years off to fight in two wars from the skies, Treuel's Trolls made history the first time. About a hundred of us vintage ballplayers, strangers and even better friends than we were at the Fantasy Camp, were introduced on the field a half-hour before a regular Red Sox game. Thousands of fans—mostly strangers among themselves and to us—ignored us. But I treated them as hero-worshippers. Deliberately bringing up the rear of the Trolls as we strolled onto the field from beneath the stands in the right field corner, I spun like an awkward dancer along the cinder track at the outfield's outer edge. First, I faced the bullpens and the centerfield bleachers, then the Celtic-green grass and the winter-brown base paths. Turning again, I saluted the Great Wall of Fenway, the Green Monster, before twisting back toward the pitcher's mound and home plate. Finally, I swiveled from the grandstands along the left field line to those along the far-off right field line, waving my cap to the fans who looked like splashy rainbow figures in baseball's version of Van Gogh's *Arena*, painted long ago in Arles, France.

Striding and turning, I waved my cap to the fans as if I knew each of them and they knew me. Or, what are strangers for? This was strange territory indeed, far different from knocking a baseball through a kitchen window in Jerusalem. My intent was to play a showy game in slow motion, to absorb each second and each minute, to capture for a lifetime in my mind's eye each faux Red Sox jersey rising in the stands and each blade of freshly mown grass bending slightly in the breeze. To be honest, my gestures were designed more to honor Treuel's Trolls than to praise the faceless and nameless fans. This was my way of keeping the occasion alive. And so it remains.

During those hours at Fenway, I thought of Michael, a Millville Little League teammate in the early fifties, more than fifty years earlier. At a weekday afternoon game in 1953, when the crowds were so sparse we Little Leaguers were allowed everywhere except in a dugout or on the field itself, Red Sox outfielder Tommy Umphlett cracked his bat while trying to go deep. A broken bat was much more rare in those days than today. Michael and I were leaning on the railing to the right of the Sox dugout when Umphlett strode back from the first-base line to pick up fresh lumber. "Hey, Tommy," Michael shouted, "How about the bat?" Silently, Umphlett walked to the railing and handed Michael his wounded weapon. What a prize! I was stunned. Bold and fearless, Michael probably expected nothing less. Within a few hours, after we taped small nails called brads in and around the wound and used black tape to wrap the handle tighter than the stitches on a baseball, the bat was better than new; it was ours. If we had only thought to sing about our beat-up gloves, taped-up bat, and brand new pair shoes, we would have beaten John Fogerty by more than three decades. Umphlett, who became our unforgettable hero, played a little centerfield during his brief career with the Sox.

Except for its provenance, which was no minor matter, wielding Umphlett's bat didn't make us feel as if we were swinging a golden rod in a field of dreams. But that notion wasn't far from our hands or our minds. Back then, some sixty-seven years ago, we played with wood bats; none of those ding-dong metal bats for us. True, a big-league bat was heavier than we were used to. That forced us to choke up higher on the handle than we otherwise did. We nailed and taped broken bats routinely, and we even wrapped old baseballs in black tape after we had literally knocked the covers off them. Taped, those baseballs and bats were no strangers to us.

Playing, even standing, on Fenway's green in 2006 was retribution of a sort. In 1951, when I was ten years old and playing for the Knights of Columbus team in Woonsocket, Rhode Island, the Boston Braves, Boston's National League team, allowed Little Leaguers to walk on Braves Field and watch their big leaguers demonstrate how to play the game. The best we ever got from the Red Sox then was to sit in the stands behind home plate and listen to manager Steve O'Neill mumble.

Unlike Ted Williams, who fished in ponds, rivers, lakes and oceans, if not at Lucas Pond with Jack Sharkey, and played a few years of decent ball at Fenway Park, I lived on the shores of Lucas Pond for months but never dropped in a line. But I did run around Fenway Park for seven hours during one day in a career that was cut brutally short by age. I was sixty-five years and five months old at the time of my debut in Fenway, the oldest park in the major leagues. From the vantage point of age, Fenway and I belonged together.

* * *

Converting worldwide reporting and a solitary life in the woods into a published book lived on after I wrote *finis* to my manuscript. Playing ball at a Red Sox Fantasy Camp and topping that off with a full day of play at Fenway Park did not end the drama or diminish the job. When a literary agent told me, "I don't just like your book, I love your book. I won't have any trouble selling it," I figured that I was in the Himalayas and the ride down would be as smooth as cruising on a beginner's slope in the old New Hampshire mountains. Then the rejections came in, as they usually do. Lots of, "We like your book, but it doesn't fit our market." Then, "We like your book, but we don't publish books about the Israelis and Palestinians." From two directors of big-league university presses came rejections that I expected, but which were encouraging. "We like your book," one of those directors said, "and if we were smart, we would publish it. But our board would never approve it because it's not an academic work."

When it comes to finding a publisher, I learned that luck is often a better ally than skill or experience. Shoe leather, my pal as a newspaperman, walked with me one Monday night in March of 2009, when I stumbled upon the publisher I would soon begin to call "my publisher." With nothing better to do on that cold night, I bundled up and headed to RiverRun bookstore in downtown Portsmouth, New Hampshire. If I had lived more than a mile and a half from the bookstore, I would not have marched into the headwinds of what promised to be more frustration.

Kismet awaited me at RiverRun, a feisty survivor among small, independent bookstores. Before long, RiverRun itself would stare into the abyss where so many bookstores, large and small, have fallen, victims of the electronic book-publishing age, economics and changing tastes, or so we're told. Just before RiverRun's apparent fall, a disparate group of local readers became independent investors when they stepped in to save the shop. Fate, for me, was borne by two women, literary midwives I would call them, whose presence that night helped transform my manuscript into a book. One of those women intended to guide writers through the self-publishing maze. But she had no idea whom she would help or exactly how. After a chance encounter, the second woman intended to help me, but could offer no guarantee that her effort would pay off.

RiverRun was and remains a pleasant place to browse and buy. Happy to be there but at the same time convinced that I was wasting my time on that Monday in early March, I arrived early. All the better, I thought, to weave through the chairs set up for the evening, stroll through the store, and search the shelves for my unpublished book. My mind was on my manuscript, my book, and how I could get it published. My eyes flitted across the shelves as I wandered, scanning memoirs, novels and history, sneaking peeks as always for titles by Russian authors.

The magnet that night was an author from Massachusetts, a woman who had spent a few thousand dollars to self-publish one of her five or six books that blind publishers refused to touch. What I thought would be the agonies of self-publishing didn't interest me, but I was impressed with the author's story, her boldness and courage. The novel she published, which has been described as comic or satirical, concerned the 2008 collapse of the real estate market, a big story by any measure. As a realtor and former stand-up comic, the author was well equipped to write a book about a business that screamed for satire, if not for gnashing of teeth. If anyone understood how tragedy and comedy go together, she would be the one, I thought. Not to be overlooked by the general listener was the fact that the self-published author had also studied dance in Paris and was a fine arts major in college. Still, that writer found no publisher for her book. As a result, she leaped into the self-publishing unknown.

A few souls like me, mixing hope, doubt and curiosity, drifted into the bookstore and warmed the seats. As we mingled and chatted, waiting for the starting bell, another woman sat next to me. Once more, I was in the right place at the right time; the woman was bubbling with joy, and soon I knew why. A publisher had just that day accepted her book. She flashed a paper, an email message as I recall, that proved it. Kathy Lockwood of nearby Rye glowed with the joy of pending publication. She also brought another lucky link to baseball and the Red Sox, and to strangers becoming instant allies because I bet on a long shot. That chance meeting was the equivalent of asking the extra question in Jerusalem, making one more telephone call in London, and pushing open the closed door in Antakya, Turkey, all in pursuit of a story. For me and my book, Kathy Lockwood's presence that night turned into the equivalent of a World Series-winning home run. It was more vital than any other baseball connection I stumbled over during my book-writing time—topping the legendary myth of Ted Williams and Jack Sharkey fishing at Lucas Pond, the Red Sox winning their first World Series in eighty-six years, my attendance at the Red Sox Fantasy Camp and my own mini-heroics at Fenway Park.

A baseball wife, Kathy Lockwood had written a baseball book about a wife's insider/outsider view of Major League Baseball. McFarland Publishing of Jefferson, North Carolina, had agreed to publish Kathy's book and she wasn't going to keep that a secret. *Major League Bride*, an incisive look at the difficulties faced by the wives and families of ballplayers, is the title of Kathy's book. Baseball wives and families, of course, function in the background. They labor as the support system for the husbands, fathers and sons who are showered with public fame and adoration and sometimes skewered with boos. Filling the spaces of known lives with unknown information provided by insiders always makes a good story. Who knows, for example, what the wives and children of ballplayers go through when their husbands/fathers are traded one day and play with another team in another city the next? So little is known about wives staying behind to help the children complete a school year or enroll in a new school the next, or about a wife playing the role of anchor to sell a house so the family can catch up to the star a city or two down the road. In such circumstances, baseball wives often stick together to survive. Kathy's book would be a great addition to baseball bibliography, I thought, filling the space on library shelves labeled Baseball Children and Wives.

When I told Kathy Lockwood the tribal story of my book, she offered help without hesitation. She gave me the name of her editor at McFarland and the link to McFarland's website: "Send your manuscript," she said. From the start, Kathy was generous with information and encouragement. Despite her own success and the optimism she tossed my way, my skepticism remained. Rejections have a way of lingering and dimming even the brightest promise. Optimism about self-publishing was the message that night at RiverRun, and the message was that it can be done. Few details about the how-to aspects of the talk remain with me. But the cost and advice left me feeling the same as when I had walked into the bookstore. At that moment, self-publishing wasn't going to be my game.

My conversation with Kathy Lockwood, however, remains vivid. Two days after we met at RiverRun, I sent my entire manuscript to McFarland. Five days after that, when McFarland wrote to say the editors loved my book and wanted to publish it, I felt the way Kathy Lockwood had a week earlier.

The full title of Kathy Lockwood's book is *Major League Bride: An Inside Look at Life Outside the Ballpark*. The groom is Skip Lockwood, who pitched for thirteen years in the major leagues, with Kansas City, Seattle, Milwaukee, the California Angels and New York Mets. Claude Edward (Skip) Lockwood pitched his final season, in 1980, with the home team, the Boston Red Sox. That was twenty years to the season after Ted Williams hit a home run in his last time at the plate and twenty-four years before the Sox won their first World Series in eighty-six years. By 1980, Williams, no longer "The Kid" of his 1939 rookie year, was the old pro angling full time for bonefish, tarpon and salmon. Even the grandest myths in Northwood, New Hampshire, wouldn't have Williams casting for those fish at Lucas Pond.

In 2010, a year after my chance meeting with Kathy Lockwood at a bookstore, McFarland published my book, *Violence, Veils and Bloodlines—Reporting from War Zones*.

***

EXTRA INNINGS

Absent another heart surgery, I've returned to James Joyce for more inspiration. Personal history, like the collective variety, is impossible to shed. So it's easy to recall again that shortly after open-heart surgery and years before this writing exercise began I read *Ulysses*. Now I'm picking my way through *Finnegan's Wake*. As I prepare to write again, time isn't on my side. With Joyce in hand, I wonder which will come first: The Kid, whole again, rising to hit more homers at Fenway Park; yours truly closing the book on Finnegan, finally spotting a deer or a cat in the woods, or finishing another book.

Appendix: Cribbage Magic

Lacking more common means of escape from writing, I often played cards, as in aces, deuces, kings and queens. That meant turning to one-man cribbage, a game I learned as a kid in Millville. In a small back room behind three pool tables, under a green-shaded lamp hung low over a round table covered with gamblers-green felt, I watched Big Louie, my grandfather; Abe, my father, and many other adults play cribbage, when the poker game was at rest. One floor below, in the back room of Ryan's Spa, the same game often graced a similar table shaded by a similar dim light. Decades later, when I needed diversions from writing, I turned to cribbage.

Counting cribbage points was at first a flight from reality, just as it was supposed to be; a way to bury time. It was a substitute for fleeing the cabin in my sporty convertible that was idling twenty-five miles to the east in Portsmouth. Cribbage became, however, a tool to help me think about writing, the reason I lived alone in the woods.

Why cribbage? The answer may be tucked away in the calendar. As years pass, humans tend to look back. The older we get, the farther back we look. As a kid, my summers were filled with bats, gloves and baseballs, and with spades, diamonds, clubs, hearts, a cribbage board and its pegs. When the sun shined in spring, summer and early autumn back then, baseball was my game. On bad weather days, cribbage pinch-hit.

Baseball and cribbage, viewed from old age, seem more similar than they did in my youth. They're both numbers games.

Numbers – fifteen, thirty-one, 121—are the essence of cribbage. Hits, runs, wins and losses, errors, strikes, balls, earned-run-averages and batting averages are baseball's lifeblood.

When I played cribbage, ideas about my book flew from my subconscious to my conscious mind and straight to a notebook. Sometimes I found the right words or phrases, the right sentence or a chapter title, but seldom an extended passage. The simplicity of those subconscious gains may have been related to the simplicity of cribbage.

Counting points while playing cribbage led to ideas for writing. Two, four, six, for example, took me to 1941, the year The Kid hit .406 after going six for eight in the final two games of the season. That's the last time anyone has hit .400 or better. The numbers inherent in cribbage reminded me of the stormy afternoon on the steppes of northern Afghanistan, where a twelve-year-old boy taught me to count to twenty in the Afghan language of Dari and I taught him to count to twenty in English.

Cribbage is essentially about simple math. It's also a visual or pictorial exercise. I learned the game so well that I could look at the cards and see instantly what my possibilities were, which cards to keep and which to toss into the crib, which is a second hand. Playing cribbage alone required little concentration. As a result, my mind wandered and opened allowing cribbage and my subconscious to fill my conscious mind with writing ideas. In that sense, cribbage was a muse.

Cribbage can be played quickly when there is only one player. The faster I played, the more my subconscious whirred. From dealing cards and counting points, I shifted quickly to writing notes about words and ideas.

Cribbage, as widely reported, was born in the 1600s, the child of Sir John Suckling, an English poet and gambler. Right there, in poetry and gambling, there may be a clue about the wizardry of cribbage. The game is usually played by two, three or four people;

played alone, it's as good, or better, a time-waster as solitaire.

Played solo, the object is to beat the game, which has fifteen points before each hand is dealt. That means I had to have sixteen points to beat the game by one point each time I dealt the cards. If I had fourteen points, I fell behind by one point. Each time I dealt, the deck dwindled by eight cards. It's difficult to average sixteen points per deal, so most of the time I lost.

With my spaghetti sauce simmering nearby, I squared off regularly against a deck of cards. After dealing myself six cards and tossing two cards into an extra hand, the crib, I decided which two of my cards to toss into the crib. After that was done, I had two hands of four cards each. Then I turned over the top card of the remaining cards in the deck to give my own hand and the hand in the crib five cards each from which to tally points in each hand. Each time I dealt a hand, the deck was reduced by eight cards. That meant I could deal six hands of eight cards each and have four cards left over from the full deck of fifty-two cards. The last four cards counted as another hand, although usually a weak one. Because I played alone, I couldn't play my cards against an opponent's and, therefore, there was no pegging—no opportunity to count to fifteen or thirty-one or to reach 121 points on the cribbage board—so I didn't need a cribbage board to tally my points. Without a cribbage board, I kept score in my head.

In those enlightened moments when my subconscious roared on, the actual writing, the composing, stood still. That came later, when guilt and pressure forced me to pull out a legal pad or ramp up the computer.

Since my year in the woods, I've urged my subconscious to reveal how the cribbage trick worked. No luck. I've tried to use one-man cribbage in the same way again. No luck with that either. So, I say, go figure.

Acknowledgments

*P*atricia Brothers Salome, my wife of fifty-five years, should stand at the beginning, middle and end of this incomplete summary of relatives, friends, strangers and astute thinkers who helped me slide home safely. Her ideas and suggestions were always helpful, even if we did not always agree. Pat encouraged me to discover the world, and she followed, sometimes to lands she would have preferred to avoid. When I roamed alone, far from sight but not of mind, she didn't object because she knew the decision was one I could not avoid. After we returned home, more or less, her support was unwavering and encouraging. Without Pat's continuing love and help, I would have been unable to live in the woods alone and write until my dreams told me I was finished.

Betsy Willeford, a superb book editor, writer, long-time friend and associate in revealing truths, now long forgotten, at *The Miami (Florida) News*, came through in the clutch, as great hitters do. Betsy's suggestions about trimming stories irrelevant to the main story were always spot-on. Even when Betsy didn't say a word, her silence was clear.

A newfound fast friend, Roland Goodbody is an especially fine writer and thinker who never surrenders. A transplanted Englishman and a better American than most Americans, Roland didn't give up on this project, although he had his doubts about baseball and cribbage. In a broad sense, Roland's criticism was a bookend to Betsy's, both being invaluable.

We walk on the shoulders of others, whether individuals or the commonwealth. My older sister Lois Salome walked ahead of me, easing my way in Woonsocket, Rhode Island, Millville, Massachusetts and at St. Mary's High School in Milford, Massachusetts. A lifelong teacher, Lois believes it's better to enlighten than to shine, although she does both with distinction and better than she will ever admit.

Acknowledgments

The leather briefcase Lois gave me when I entered the woods still houses the computer I pounded on after book dreams woke me in the middle of each writing night.

Word of mouth often brings great rewards. My younger sister Mary Lou Salome Etheredge and her husband Rob told their friends, Mirtha Crisóstomo and Mirtha's husband Al Dragon, that I was looking for a cabin in the woods. Mirtha and Al lived near Paul and Karen Dale, who owned a cabin at Lucas Pond in Northwood, New Hampshire. Presto. Before long I rented the Dales's cabin and moved in, first to freeze and then to warm to the writing. No cabin. No book. If better landlords than Paul and Karen Dale exist, they are in fairy tales.

Joy True, curator of the Epping (New Hampshire) Historical Society, was especially gracious and helpful. She turned over the society's thick file on boxer/angler Jack Sharkey and let me fish. The staff at the Northwood (New Hampshire) Public Library never showed me the door when I entered with questions about Ted Williams.

For the people around Lucas Pond who wondered but never asked what the crazy geezer in the woods was really doing I have a special fondness. But no one is more special than Jody and Bill at Demmons Country Store. Their quiet wisdom informed me more about New Hampshire and its people than any university class ever could. An especially good reader, Jody measured friendship in quiet courtesy and helpfulness.

Special thanks to the motley crew who worked in and visited Susty's Vegan restaurant in Northwood, New Hampshire. I'm no vegan, but I came to enjoy Susty's food.

To the countless people in the world who helped me, the strangers who fed me and gave me a blanket to sleep on, I owe boundless thanks. All those who left me alone are beyond praise. A special love is reserved for those who didn't shoot first and doubt their decision later.

Thanks also to Paul Donnelly, another teacher and lifelong resident of Millville, who dug out the proper spelling of Kimieck's Pond. If you think that's easy, Kimieck's is pronounced something like Kamidjiks. Paul still lives between what was known as Upper Kimieck's and Lower Kimieck's ponds, although no one I knew could spell Kimieck's.

When I sought a map of the Blackstone River corridor, Bonnie Combs came to my rescue with surprising speed. Thank you, Bonnie, who is the marketing director at the Blackstone River Valley National Heritage Corridor. Her office is in Whitinsville, Massachusetts. Via the Internet and by post, Bonnie sent maps that were easy for publisher Grace Peirce to work into the text.

Finally, I'm especially grateful to the creative rescue efforts of Grace Peirce at Great Life Press in Rye, New Hampshire. A wizard on all matters related to book design and book publishing, Grace made all the photos and maps integral to the stories, while adding ideas of her own.

About the Author

Retired journalist **Louis J. Salome** is the author of *Violence, Veils and Bloodlines—Reporting from War Zones* (McFarland 2010). His 35 years as a newspaper reporter and editor include seventeen years at The *Miami* (Florida) *News*, where he was the editorial page editor for ten years; more than nine years overseas with Cox Newspapers, Inc.; five years with The *Palm Beach* (Florida) *Post* and three-and-a-half years with the *Worcester* (Massachusetts) *Telegram & Gazette*. His numerous awards and prizes for reporting and editorial writing include the National Society of Professional Journalists (Sigma Delta Chi) Award for Editorial Writing, which he won twice. He lives in Dover, New Hampshire with his wife Patricia Brothers Salome.

www.ingramcontent.com/pod-product-compliance
Lightning Source LLC
Chambersburg PA
CBHW071656090426
42738CB00009B/1542